SO SUE ME!

The All-American Solution to the Israeli-Palestinian Bloodletting.

L. Meier
D. Cellini

SO SUE ME!

Copyright © Belmar Publications 2004
        Second Printing: September, 2004:
                        Adds Chapters VIII and IX, plus Postscript.
                        Reduces portions of State Department Reports

ISBN -   0-9746366-1-4

LCC -   2004107278

See updates on the book at: *so-sue-me.com.*

Other books by Belmar Publications,
    Liberating Korea ? by Arthur J. Paone (2003) at
    liberatingkorea.com

Dedicated to

ANONYMOUS*

*[The first person we approached with this Honor declined and unexpectedly left the country. The next person agreed, but only if done anonymously and provided we help him/her/it get into the Witness Protection Program.]

ACKNOWLEDGMENTS

We cannot possibly thank individually each and every person and group that helped us put this project together. But we would like to mention a few of the more important ones.

First of all we would like to thank XXXXXXXXXXXX, without whom this book would have been impossible. Almost as important to the development of this book was XXXXXXXX and XXXXXXXXXX. Thanks also to the librarians at the University of ZZZZZZZZZ and the archivists at XXXXXXX. Finally, our heartfelt appreciation to XXXXXXX and ZZZZZZZ who read early drafts of this work and made such vital contributions by their comments that we can honestly say that this book is not the same one which they first read. As always, we pay tribute to XXXXX and WWWWW who proofread the manuscript and put it into final shape.

LM & DC

CONTENTS

INTRODUCTION

The US Federal Courts

The most effective way to slow down and maybe even defeat the outlaw Israeli juggernaut that is crushing the Palestinian people is through the United States Courts.

Federal judges in the United States are appointed for life. They are the only individuals in the United States Government who could withstand every kind of pressure – from the Executive Branch (the President), the Legislative Branch (Congress) and the Fourth Branch of government (the Media). The Federal Courts in the US have a history of independence and of ultimately doing the right thing in most cases.

The Palestinians therefore would be wise to seek redress for their wrongs in the US Courts -- the only governmental power in the United States that is capable of thinking and talking rationally about the Middle East situation. The judges don't have to run for office. They don't have to raise funds. They are immune to media condemnations. The other two branches of government have been paralyzed when it comes to the Middle East. The President, and everyone who is trying to take his job, has become shrill and hoarse trying to out- shout the others in declaring his loyalty and love for Israel. And at any given time the Congress could be counted on to approve almost unanimously any sort of resolution or law in favor of Israel.

A preliminary requirement for any search for possible solutions to the Palestinians' present condition of humiliation and subjugation is that they recognize and accept two fundamental truths.

The first is that Israel and the United States are joined at the hip. The United States will defend and support Israel as if it were another State of the Union. Israel's enemies need to forget about ever being able to put a wedge between the US and Israel. The people of America are devoted to the survival of Israel and nothing will ever change that.

There are many reasons for this, most of them sensible, some of them not. Israel, like America, is a land of immigrants. But also, the Israelis, like the Americans, had to chase the natives off the land. In fact, one of America's greatest folk heroes is Andrew Jackson, a General, and later President, who was legendary not only for his hatred of Indians but for his relentless campaign to drive them off the good land in the East. As long as he lived his crusade was to push the Indians farther and farther into the barren deserts and wild mountains of the West, which the English settlers in those days had no use for. In the same fashion is the crusade of people who lead the Likud Party in Israel, like Ariel Sharon and Binyamin Netanyahu, who will for their entire lives try to leave only what they consider usleless parcels of land for the natives.

Then there is the Holocaust and the famous American sympathy for the persecuted. But there is also Einstein, Freud, Richard Tucker, Al Jolson, Jascha Heifetz, Houdini, Fiorello LaGuardia, and so on in a glorious line of great people who have made our lives better and have become molecules in our blood and fibers in our muscles.

The second fundamental truth is that America is today's Rome – all roads lead to Washington DC. The rest of the world is America's Province. Those seeking redress for wrongs in the provinces must come to Washington with their petitions in hand.

As only the Americans have the military power and the money to resolve the Israeli-Palestinian battle, and as only the US Federal Court system is capable of acting rationally on this issue, the Palestinians must make their case to the US Courts. The Palestinians, like the provincials in the time of ancient Rome, must come with petitions in hand, and file them in the Federal Courts of America. Sue, and sue often and everywhere. Take your pick of judges, the more the better as there will be those even with lifetime appointments who will become paralyzed upon reading your pleas for redress.

Now, please understand, the US Courts do not *make* the laws or our foreign policy. Nor can they directly curtail the billions being granted to Israel by Congress. Nor can they themselves on their own order the President to restrict Israeli use of American aid or weapons. But they do interpret laws and the Constitution. They can award monetary damages. They can enjoin illegal behavior by corporations as well as by federal and state agencies. US Presidents and the Congress, at least as of this writing, have generally abided by rulings from the highest of the Federal Courts, our Supreme Court.

The International Rule of Law

The international community, not the Israelis, divided the land of Palestine. It was the international community, acting first after World War I and then again in 1948 after World War II, which created the State of Israel. The United Nations gave the Israelis the land that up to then had belonged to the Palestinians. To seek redress from the US Courts based on international law, therefore, that decision of the international community to give the Israelis that land in 1948 must be accepted as a given fact by the Palestinians. Careful distinction must also be made between the right of millions to return to their homes in what is now Israel, on the one hand, and the entirely different issue of compensation to those millions for having taken their homes from them. Since 1948 the world has been promising such compensation, but though billions have found their way into building the modern State of Israel, the refugees are still waiting for their promised compensation. But as far as actually returning to the areas of Palestine that are within the internationally recognized 1948 borders of Israel, forget about it. The sooner that fantasy is put aside, the sooner the Palestinians can get down to the business of seeking redress – for the wrongs done to them.

On the other hand, while the international community gave Israel its existence, the Israelis must live by the law of nations — those rules of behavior that have become customary among the civilized nations of the world. Such rules are embodied in the United Nations Charter and the various treaties that have been accepted by most nations. That is where the US Federal Courts come into play. The "law of nations" is part of the federal law of the US. The courts, from the very beginning, have had jurisdiction to enforce the law of nations and treaties entered into by the US as the supreme law of the land.

The international community recognizes the land which became the State of Israel in 1948 as belonging to Israel. But the international community does *not* recognize the taking of land by conquest. So it is to the US Courts that the Palestinians must come to get back every inch of land that the Israelis have been taking, by force or by trick, since 1948. Rules interpreting the Statute of Limitations clearly would toll the period limiting a remedy so long as the taking remains illegal. Therefore the statute of limitations, on the actual right to the confiscated lands since 1948, would never toll. In addition, the parts of the Barrier Wall now being erected by Israel on lands in the Occupied Territory are likewise illegal confiscations under international law and they must be returned.

Just as clearly, modern customary international law prohibits *colonization* of territories taken by force. It does not allow a nation that wins a war and then occupies the enemy territory to settle its own people in the occupied lands. Instead, international law even sets up a series of rules for the behavior of the Occupying Power with respect to the land and the people in those enemy lands. Many of those rules are embodied in the Four Geneva Conventions of 1949, to which Israel and most other nations of the world are signatories. Therefore each and every Israeli settlement, in the West Bank as well as in Gaza, the Golan Heights and East Jerusalem, is illegal and must be dismantled. The Israelis knew from 1948 that any attempt at colonization would be an illegal taking, so they have themselves set the stage for the anguish that will be caused to their "settlers" who must eventually be removed.

Directly, or indirectly, that can be done through the US Federal Courts. The Courts will not change US policy on this. They cannot directly order the settlements be dismantled or the land given back. But they could prohibit the disbursing of monetary and military aid to Israel in support of the Barrier or the settlements. The courts can also do other things. For instance, they can enjoin the Ford Motor Company from sending any of its vehicles to Israel for illegal uses. They can punish Boeing if it's fighters and helicopters are used by the Israelis to destroy Palestinian homes or assassinate individuals. The can stop Caterpillar Inc. from shipping to Israel those bulldozers that are demolishing Palestinian homes. Eventually these cumulative remedies should modify the behavior of the Israelis – and the American Government.

Customary international law prohibits extrajudicial or targeted murders. Israel's policy of assassination is illegal under a number of treaties and international principles. The legal representatives and the next of kin of those who were killed, and those who were wounded, by Israel's targeted assassinations, can seek redress in the US Federal Courts. While the United Nations and its various organizations have the theoretical authority to help the victims, they have been castrated by the United States. In the Security Council, where the only Resolutions that are binding on all Member States can be passed, the US has exercised its Veto numerous times to prevent any real enforcement of international law -- or for that matter of the Council's own Resolutions. The ironic consequence is that the US alone has the ability to enforce the very international law which it is not allowing the UN to enforce. But in the US, the President, whoever he or she is, will not. Congress will not. But the Courts *might*.

So come, Palestinians, come and sue. Sue often and everywhere.

ISRAEL FOREVER — — ?

The almost universal condemnation of the Israeli state policies of assassination, home demolition and colonization signals the path that the Palestinians must travel to escape from the prison Israel is constructing for them. The most spectacular of those policies, assassinations, can alone serve as a weapon. Every nation in the world, except the United States, has condemned the Yassin and Rantisi assassinations as "immoral" and "illegal." If the Palestinians organized a careful international legal offensive, they could turn the tables on their tormentors and make Israel itself a prison for them.

The uniform international condemnation of Israel's targeted killings means that from the day they leave their official positions, every individual who had a hand in the assassinations will not be able to leave Israel. Let them land in Frankfurt or Paris or Rome; the Riviera, the beaches of South America or the streets of New York – they could be served with legal papers to account for their illegal actions. The lucrative speaking tours and TV appearances for retired Israeli politicians and military officials in the US will be closed off. The beaches on the coasts of Europe will be out of bounds. The casinos of Monte Carlo as well as South Africa will present dangers of legal entanglements. Even escape to New Zealand will be out of the question, as that country has especially condemned the assasinations. The politicians in Sharon's Cabinet who approved of the assassination; the Generals in the Army and Air Force who gave the orders; the pilots who pulled the triggers. Each and every one of them could be pursued relentlessly in almost any corner of the world – except Israel. So these folks had better plan to retire and die of old age in Israel and never see another part of the world, except on television.

COMING TO AMERICA : Part I

Much of the anti-American hatred throughout the world is fueled by America's apparently blind support for the repressive measures used by the Israelis against the Palestinians. The more atrocities committed on the Palestinian people by the Israelis, the more hatred is generated against America around the world. Israel exists today, both in fact and in the imagination of the world, solely because of American military and economic support. People generally believe that just one word from America would curtail the Israeli excesses, including its targeted killings and it land grabs. That word will *never* come from the politicians; the Americans are speechless.

So the higher and more effective the Israeli Barrier grows, the more tempting the erstwhile far away American targets will become. The desperate and helpless Palestinians and their allies, unable to strike Israel itself, will seek to change things by blowing

themselves up in the subways and tunnels of New York; by destroying the bridges of San Francisco, the buildings in Des Moines, Dallas and Miami. The harder it becomes to get across the Israeli Barrier, the easier it will seem to be able to get into America's heartland. Then we will see the student becoming the teacher, as Americans begin building various forms of their own Barriers to keep "them" out. Main Street will slowly take on the appearance of the closely guarded settlements in the West Bank and Gaza.

MAPS

MAP A: Courtesy UT Perry-Castaneda Library

x

The Separation Barrier in Jerusalem

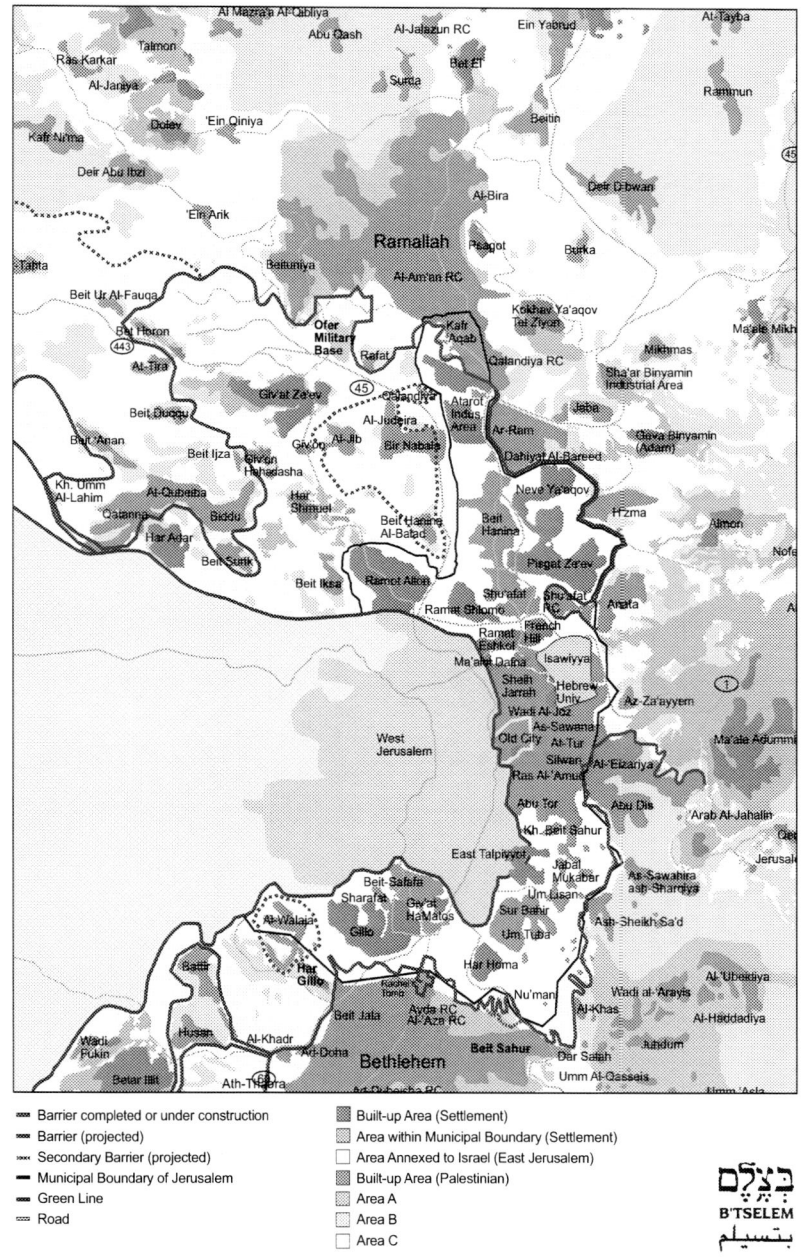

Barrier completed or under construction — Built-up Area (Settlement)
Barrier (projected) — Area within Municipal Boundary (Settlement)
Secondary Barrier (projected) — Area Annexed to Israel (East Jerusalem)
Municipal Boundary of Jerusalem — Built-up Area (Palestinian)
Green Line — Area A
Road — Area B
— Area C

בצלם
B'TSELEM
بتسيلم

MAP B: Courtesy of B'Tselem (The Israeli Information Center for Human Rights in the Occupied Territories)

The West Bank
Jewish Settlements and
the Separation Barrier

January 2004

Dead Sea

B'TSELEM
بتسيلم

B'TSELEM - The Israeli Information Center for
Human Rights in the Occupied Territories

MAP C: Courtesy of B'Tselem

Map D: Courtesy UT Perry-Castanda Library

— I —

EXTRAJUDICIAL KILLINGS AND THE "TORTURE VICTIMS PROTECTION ACT OF 1991" (TVPA)

Glossing over a lot of history and law, we come to 1991 and to Senator Joe Biden's US Senate Committee on the Judiciary. The Committee determined that a law had to be passed to give individuals, *any* individuals in the world, an expressed cause of against other individuals who "under actual or apparent authority or under color of law of any foreign nation" subjected that person to torture or extrajudicial killing. Those who would qualify as the legal representative or the beneficiary in a wrongful death action according to American law were to be given an expressed cause of action against individuals who had wrongfully caused the death of that individual. This law was being passed, according to the related

House of Representatives Report, "to carry out obligations of the United States under the United Nations Charter and other international agreements pertaining to the protection of human rights by establishing a civil action for recovery of damages from an individual who engages in torture or extrajudicial killing."

The House Committee Report also stated that the purpose of the Act was "to provide a Federal cause of action against any individual who, under actual or apparent authority, or color of law, of any foreign nation, subjects any individual to torture or extrajudicial killing." According to the Congressional Committees that enacted this law, called the "Torture Victims Protection Act of 1991" ("TVPA"), this Act incorporated into US law the definition of extrajudicial killing found in "customary international law," namely, in the Geneva Convention for the Amelioration of the Wounded and Sick in Armed Forces in the Field, August 12, 1949. Extrajudicial killing is defined in TVPA as

> *"a deliberated killing not authorized by previous judgment pronounced by a regularly constituted court affording all the judicial guarantees which are recognized as indispensable by civilized peoples."*

Of the dozens of targeted killings of Palestinians, as far as we know, not one was "authorized by previous judgment pronounced by a regularly constituted court affording all the judicial guarantees which are recognized as indispensable by civilized peoples."

True, each one apparently was approved by the validly constituted Israeli Cabinet which condemned these people to death. In fact, the Prime Minister at the time, Ariel Sharon, declared that : "We will not let up on them [after the killings of Sheikh Ahmad Yassin and Abdul Aziz Rantissi]. We got rid of murderer number one and murderer number two and it isn't over, and the list is not short."

The question raised by these events is whether a democratic State, by express and open state action, can lawfully, under the laws recognized by civilized nations, merely draw up a list of hundreds of individuals selected secretly by its own intelligence agencies and then sentence them to death?

Was Yassin and Rantissi, together with the people who died as bystanders or assistants, killed by authorization of a "previous judgment pronounced by a regularly constituted court affording all the judicial guarantees which are recognized as indispensable by civilized peoples"? No mention of any court order, much less of a hearing in which Yassin or Rantissi could present evidence, was mentioned in these assassinations. The only authority ever cited was the Israeli Cabinet. Can the Israeli Cabinet legitimately authorize the death of any individual under international law? Does a killing sanctioned by the Government of Israel automatically take the killing out of the category of "extra-judicial?"

Aside from the world headlines on the assassinations of Sheikh Ahmad Yassin and Abdul Aziz Rantissi, almost on a daily basis the Israeli Defense Forces or some related Israeli military agency announces the elimination of other "terrorists." Are these considered under international law as extra-judicial killings, and therefore illegal, or are they properly sanctioned state executions?

According to the Israeli Information Center for Human Rights in the Occupied Territories ("B'Tselem"), among the 200 Palestinians assassinated by Israel upon orders of the Israeli Cabinet in the period from 2000 to March of 2004, some of those identified were the following:

> 9 November 2000 – Hussein Muhammad Salim 'Abayat, 34, killed by Israeli helicopter missile fire in Beit Sahur, Bethlehem, along with two bystanders: Aziza Muhammad Danun, 52, female of Beit Sahur and Rahameh Rashid Sahiin, 52, also female of Beit Sahur who happen to be near the car hit by the missile.

If Hussein was the target and the Israeli Cabinet decided that he must die, was this a properly sanctioned state killing, "authorized by previous judgment pronounced by a regularly constituted court affording all the judicial guarantees which are recognized as indispensable by civilized peoples"? What of the two 52 year-old female bystanders?

The B'Tselem list continues:

12 December 2000 — Yusef Ahmad Mahmud Abu Sawi, age 28, Bethlehem, killed by IDF sniper gunfire when standing outside his house.

5 April 2001 — Iyad Mahmound Nayet Hardan, 24, Henin, killed in an explosion in a booby trapped phone booth in Araba.

31 July 2001 — Eight people killed in Nablus, mostly by helicopter-missile fire at homes and offices. One killed was Omar Mansour Muhammad Mansour, 28, along with bystanders Ashraf 'Abdel-Mun'em Khalil Abu Khader, age 8, Jenin and Bilal 'Abd al-Mun'em Khalil Abu Khader, age 10, also Jenin.

Was this summary execution of 28 year old Omar Mansour Muhammad Mansour "authorized by previous judgment pronounced by a regularly constituted court affording all the judicial guarantees which are recognized as indispensable by civilized peoples"? What of the killing of the 8 year old and the 10 year old who happen to be with him at the time of his murder?

A fundamental legal principle is that one is charged with the obvious consequences of one's acts. Did the Cabinet ordering the killings, and the pilot pulling the trigger, have reason to believe that a missile fired at a great distance from a helicopter into a building would possibly kill and injure innocent bystanders? Only if we assume that *every* Palestinian by membership in the *Arab race* was per se guilty of terrorism, could we say that no "innocent" bystanders were killed. The Israel Cabinet as of this date has not gone that far. But after the killing of Yassin and Rantissi, the Israeli Government announced that it would continue to kill anyone it thought was a risk to Israel, a "terrorist." In fact, the duly elected leader of the Palestinian Authority, Yaser Arafat, was mentioned by name as another prospective target. Did we miss the trial of Arafat, as we had missed the trial of those other 200? Was the announced intention of executing Arafat "authorized by previous judgment pronounced by a regularly constituted court affording all the judicial guarantees which are recognized as indispensable by civilized peoples"?

In the United States we are very familiar with "guilt beyond a reasonable doubt." Was each of the 200 Palestinians properly put to

4

death — after a fair trial, with a finding by a jury of guilt beyond a reasonable doubt? Was each confronted with evidence of crimes worthy of death and not rebutted by evidence submitted to the contrary by the accused in open court? Were these 200 allowed to face their accusers? Was the chance of error reduced to the absolute minimum, because, after all, death was the absolute punishment? Were the deaths of the 100 or so innocent bystanders, like Ashraf 'Abdel-Mun'em Khalil Abu Khader, age 8, Jenin, and Bilal 'Abd al-Mun'em Khalil Abu Khader, age 10, in the Omar Mansour execution, which the Israeli Cabinet knew was inevitable, "authorized by previous judgment . . . recognized as indispensable by civilized peoples"? Could the execution of 8 and 10 year olds under any imagined circumstances ever be justified among "civilized peoples"?

One must also admire the seemingly miraculous ability of the Israeli secret service, border guards and just plain soldiers who are successfully shooting and blowing up moving figures in the dark who turn out to have been "wanted" terrorists. An example of how brilliant these men must be was reported in the New York Times of April 24, 2004. Ending a week in which Israeli forces had already killed 25 Palestinians in various search and destroy operations in Gaza towns and villages, Elissa Gootman of the Times wrote that Israeli military officials said its forces had opened fired on "three armed men from the Hamas faction in a field in the village of Taluza, north of Nablus. One man was killed while the other two escaped . . . ." The three men were supposed have been armed, according to the Israeli military, and also were "from the Hamas faction." Presumably the fact that they were "armed" and that they were males could be verified by eyesight. But how did the soldiers in the dark of night determine that these people were "from the Hamas faction," particularly the two that escaped. Such is the trustworthiness of much of the reporting from the occupied territories.

Gootman further reported that the Palestinians identified the man who *was* killed as Yaser Ahmed Abu-Laymoun, 33. Israeli security had said he was an armed member of the Hamas faction. Yet it turns out upon further investigation by the reporter that this gentleman had been a lecturer at the Arab American University in Jenin. The president of that university, Dr. Waleed Deeb, cautiously wondered out loud why this teacher, who had given courses on hospital administration, and who had earned his master's degree at Philadelphia University in Pennsylvania, and who had spent all his time on his family and school work, would have been targeted by the Israeli security forces. "If he's really wanted [by Israel as a terrorist]," Dr. Deeb is reported to have said, speaking in shock as if his friend were still alive, "he would not be able to cross checkpoints on a daily basis to come to the university."

Is it likely that this teacher, killed in his own home town, had been properly identified, tried and convicted before his execution? Was his death "authorized by previous judgment pronounced by a regularly constituted court affording all the judicial guarantees which are recognized as indispensable by civilized peoples"?

In the same article by Elissa Gootman she relates that Israeli military officials recounted another instance where "undercover forces" had entered into the West Bank town of Qalqilya "to arrest four wanted operatives of Al Aksa Martyrs Brigades." Again, rather miraculously, somehow or other the undercover forces moving into a densely populated Arab town were able to confront these 4 men all at the same time; then when the four men tried to flee and "did not heed repeated warnings to stop," they were fired upon — three being killed and one wounded and escaped.

Were the fortuitous executions of these three residents of Qalqilya also "authorized by previous judgment pronounced by a regularly constituted court affording all the judicial guarantees which are recognized as indispensable by civilized peoples"? This is somewhat doubtful considering the seemingly random slaughter. Amos Harel, an Israeli reporter for the Haaretz Daily (4/23/04), also reporting on the same incident, quoted the army as saying that all the dead "were *wanted* militants who were shot while trying to *escape* arrest." But the serendipitous way these "suspects" were found would suggest otherwise. Amos Harel cited Palestinian witnesses who reported that "the troops entered the town in a civilian car and in a refrigerator truck and then opened fire from close range on a group of eight men standing outside a house." Only if one can assume that *any* male Palestinian between the ages of 10 and 70 is a militant and therefore "wanted," could we conclude that these undercover forces had really found wanted targets. If *everyone* is a target in an Arab town, then this shooting gallery form of execution would make sense.

According to international law, would such openly sanctioned state executions be exempt from the prohibition against extrajudicial killing? Would those killings be excluded from this definition because they are "lawful state sanctions"? The Congressional Committees introducing the Torture Victims Protection Act addressed that issue specifically in 1991. The United States Senate Committee noted "that a State Party could not through its domestic sanctions defeat the object and purpose of the Convention . . . ." In other words, the Committee stated, the US Government "does not regard authorized sanctions that unquestionably violate international law as 'lawful sanctions' exempt from the prohibition. . . ." This principle is the same principle recognized at the Nuremberg trials; the trial of Adolph Eichmann; the legal pursuit of Pinochet; the current hunt of the Argentine Military involved in the "dirty war" and the "disappearances;" and the trials before the International Court of Justice of the leaders of the genocide in Kosovo, Serbia, and the rest of the Balkans.

Was the targeted killing of this teacher in Taluza lawfully sanctioned and so exempt from the prohibition or did it "unquestionably violate international law"? The answer is quite simple. Article 3 of the Fourth Geneva Convention Relative to the Protection of Civilian Persons in Time of War states that "persons taking no active part in the hostilities . . . shall in all circumstances be treated humanely." This, the Article provides, prohibits "at any time and in any place whatsoever . . . the passing of sentences and the carrying out of executions without previous judgment pronounced by a regularly constituted court, affording all the judicial guarantees which are recognized as indispensable by civilized peoples."

This teacher, Yaser Ahmed Abu-Laymoun, was said by the Israeli officials to have been an armed member of Hamas when he was shot and killed in his village. Therefore it was not required that he be tried and convicted, since he was engaged "in the hostilities."

But most of the targeted killings were of people standing in front of their homes in villages far from any hostilities; people in their offices visited suddenly by Israeli missiles; an old man in a wheelchair being pushed to his home from a mosque; a man and his family in their car on the way home; an individual making a phone call outside of a hospital where he had just dropped off his sick mother. Death by unseen hands; sniper shots in the dark; missiles from afar; booby traps in public telephones. Could these people have been engaged "in the hostilities" and therefore not entitled to prior trials and convictions? The term "engaged in the hostilities" is used frequently in statutes and in treaties. Usually, there would be no difficulty in determining what that means in the context of justifying an exception to the rule that one must be fairly tried before being killed. Very little information is needed beyond the basic facts as even reported by the Israeli Press to conclude that those eight unarmed men, who had been standing in front of a house in their small town and just chatting, were not "engaged in the hostilities."

No one, except the Israelis and the Americans, had any difficulty in finding that these killings "unquestionably violate international law."

The Secretary General of the United Nations, Kofi Annan, when asked what his reaction was to the assassination of Sheikh Yassin, stated: "I must say, I do condemn the targeted assassination of Sheikh Yassin and the others who died with him. Such actions are not only contrary to international law . . . ." What better authority could there be about international law than the Secretary General of the UN?

A few weeks later the Secretary General was given the opportunity to repeat this opinion upon the Israeli assassination of the man who had just replaced Yassin, Abdel Aziz Rantisi. The Israel Defense Forces on April 18, 2004 issued a brief statement: "This evening, in a security forces operation in the Northern Gaza Strip, the IDF targeted a car carrying the leader of Hamas. Abdel Aziz Rantisi. . . ." An equally brief press release from the UN stated:

> *"The Secretary-General condemns Israel's assassination of Hamas leader Abdelaziz Rantissi. He reiterates that extrajudicial killings are violations of international law and calls on the Government of Israel to immediately end this practice."*

Far from ending "this practice," the Israeli Foreign Ministry spokesman, Gideon Meier, bragged: "We tried to do (this) a few months ago. At that time, he managed to run away. This time we got him." Death is not enough for a man like Rantisi, they need to mock him as a scurrying cockroach. Sharon himself followed this up with announcing that Yaser Arafat was now also on the still very long target list.

Yet even our close allies, the British, were quick to find the killing illegal under international law. Foreign Secretary Jack Straw called the Yassin assassination "unacceptable, unjustified and unlawful." A month later, he likewise condemned the killing of Abdel Aziz Rantisi: "The British government has made it repeatedly clear that so-called target assassinations of this kind are unlawful, unjustified and counterproductive."

The European Union's High Representative for Security, Javier Solana, spoke for Europe: "The European Union has consistently condemned 'extra judicial killing.' In this particular case [the Yassin killing] the condemnation has to be even stronger." At the United Nations, the European Union's Ambassador, Richard Ryan, made a statement to the Security Council which read in part:

> *"Extra-judicial killings [are] contrary to international law. . . . The EU recognizes Israel's right to protect its citizens against terrorist attacks. Israel is entitled to do this under international law. Israel is not, however, entitled to carry out extra-judicial killings."*

The United Nation's Commission on Human Rights discussed and passed a resolution, over American objections, which "strongly condemned the continuing grave violations of human rights in the occupied Palestinian territory, in particular the tragic assassination of Sheikh Ahmed Yassin on 22 March 2004, in contravention of the Hague Convention IV of 1907. . . ."

At the United Nations itself, the United States exercised its veto to kill a Resolution condemning the Yassin extrajudicial killing. But not before a parade of speakers representing practically the entire world denounced the killing as illegal and counterproductive. Ambassador Ryan, on behalf of the European Union, stated:

> *"The action by the Israeli armed forces is in complete violation of international law. There can be no justification for targeted assassinations and extrajudicial killings as an instrument of State policy.*

"This is also in direct conflict with Israel's obligations as the occupying Power under the Fourth Geneva Convention. The logic of self-defense cannot be extended to justify extrajudicial executions. Even suspected terrorists should be subject to the rule of law, especially by a country that prides itself as a democracy."

Ambassador Munoz of Chile stated: "My delegation condemns this act of violence: the assassination of Sheikh Ahmed Yassin and a number of companions. . . . Extrajudicial executions are reprehensible acts that constitute an assault on international law. . . ." Similar language was used by the Ambassadors from various other countries, including, Angola, Russia, China, the Philippines, Spain, Brazil, Benin, Romania, Germany, France, Japan, Senegal, Cuba, South Africa and Norway. Much more passionate denunciations, as expected, were voiced by every Arab and Muslin country in the world.

The universal condemnation as expressed by those Delegates was answered by Israel with a follow-up assassination of Rantisi. Those Delegates and others stood up again and essentially repeated their disgust with the Israeli intransigent defiance of the law of civilized nations.

The targeted killings are unquestionably contrary to well-established principles of international law, and therefore cannot validly be sanctioned by the Government of Israel. Thus the Palestinians clearly have valid causes of action under the Torture Victims Protection Act of 1991.

— II —

SOME OF THE MECHANICS

Who Can Sue

Under the Torture Victims Protection Act of 1991 ("TVPA") a civil suit may be brought by the legal representative of an extrajudicial killing victim or any person who may be a claimant in an action for wrongful death. It is expected, according to the Committee Report, that "courts may look to state law for guidance as to which parties would be proper wrongful death claimants." Also, unlike the much older (1789) Alien Tort Law, which limits the plaintiff class to foreign aliens, the remedies of the TVPA are available to citizens of the United States as well.

If, for example, there happens to be an American relative of Sheik Ahmed Yassin or Dr. Abdel Aziz Rantisi, who also qualifies as a representative (see below), he or she could bring an action under TVPA. American relatives who qualify as representatives of the 200 plus others targeted and killed in the Israeli assassination program would also be able to bring suits.

In addition to the heirs of the targeted victims of extrajudicial killings,is there any other class of claimants? What of the heirs and representatives of the innocent *bystanders*. They were not the targets per se, but for the most part their deaths could have been reasonably foreseen. It is estimated that somewhere along the line of 100 others were killed when the intended targets were hit. So in Yassin's case there were seven other people killed. Among them were bodyguards, relatives, medical assistants and simple bystanders. When Rantisi was eliminated, his driver and bodyguard were also killed. One report further raised the possibility that his wife may have perished in the car with him.

Then there are people like Aziza Muhammad Danun, 52, female of Beit Sahur, Bethlehem, and Rahameh Rashid Sahiin, 52, also female of Beit Sahur who happened to be near the car hit by the missile killing the targeted Hussein Muhammad Salim 'Abayat on 9 November 9, 2000. Or the relatives of bystanders Ashraf 'Abdel-Mun'em Khalil Abu Khader, age 8, Jenin and Bilal 'Abd al-Mun'em Khalil Abu Khader, age 10, also Jenin, who died in the missile attack on the targeted Omar Mansour Muhammad Mansour, 28. Would relatives of these reasonably anticipated incidental victims of extrajudicial killings have redress under TVPA?

Under American law if someone murders another person, he would be charged with that murder. If he also kills someone else, even accidentally during that murder, he would be liable for that additional murder charge as well. This type of principle runs throughout other areas of American law. It is not unreasonable, therefore, to assume that the same principle would be applied under TVPA to give the relatives of bystanders killed during extrajudicial killings a remedy.

In addition to the 200 targets and the 100 bystanders (a conservative count by B'Tselem up to March, 2004), there were reportedly hundreds of others wounded in these attacks. Would they have redress under TVPA? Again, if basic principles of the American law on liability are applied, they also should have causes of action under this Act.

Who Can be Sued

"*An individual who, under actual or apparent authority, or color of law, of any foreign nation . . . subjects an individual to extrajudicial killing. . . .*"

Only an *individual* can be sued under this Act, not any government or organization, company or other artificial entity. This personal liability would apply to every individual down the entire chain of command – from the members of the Israeli Cabinet, to the Chiefs of the Defense Forces, to the commanders of the units carrying out the killing, to the radar operators tracking the victims, to the informants helping to locate the victims, to the pilots flying the helicopters, to the soldier who pulls the trigger, to the airman who sends the missile on its way, to the technician who plants the booby trap in the roadside telephone and to the Military Spokesmen who brag about the killings. Every individual who had anything to do with the murder, directly or indirectly, would be subject to civil suit for damages under TVPA. This is not a criminal statute, but a civil statute, so the net for civil liability stretches far wider than that of a criminal law.

In addition to being an individual, and having something to do with the killing, the individual must also be acting "under actual or apparent authority, or color of law, of any foreign nation." Israel of course is a foreign nation. American law, particularly in the field of civil rights, has a well developed body of guidelines to determine if someone was acting under actual or apparent authority or color of law. Certainly the soldier and the pilot taking orders to kill would be included. Sharon and his fellow Ministers undoubtedly are included. The informants on the ground and the radar technicians tracking the victims would be acting under color of law. This requirement, then, would be relatively easy to determine and there would be few gray areas under it. At the present time the Israeli Government is so defiant of the international community and the standards of international law that it is not hiding much. The targets are announced and claimed. The killings have become reasons to brag. Prospective victims are threatened. The overwhelming military power of the Israelis and their ability to track down and kill individuals not only in the Gaza Strip and the West Bank, but in foreign countries as well, is deliberately held out by the Government in what it must believe will be a deterrent to its enemies. Consequently there will be few questions in any case in the US involving assassinations about whether the defendant was acting under official auspices as required by the statute.

This requirement, on the other hand, would *exclude* killings by individuals who are not acting in any way on behalf of a government. Someone may kill for political reasons, but unless it is somehow connected with the government, this statute would not apply. An interesting category of killers would be the Israeli settlers who sometimes kill Palestinian civilians. The Israeli Government encourages them in the first place to swim in among the Palestinians, offering them "free" land and other financial incentives, along with military protection, separate roads, water, gas and electric, etc. A settlement is in itself such a provocation that any reasonable person would assume the result would be violence, then retaliation, then more violence, then retaliation, and on and on. Would the Government's turning a blind eye to the killings by settlers then make the settlers' activities come under the color of law? Congress intended this issue to be interpreted along the same lines as the civil rights statute, 42 US 1983. Under such reading it is clear that the settlers in this regard are the agents of the Government of Israel, carrying out it policy of colonizing Arab land. Being agents for colonization, they are also agents for whatever inevitable activities flow from that — including chasing and annihilating the natives.

While this may be an interesting question, however, it may not be of any significance. The settlers will unlikely ever be in the United States subjecting them to jurisdiction of our courts. Nor would they be likely to have any worthwhile assets here. So this category of defendant would not seem to be of any value under TVPA.

When Can They Be Sued
The Prime Minister of Israel visits the US often enough. Could he be handed a subpoena next week, for instance, when he lands in Washington or New York? The equivalent of the Israeli military Chief of Staff also visits the Pentagon frequently, as does his subordinates. Can they be served while driving over the Potomac? There are Israeli ambassadors and other officials otherwise always in the United States. Can the claimants under TVPA get their hands on them?

The simple answer is: No. Various international treaties, domestic laws and procedural regulations clearly exempt these individuals so long as they are in official positions. As the Senate Committee which introduced this Act reported, none of the traditional diplomatic immunities that prevent the exercise of jurisdiction by U.S. courts over foreign diplomats are intended to nor could be overridden by the TVPA. Heads of state could neither be served with process nor sued under this Act while they are on official visits.

The immunity ends, however, promptly upon the officials leaving office. As the Senate Committee stated: "The committee does not intend these immunities to provide _former_ officials with a defense to a lawsuit brought under this legislation." Similarly, "the committee does not intend the 'act of state' doctrine to provide a shield from lawsuit for former officials." By definition, both torture and extrajudicial killing cannot be a valid state doctrine, so the "act of state doctrine," ipso facto, does not apply. Even though the Israeli Government in its arrogance has repeatedly pronounced that the targeted killings were indeed state policy, this fact will not be relevant since such a policy is against international law and therefore cannot be a defense under this law. Both the Senate and House Committees made this clear in their Reports.

All the rules for personal jurisdiction, however, apply. Consequently the former official has to be caught where he could be served with process to bring him under the jurisdiction of the federal courts. Essentially this would require that he or she be served with process while in the United States. This of course greatly limits the pool of potential defendants under the TVPA – primarily former officials, soldiers and airmen of Israel who for some reason come to the United States. Congress did not intend to flood the courts by providing every political killing victim in the entire world and their families with a cause of action in the United States. So this limitation is real and significantly limits the redress under this statute.

However, the people with the most assets, and therefore the best type of defendant, are the most likely to come to the United States after they leave office. The number of former Israeli politicians and military officers who engage in business transactions in the US, travel the lecture circuit, visit vacation spots, etc., should afford a large enough and lucrative target list themselves for action under the TVPA.

Finally, another limitation is that an action can be brought only within 10 years of the killing. Like most remedies provided by law, the legislature puts a time limit on when plaintiffs can come into court. The reason is primarily administrative — as memories fade over time, evidence becomes difficult to gather, witnesses die or disappear, etc. So the Statute of Limitations is intended to strike a balance between providing a remedy to the victim and allowing for an efficient adjudication. Ten years is somewhat short for a murder, but it is longer than most tort statutes of limitations in the US.

— III —

THE SUDETENLAND AND THE WEST BANK OR ...
JESSE JAMES AND *BILLY THE KID* MAKE A DEAL

First – the Bandits: Jesse and Billy

On April 22, 2004, at a good-old-boy gathering at the White House, Sharon and Bush, two democratically elected leaders (so we cannot say they were renegades) gave each other letters (carefully negotiated over several months) signaling their understanding that an as yet undetermined part of Arab land in the West Bank (the Israelis to make that determination at some future date, depending on their needs and wants from time to time) would become Israel's. No specifics were given as to how much West Bank land would become Israel's, it was just agreed that the West Bank was only a little pregnant with an Israeli baby. At the same time Israel would disentangle its 7,500 settlers from the 1,300,000 Palestinians in Gaza and relocate them beyond the Gaza Strip.

Sharon had immediately recognized a fellow *Bandito* when Bush stole the Presidential election in 2000. The "Law" had no sting to these two outlaws. Both would have no part of international law; in fact they partnered up to change the world back to the lawless Old West, where a man was a man. Neither would allow his country to join the International Court of Criminal Justice — and for good reason; Bush even threatened to do harm to any nation that assisted the International Court.

Would Americans want to see their soldier-sons and daughters judged by foreigners? Would those foreigners perhaps have found something disgusting with the pictures of naked Iraqi prisoners piled on each other like slaughtered cattle? If the President could make a person legally invisible by saying the magic words: "enemy combatant," or "illegal combatant," why couldn't a female US soldier drag naked Iraqis along the prison floor with leashes tied around their necks? If they were doing this to prisoners of war supposedly protected by the Geneva Convention, imagine what they have been doing to the legally invisible "enemy combatants" at Guantanamo these last few years? To top it all they brought in that sick individual, General Geoffrey Miller, from Guantanamo Bay to "solve" the mess at the Iraqi prison camp,
,The Bush-Sharon exchange of letters does have an American historic precedent. We must first assume that Jesse James and Billy the Kid were not illiterate, or, that if they were, they used a Doc Watson (similar to the Elliott Abrams role) to write the letters for them. Then we need to imagine a young and energetic couple today renovating a long-abandoned brothel in an area of Dodge City undergoing gentrification. To their utter astonishment, they come upon an old chest belonging to the famous Madame, Miss Candy, containing the correspondence of Jesse James and Billy the Kid.

Jesse and Billy's letters were as simple as the Bush and Sharon letters. The money in the Bank in Dodge City, they agreed mutually, was there for them, mutually.

Then — the Sudetenland

We wonder if the Americans at the time of the Bush and Sharon exchange of letters which determined, mutually among themselves, the fate of Arab land, had the same grace as the French did after they had given away Czech territory at Munich. The European Powers at the time, Britain, France and Italy, on September 29, 1938, had agreed to cede a large chunk of Czechoslovakian land bordering Germany, called the Sudetenland, to Germany to avoid a war. Then the French Minister at Munich, Edouard Daladier, instructed his office in Paris immediately to convey to the Czechs in Prague the terms of the deal worked out by himself, Neville Chamberlain, Benito Mussolini and Adolph Hitler.

> *As a matter of extreme urgency get in touch with M. Benes [Edvard Benes, Czech President] in order to make sure of his agreement. I request you to express to him my deep emotion at the end of these negotiations and to assure him that it was not by my choice that <u>no representative of Czechoslovakia was present</u>.*

Bush and Sharon had convinced themselves of the self-fulfilling prophecy that there was no one on the Palestinian side that they could talk to – notwithstanding the dozens of professional Palestinians who represent the Palestinian Authority in various UN and other international bodies. So they divided the occupied territories without any representative from the natives, or even friends of the natives.

Nor have we seen any condolences sent to the Palestinians by the Americans, the "honest brokers," for the pain the Bush-Sharon deal will cause. Again, the French in 1938 were more considerate. The French Foreign Minister, Georges Bonnet, instructed his Minister in Prague: "Please make an immediate communication to M. Krofta [Czech Foreign Minister] to express the sentiments of profound sympathy with which, from hour to hour, I have followed his noble and courageous personal handling of the situation during so painful a national trial. . . . Will you assure him of my most loyal personal friendship and of my desire to help him to the best of my ability *in the constructive task which now lies before him*." The "constructive task" for the Czechs was to evacuate pell mell in 10 days the entire area of the Sudetenland of any ethnic Czechs, making sure to leave their homes and businesses intact for use by the incoming Germans. The Munich Agreement was signed on the 29ᵗʰ of September and the Czechs were told to cleanse the entire area of Czechs by October 10ᵗʰ.

The Czechs had been counting, in turns out vainly, on their British and French allies to resist Hitler's demands. Hitler had promised in a speech just a few days earlier that the Sudetenland would be "the last territorial claim which I have to make in Europe. . . . the German people want nothing but peace. . . ." England and France thought that the sacrifices to be made by the Czechs was a fair price to pay for peace. Likewise, the Palestinians have been vainly counting on the Americans, the "honest brokers." The Bush Administration, however, without having signaled that it had given up the traditional American role of the honest broker, unilaterally decided on the sacrifices that the Palestiniansmust make for peace. This was done without Sharon even having to promise that this would be his last demand.

Bush went even further: he tried to give away the bargaining chip of the Palestinian "Right of Return;" he agreed to the Israeli taking of whatever West Bank lands they wanted; he blessed the continued building of the Barrier on West Bank land and tacitly, at least in public, consented to the extra-judicial killings being carried out by Israel. Somewhat similar to the handing over of Czechoslovakia to the Germans – yet we have not seen any note of condolence to the Palestinians from the "honest broker," nor words of encouragement for the grim future the lies ahead for them. The art of diplomacy must have changed in 70 years.

Of course there are limits to analogies. How could one legitimately equate President George Bush's ceding the West Bank to Ariel Sharon with the ceding of the Sudetenland to Hitler? It is utterly foolish to compare Sharon to Hitler or Bush to Mussolini – though, in truth, Bush's heroic strutting on the naval carrier in a somewhat premature victory march over Iraq did bear some resemblance to Il Duce's antics. In addition, one is forced to admire the decades-long determination that Sharon has displayed to achieve his goals. International condemnation and multiple setbacks have never deterred him. In that way he possesses the same kind of rare steadfastness that Hitler showed. Even from his jailhouse cell in his early days, Hitler, in writing his Mein Kampf with its long-term ambitions for the *Anschluss* (union with Austria) and *Lebensraum* (living space for Germans), knew where he was going. Goals and ambitions only thinly veiled with doubletalk over the years. This trait Sharon also shares with Hitler. Even now Sharon has shown his mastery of the promise that is not a promise. Remember his promise last year to begin negotiations with the Palestinians as soon as there were seven days of absolute peace. An illusory promise, of course, since that merely was an offer that could not be refused to any single fanatic on either side to scuttle things — as they did. Now, in his letter to Bush, Sharon states that

> "my plan *will create* a new and better *reality* for the state of Israel. And it also has [1] *the potential* to create the [2] *right conditions* to [3] *resume negotiations* between Israel and the Palestinians." [Numbers and italics added.]

Sharon immediately, in the here and now, *creates* the reality on the ground for Israel by brute force and with American weapons, namely, the taking of whatever portions of the West Bank that he found attractive. But for the Palestinians , in Sahron's vision there is only a long and wandering dark path that *may* have "potential," and then, if that potential develops, they may finally arrive at the "right conditions" (to be named later by Israel) and then finally, back to square one, there is the *possibility* of "resuming" negotiations. Can one envision that this could all happen in our lifetime, or even in the lifetimes of the next two generations? The Israeli leaders are bestowing mayhem on their descendants for 100 years. Meanwhile, what other "new realities" that so impressed Bush this time will there be on the ground? The Sharon maneuver in these "exchange of letters" tells us that those in control of the Government of Israel in 2004, like the Germans in 1938, have no intention of altering their plans. They will say whatever the world wants to hear, but with utterly no sincerity and only to camouflage and disguise their ultimate goals.

Finally, the Munich Agreement and the Bush-Sharon Agreement bear similarities in that both were contrary to international law and various treaties signed by the parties. Articles 45 and 46 of the Laws and Customs of War on Land (Hague IV) state that in any territory occupied by a belligerent,

> *Family honour and rights, the lives of person, and private property . . . must be respected.*

Private property cannot be confiscated.
Pillage is formally forbidden.

Article 49 of the Fourth Geneva Convention (1949) states:

> *The Occupying Power shall not deport or transfer parts of its own civilian population into the territory it occupies.*

These rules follow a fundamentally recognized principle of modern international law: -- there can be no legitimate taking of land by conquest.

"Family honor" has been interpreted by the Israelis as making anyone in the family, grandmothers to grandsons, liable for the transgressions of the individual. Bulldozers made by Caterpillar in US cities are used to raze the homes of these families and push them, again, into the growing pool of homeless Arabs.

Numerous UN resolutions, many joined in by the United States, and many others supported by almost the entire international community, except the United States, have declared the settlements illegal and warned Israel *against changing the facts on the ground.* Nevertheless Bush has attempted to reward the decades-long Israeli defiance of international law by his agreement with Sharon.

In 1967, after the cease fire, the UN Security Council, including the United States, passed **Resolution 242**, which emphasized "the inadmissibility of the acquisition of territory by war" and stated that a lasting peace in the Middle East should include various principles, one of them being: "Withdrawal of Israeli armed forces from territories occupied in the recent conflict. . . ."

Ten years later not only had the Israeli troops not withdrawn, but Israel had moved some of its own civilians into the Arab territories and set up colonies on confiscated private land. Still at that time there were only about 6,000 Israeli settlers in the Arab territories. On July 20, 1979, the United States signed on to UN Security Council **Resolution 452**. That Resolution "strongly deplored the lack of co-operation of Israel;" repeated that "**the policy of Israel in establishing settlements in the occupied Arab territories has no legal validity and constitutes a violation of the**

Fourth Geneva Convention;" and stated that the Security Council was "deeply concerned by the practices of the Israeli authorities in implementing that settlements policy in the occupied Arab territories, including Jerusalem." Finally, the Security Council called "upon the Government and people of **Israel to cease**, on an urgent basis, the establishment, **construction and planning of settlements** in the Arab territories occupied since 1967, including Jerusalem . . . ."

Thus the world community in 1979, in what was supposed to be a "binding" Security Council Resolution, ordered one of its members, who had just 6,000 colonialists on Arab land at the time, to cease and desist from this outlaw practice. The United States, a member of the Security Council, was part of the world community voicing this demand at that time.

Yet, another twenty years later, when the UN General Assembly's Special Committee to Investigate Israeli Practices in the Occupied Territories made its report in July 1999, reaffirming "that Israeli settlements in the Palestinian territory, including Jerusalem, and in the occupied Syrian Golan are illegal and an obstacle to peace. . . .," the number of Israeli settlers transported to the West Bank and Gaza, financed by Israel and protected by the Israeli Army, had grown to over 200,000.

And more recently, when the UN Commission on Human Rights adopted a Resolution on April 15, 2003, (Resolution E/CN.4/2003/L.18 which passed with 50 nations voting in favor and only the United States voting against) expressing

> *"grave concern . . . at the continuing Israeli settlement activities, including the illegal installation of settlers in the occupied territories and related activities, such as the expansion of settlements, the expulsion of Palestinians and the construction of bypass roads, <u>which changed the physical character and demographic composition of the occupied territories</u>, including East Jerusalem, as settlements were a major obstacle to peace and to the creation of an independent, viable, sovereign and democratic Palestinian State . . . .*

--- the number of settlers in the West Bank, Gaza and East Jerusalem has grown to about 326,000.

Though the Israeli spokesman at the time railed against this Resolution, Sharon could only smile at the impotence of the world community. He of course understood that his settlement policy indeed was making it impossible ever to create, as the Resolution stated, "an independent, viable, sovereign and democratic Palestinian State." That precisely was his purpose.

It can be said in fairness to Bush that he was doing no more than recognizing the realities on the ground that had been created by the Israelis – just as Chamberlain, Daladier and Mussolini had to recognize the realities of the German troops massing on the Czechoslovakian border. What was the alternative? For the European Powers it would have meant a devastating war in 1938 with the consequent killing of millions. For the Bush White House, it means the possibility of gaining another 10% of the pro-Israel vote with which to capture the swing states of Pennsylvania, Ohio and Florida. But Bush may have trouble converting this into votes. The logic of American politics is such that once Bush has offered 20 or 30% of the West Bank to Sharon, the Democrats will come back and find compelling reasons to raise the ante to 40 or 50% of the West Bank that must be offered to Israel.

Dark humor hovers over the Bush-Sharon meeting and exchange of letters. Bush congratulates Sharon on his courageous and historic decision to pull the 7,500 settlers out of Gaza at some vague, future, indefinite date —— settlers whose own courage to live in such provocative fortified villages amidst one million three hundred thousand hostile Palestinians must also be admired, or their sanity questioned. The Israeli objective for the civilian pullout from Gaza, according to Sharon's plan of disengagement which he sent to his Ministers upon his return to Israel "as coordinated with US President George W. Bush," is to eliminate any "basis to the claim that the Gaza Strip is *occupied territory*." Sharon then described that the security "reality" in the plans for this erstwhile "occupied territory" would include the following:

> *"Israel will supervise and secure the outer envelope of the geographical land mass [of Gaza], will exclusively control the airspace of the Gaza Strip, and will carry out military operations on the territorial waters of the Gaza Strip."*

In addition, Israel will maintain and even enlarge its military presence in Gaza on Gaza's border with Egypt and retain "the basic right to self defence, including preemptive steps and response, with the use of force, against threats emanating from the area."

Sharon's point is to get from under the endless carping from the international community. As an Occupying Power it is responsible by international law for the safety and well-being of the civilian population – food, shelter, water, jobs, education, etc. What a nuisance – not only were they theoretically not to kill the Palestinians, but Israel was supposed to feed them and educate their children! As the Occupying Power in Gaza, therefore, it theoretically had to live with the restraints and obligations of the Fourth Geneva Convention – restraints and obligations it has never complied with in any event. Well – like magic, this 27 by 3-7 mile odd stretch of impoverished and valueless land surrounded by Israeli troops ready to pounce in with "preemptive" strikes, is no longer an "Occupied Territory." What other descriptions would suit the situation: . . . An Indian Reservation? . . . A cheap labor force? . . . . A prison? . . . . A concentration camp?

Leaders around the world began describing the Sharon plan as the "bantunizing" of the Occupied Territory. Bantustan refers to the all-black enclaves in the old Republic of South Africa that were given a limited degree of self-government. Meron Benvenisti in an article entitled "Bantustan Plan for an Apartheid Israel" (The Guardian (UK)), April 26, 2004) even thinks that "the Bantustan model for Gaza as depicted in the disengagement plan, is a model that Sharon plans to copy on the West Bank." Benvenisti thinks that none of the Gaza settlers will be moved until Israel has finished construction of the fence or Barrier which would be along a route to include all settlement blocks. The result will be that the fence or Barrier would create "three bantustans on the West Bank — Jenin-Nablus, Bethlehem-Hebron and Ramallah."

Others called it the ghettoization of the Occupied Territories, recreating the Ghettos of the Middle Ages. Yet even this was not enough for some Israelis. The Butcher of Lebanon, their own Monster, evidently had determined that he could not kill all the Arabs in the occupied territories. So he was hoping to do the next best thing — bottle them up into slave camps. You would think that his supporters would accept this determination. But soon after the Bush-Sharon Agreements 70,000 Israeli die-hards marched into Gaza, objecting to this "give away." Then a strong majority of Sharon's own party rejected this plan.

What else would these die-hards do with the one million three hundred thousand Arabs in Gaza? Prisoners on their own impoverished land is too good for these people? God has destined them for something else? What *else* could you possiblye do with this mass of humanity which is now in the world's spotlight?

That the settlers are really the agents of the Israeli Government was recently highlighted by a report by the Israeli State Comptroller, Eliezer Goldberg. Notwithstanding all the public promises from time to time, of the Israeli Government that it would freeze settlements or not allow vigilante settlements and even dismantle some of the unauthorized outposts set up by renegade settlers, as a matter of fact the Israeli Government has secretly funded even the "unauthorized" settlements and outposts over the years – providing money for housing, encouraging settlers to go there, building roads and supplying the other essential elements of the infrastructure, like water and electricity (Haaretz Daily, May 5, 2004, reports by The Associated Press and the Haaretz staff). Yariv Oppenheimer of Peace Now is quoted as saying that there were, between January 2000 and June, 2003, 102 unauthorized settlement outposts built, and just 21 were removed, many of them later rebuilt.

This Report by Goldberg, giving the fine details of the continuing financing of settlements considered "illegal" and "unauthorized" by the Israeli Government, reminds us of the details of human rights abuses frttailed each year in the US State Department's Annual Report on Human Rights in Israel and the Occupied Territories. The facts are given — then nothing is done about them. The following year, the facts are repeated. Then, again, nothing is done about them.

Clearly, the Palestinians cannot count on either the Israeli or the American Government even doing the minimal of what they promise to do. In fact, the Israelis and the Americans seem very often to be working in tandem. Israel assassinates Yassin and Rantisi with no rebuke from Washington. At the same time the Americans announce that they have halted work on water development projects in the "overcrowded, poverty-stricken seaside territory" of Gaza, partly in retaliation for attacks on US diplomats (Haaretz Daily, May 7, 2004). The Israelis kill the leaders of Gaza; then the Americans punish the population of Gaza.

Are the "die-hards" who are insisting on expanding settlements, even in impoverished and overcrowded (by Arabs) Gaza, really *fringe* elements? Or are they the pit bulls of the true Israeli policy stretching over many years and regardless of who is Prime Minister and who promises what "freeze." It has all been pretense — while the facts on the ground have been changed.

Israel in its agreed plan with the United States also demanded compensation from the World Bank (aka US taxpayers) for the "assets" it will be leaving behind in Gaza (which was probably financed in the first place with US aid). However Sharon, soon after making this demand and returning to Israel, could not contain himself and threatened to destroy all the homes to be (at some future date) evacuated by the 7,500 settlers if the Palestinians put any families in them who may be on Israel's extensive "hit list." The World Bank, for its part, later sheepishly announced that it could not join the party — the Israeli's were too rich to qualify for World Bank subsidizing.

Aside from being paid to leave and give back the Arabs the land they originally took from them, someone has to pay to resettle yet again these illegal settlers. Not expressed in so many words in the exchange of letters is the means of financing the plan's goal to take care of these 7,500 Gaza settlers and the 500 to be evacuated (at some future date) from four minor outposts in the West Bank. However, we do get a preview of who will be paying for that in Bush's letter to Sharon: "We also understand that . . . Israel believes it is important to bring new opportunities to the Negev and the Galilee." Who but the American taxpayers would be anxious to finance these new "opportunities" in the desert?

The United States for its part in these letters does promise to deal with the vanquished Palestinians – but only *after* the Palestinians have a new leadership *acceptable* to the US *and* Israel; and only after the Palestinians have learned to *behave* themselves; and then only after they have become a **peaceful**, progressive and democratic society. Likewise, Sharon promises to deal with the

Palestinians and help in developing a **peaceful** Palestinian state. The emphasis always in all these promises is on the world "peaceful," as in the "pacified" towns and villages of Korea and Vietnam, and now Iraq.

The Prime Minister's message to his fellow Ministers also advised them that the Security Fence (the Barrier, as called by others) would continue to be built "in accordance with the decisions of the government." This means that Bush had agreed that Israel could include on the Israeli side of the Barrier as much of the West Bank as it wanted for "security" purposes to ward off "terrorists," provided only that Israel designate the Barrier as "temporary." This "temporary" is the same term used by the Israelis when they confiscate Palestinian lands. By Israeli law (Israel prides itself on pretending to be a democratic country and subject to the rule of law) the taking for security purposes is temporary only, meaning for a 5 year period. Of course there is no restriction on how often this 5 year period could be renewed and, in fact, on some older confiscations so far it has been renewed repeatedly. Eternity could be divided, if necessary, into 5 year periods. Again, all the right words used — to get to the wrong result.

As for assassinations, Sharon's and Bush's letters and the Sharon letter to his Ministers are silent. But silence is often as frightening as the roar of a tiger. This meeting was followed promptly by the assassination of Abdel Aziz Rantisi upon Sharon's return to Israel. Are we supposed to believe that Sharon did not clear this with Bush the day before? The international community again condemned this illegal killing (various international treaties prohibit extra-judicial killings), but the United States limited itself to *warning the Palestinians* not to over-react. What possibly could qualify as an "over reaction" to the killing of their leaders, their sub-leaders and their sub-sub-leaders and dozens of innocent bystanders and the wounding of hundreds in these targeted killings? Could Bush and Sharon, and those like them, be blind to the truth expressed by Alexander Solzhenitsyn:

> *"You only have power over people so long as you don't take everything away from them. But when you're robbed a man of everything, he's no longer in your power – he's free again."*

Free people, of course, with nothing to lose, always make trouble.

IV

THE SHARON/BUSH WITHDRAWAL FROM GAZA – STEP ONE THE HOLOCAUST OR THE NAKBA

The old woman on the TV screen, crawling on her hands and knees, reminded Yosef Lapid, himself already 71, of his own grandmother. The woman, dressed in black, was searching for her

medicine through the debris of her bulldozed home in Rafah, Gaza. Lapid's grandmother had died in a German concentration camp some 60 years earlier. *These are war crimes*, he thought, *and the world will think we are monsters. . . . There will be no forgiveness.*

(Photo: *Al Jazeeza*, May 2004)

The next day Lapid shared his thoughts with his colleagues at work – and then all hell broke loose over his head. Yosef Lapid was the Justice Minister in Ariel Sharon's Cabinet. His colleagues were Sharon and his other Ministers.

Everyone at the meeting understood the veiled reference to the Holocaust – a taboo subject in Israeli politics. Health Minister Dan Naveh told Israeli Army Radio that the reference to the Holocaust was unmistakable and was "not a legitimate analogy."

"Unacceptable," shouted Sharon, who was joined by Finance Minister Benjamin Netanyahu in demanding that Lapid retract his comments. Yet the Justice Minister went on, speaking over the uproar. "The demolition of houses in Rafah must stop. It is not humane, not Jewish, and causes us grave damage in the world." (Haaretz Daily, May 23, 2004.) Lapid said he did not intend to compare the Israeli demolition campaign in Rafah to the Germans, but "when you see an old woman, you think of your grandmother." Israel that week had been on a punitive expedition in Gaza to avenge the killing of 13 soldiers who themselves had been in Gaza as part of an earlier force demolishing 200 homes in the Block O neighborhood of Gaza.

While Lapid was reminded of his grandmother, there were other scenes on the TV that week which would remind viewers of their own children. Three and four year old children were being shot down by Israeli snipers for sneaking out during curfew in Rafah to buy candy or play with friends; a 12 and 14 year old brother and sister were shot in their heads by snipers while hanging out laundry on their balcony. The Colonel leading Operation Rainbow, as it was called, identified only as a "Colonel Erez," sought to justify killing *anyone* who opened his or her door in Tel al-Sultan during the weeklong 24 hour curfew.

> *Someone who exits is obviously someone who is looking for trouble, someone who's looking to carry out a terrorist attack, and therefore they are legitimate targets.*
> (<u>New York Times</u>, May 20, 2004.)

The three or five year old girl shot in the head, Rawam Abu Zaed, according to her family had just opened her front door when the sniper caught her with two bullets, one in the head and one in the neck (<u>Haaretz Daily</u>, May 22, 2004).

The Israeli Defense Forces adamantly denied that their snipers would put a child in their crosshairs, and suggested instead that these deaths had been caused by the terrorist Palestinians themselves with their own booby traps and planted bombs.

As it happened, these same reporters, however, were able to actually find the bodies of these children in makeshift morgues. While the Muslin religion called for immediate burial, these children could not be buried because their families were still pinned down in their homes by a 24 hour curfew imposed by the Israeli Army. Thus their bodies were being stored in refrigerators that had previously served as flower and vegetable coolers. The reporters got to the bodies of these children, had them identified, and confirmed that they had been killed by bullets into their heads and necks – snipers, and not explosions. (Guardian (GB) May 21, 2004; The Observer (GB), May 23, 2004; New York Times, May 23, 2004). An Israeli sniper, looking through his powerful telescope, could not mistake a five year old girl for anything other than a five year old girl. These facts, as described by the Western reporters who this time were fortuitously on the scene, verified what human watch groups and other reporters had been told by the relatives of the children, and contradicted the accounts given by the IDF.

This was an unusual news event, as in normal course the Western Press had to rely solely on the statements of the IDF as to what was happening in the "Combat Zones." It serves as a warning about taking IDF statements without a graim of salt.

The Israelis had surrounded the town of Tel al-Sultan, with a population of 25,000 on the outskirts of Rafah, after cutting off Rafah itself from the rest of Gaza with a long line of tanks, bulldozers and armored vehicles straight across the width of Gaza. At Midnight

Sunday, May 16/17 the residents were stunned by bright lights, flares and the announcement on loudspeakers that their town was being declared a "Combat Zone" by the Israeli Army; that a 24 hour curfew was being imposed; and that *anyone* leaving his or her home would be killed. The water and electricity to the residents were cut off. Patrols took over the tallest buildings in town, broke holes in the concrete walls near the top of the buildings and set up their sniper nests.

For the next week the residents of Tel al-Sultan, a quiet community that would offer little resistance, were locked in their homes, without water or electricity. To show they meant business, during the next week Israeli snipers shot at anything moving in Tel al-Sultan, including three year old Rawam Mohammed Abu Zaed as she left home to buy some candy (<u>Haaretz Daily</u>, May 22, 2004).

What could serve as a better lesson to the natives than shooting down children in cold blood? At around the same time another child, three year old Samer al-Arja "died from shock when IDF tanks fired shells at a residential building" (<u>Jerusalem Post</u>, May 21, 2004).

Sixty to 100 homes were bulldozed – in addition to the 200 homes demolished in Gaza the week before. Children were gunned down in peaceful demonstrations by fire from Israeli tanks and helicopters. Chaos and bedlam was the order of the day. STEP ONE in the "evacuation" of Gaza.

President George Bush and Prime Minister Ariel Sharon had agreed on a program at their meeting in April. The details had been laboriously worked out over many months by Sharon for the Israelis and Elliott Abrams in the State Department for the United States. Bush, in accordance with his mantra policy on the Middle East, "Israel is entitled to defend itself," signed off on the plan. In the plan it was stated:

> *Israel will continue to maintain a military presence along the length of the border line* [4.50 miles] *between the Gaza Strip and Egypt (The Philadelphi Corridor). This military presence is an essential security presence. In certain areas, it may be necessary to physically enlarge the area in which military operations are conducted. . . .*

One has to assume that during the months of negotiations between Sharon and Abrams that each side had explained fully every element laid out in the written plan. This particular component would call for Israel, in the first stage (itself an indefinite length of time) to maintain a presence in the Philadelphi Corridor and in fact would have to "physically enlarge the area." What did it mean to the negotiators that the area in Gaza on the Egyptian border would have to be enlarged? As it happened, the Israelis already had a 2 year old proposal calling for widening the four and a half mile Gaza/Egyptian border (the "pink" zone or the Philadelphi Corridor) by another 250 or 350 feet. This must have been disclosed to the Bush were leveled with no compensation. The fear felt by the residents for the Israeli Forces was so great that when the Army announced on May 16th that it would begin demolitions, hundreds of frightened families packed up, abandoned their homes and took to the roads.

The first wave of Israeli troops and bulldozers entering the Rafah area caused the deaths of 19 Palestinians, most of them innocent civilians. Human Rights groups, the UN, the European Union and many other nations called the punitive expedition an outrage and against international law. Not so the United States, whose officials either remained silent or spoke the magic words: "Israel has a right to defend itself."

The one official who did take to the podium, however, in actually trying to capitalize on the slaughter was none other than the President himself. On the very day after the incursion resulting in the 19 deaths, and after reports of them had reached Washington, Bush delivered a rousing speech to an Israeli lobbying group, AIPAC or the American Information Pubic Affairs Committee. To raucous shouts of "Four More Years" he presented an over-the-top speech in support of whatever Israel was doing. His speech was interrupted 67 times by thunderous applause. Sharon, he said, was doing no more than fighting terrorism, just as the United States was doing. The fault lay in the intransigence of the Palestinians. "Again and again, Israel has defended itself with skill and heroism. . . . Israel is a democracy and a friend, and has every right to defend itself from terror" (New York Times, May 19, 2004). The President of the United States thought that the Israeli incursion, killings of innocents and home demolitions were "skillful and heroic." Yosef Lapid thought it was monstrous, unforgivable and a war crime. The President's political opponent, Senator John Kerry, for his part found it simply impossible to trump Bush on support for Israel, so he just kept quiet.

Bush's approval of the mayhem in Gaza contrasted sharply with the reaction of the rest of the world. Javier Solana, the European Union's high Representative issued a statement: "I am deeply distressed by the recent Israeli action in Gaza which appears to have left a large number of casualties among Palestinian civilians, including children. I condemn such indiscriminate action. The steadily mounting death toll and the continuing destruction of houses in Gaza cannot but disturb . . . ." (European Union Press Release, May 19, 2004). Equally forceful was Ireland's Foreign Minister, Brian Cowen, who spoke for the European Union as its President: "It is clear the [Israeli] action was completely disproportionate . . . and that Israeli forces showed a reckless disregard for human life. . . . I would once again remind Israel, the occupying power, that the Fourth Geneva Convention . . . is fully applicable to the Gaza Strip" (Jerusalem Post, May 20, 2004).

Analysts speculated that this movement into Tel al-Sultan, until then a relatively quiet community compared to the town of Rafah itself, was intended to lure out the militants from Rafah so the snipers would have better shots at them. Overall, it was a program to soften up the Palestinians and cower them for the more serious business of massive house demolitions. The Palestinians might get it into their heads that they should resist the planned destruction of another 2,000 homes in a densely populated neighborhood. Hence, the need to reduce the population to fear and trembling before the wholesale demolition itself in the pink zone.

Besides the pictures of bloody children being dragged out of demolished buildings, the wantonness of the Israeli punishment of the civilians was best symbolized by the mangled bodies of the animals at a zoo gratuitously destroyed by the IDF.

Dead ostriches, ducks, snakes, monkeys and such were all that was left of Muhammad Juma's little zoo. When he had seen the Israeli tanks and bulldozers coming, he assumed that they had made a mistake, and once realizing it was just a zoo, they would stop. But they did not. He watched from a window of his nearby house as the tanks and bulldozers crashed through the gates, broke down the walls, dug up the ground and climbed up over cages and crushed everything before them. Juma showed reporters the bodies of some of his animals, a few birds that had survived and a terrorized kangaroo hiding in the basement. The rest of his 80 animals, monkeys, birds, etc. were gone or dead. A military spokeswoman, Maj. Sharon Feingold, said that the army had to go through the zoo as the Palestinians had blocked the intended road. Since the zoo was being destroyed anyway, the troops released the animals for their own safety so they would not be in a combat zone (Guardian (G.B.), May 22, 2004; New York Times, May 22, 2004).

The person appointed by the UN to oversee refugee relief in Gaza, Peter Hansen, called these activities "war crimes." The independent organizations that concerned themselves with these matters, like Amnesty International, also declared the house demolitions as war crimes and in every respect violations of international law. Israeli human rights groups, like B'Tselem filed petitions, vainly, with the Government and with the Israeli courts to stop the demolitions.

But then the Israelis took that extra step — they went too far. At the same time the Americans suddenly found themselves besieged by revelations of torture and humiliations of prisoners at Abu Ghraib and a bombing of an Iraqi wedding party resulting in 40 deaths. The front pages of the newspapers had competing photos of naked Iraqi prisoners piled up in a pyramid like so much dirt, and Israeli bulldozers piling up the debris of Palestinian homes.

Assuming they had the Americans boxed in, particularly during this election year, the Israelis began to engage in the open slaughter of citizens while the world watched on TV. During a demonstration of 3,000 Palestinians against the curfew at Tel al-

Sultan and al-Brazil, the Israelis fired on men, woman and children demonstrators with tank fire, machine guns and helicopters. Ten people were killed, half of them children. Dozens were wounded. New international condemnations ensued. Bush was asked about the killings, and declined to comment until he had heard more details from the Israelis. But the rest of the international community did not need to hear anything else from the Israelis, it had all happened on TV and was witnessed by reporters and human rights groups. The Israelis tried to claim that there were armed gunmen among the marchers, and the Israeli Delegate at the UN even said there were — but the actual films of the demonstration and the numerous outside witnesses, including the UN's Peter Hansen, gave the lie to these claims.

Finally, in the UN that afternoon the issue was joined. While delegates were demanding that a Resolution be passed to stop the Israeli onslaught, the Bush Administration was itself under siege by public opinion because of the Iraqi prisoners scandal and the bombing of the wedding party. The decision was made to step back a bit and get some distance from the Israelis. In any event it would have been difficult to argue against a Resolution demanding that Israel stop killing woman and children and making additional thousands homeless. The Resolution (No. 1544) condemning Israel's activities in Rafah and its plans for further demolitions passed unanimously, with the United States quietly abstaining. This was the first time in years that the US had withheld its veto and allowed a Resolution critical of Israel to pass. Israel had gone too far, and the Americans were momentarily distracted.

Apparently the US abstention was enough to make the Israeli Government hesitate. It put a temporary halt to its plans for demolishing another 2,000 homes in Rafah to widen the Philadelphi Corridor. On Monday, May 24th, it pulled its troops, tanks and bulldozers to the borders of Gaza, though warning on the Army Radio that this was just to re-energize the troops and that the Palestinians "can't breathe easy yet."

As the Israelis pulled out, the 25,000 residents of the Tel al-Sultan district finally were able to leave their homes without risk of being shot. They immediately gathered by the thousands in a soccer field to bury 16 victims of the Israeli incursion. These 16 had been kept in a vegetable refrigerator during the week as their relatives could not comply with their religious custom of prompt burial.

The other immediate task that the newly freed residents attended to was to salvage what they could of their crops. Reporters noted dozens of people crawling through what once had been gardens and groves trying to unearth vegetables that had been buried by Israeli tanks and bulldozers.

These two scenes alone gave substance to the term "wanton" that had been used all week by the UN Commissioner General for the Palestinian refugee camps, Peter Hansen. He had seen the demonstrators shot down. He had heard the snipers who had killed the children. He had seen the rows and rows of homes bulldozed by the Israelis on the pretext of searching for militants. Electric, sewer and water connections had been destroyed in addition to the roads and homes. Thousands upon thousands of newly homeless people now swarmed out of the embattled neighborhoods seeking shelter. Peter Hansen declared that these scenes of collective punishment indeed put Israel "in grave breach of international law."

The Israelis, though, were having some fun in their perch of power over the defenseless civilians. Why, said one legislator, we are being about as careful with the civilians as the Americans were in Iraq. Another Minister suggested that the displaced Palestinians be provided with substitute pre-fabricated houses – but in Canada or some other such country.

While every American schoolchild is familiar with the Holocaust, most have not heard of the NAKBA. This was the word on the lips of many Arabs around the world as they watched the wholesale abandonment of homes by the Palestinians in Rafah upon the approach of the Israeli tanks and bulldozers. It was in 1948 when the roads were filled with hundreds of thousands of Palestinians fleeing their homes before the forces of the Israelis. Now in 2004 the children and the grandchildren of those refugees had become refugees again at the hands of the Israelis. (Meron Benvenisti, "An Old Refrain That Stabs the Heart," Guardian (G.B.) May 22, 2004). It was all back to the beginning as if nothing had been learned, and with no end in sight.

The survivors of this incursion into Rafah would have the most excellent chance for recovering in US lawsuits. The family of those 3 and 4 year olds who were killed, the owner of that private zoo in Ramah, and each of the others who suffered any loss during or before Operation Rainbow can seek redress in the US. Not only did the international community clearly define the calamity as a war crime, and an Israeli Minister called it such as well, but most importantly, the US had abstained from the UN Resolution condemning the destruction. A court would have a difficult time trying to find a way around such lawsuits – neither the facts nor the law would be in any doubt, nor could it resort to the expediency of calling the catastrophe a "political question" when even the US Government under George Bush would not touch this despicable and vile abuse of power.

Some potential targets or defendants of the lawsuits could be:
- the American companies that produced the bulldozers (Caterpillar Inc.) and the helicopters (Boeing Company) (the deepest pockets);
- the Government officials and top military leaders;
- the men and women of the
  - Givati Brigade;
  - Golani Brigade;
  - Beduin Desert Patrol;
  - Shin Bet;
- Armored Corps Brig. General Avigdor Klein;
- Brig. Gen. Shmuel Zakai (Gaza division commander: "none of them is starving");
- Colonel Fuli Mordechai and ;
- General Dan Harel (Chief of Israeli Southern Command).

44

Distr.: General 19 May 2004

Press Release

SC/8098

SECURITY COUNCIL CALLS ON ISRAEL TO STOP DEMOLITION OF PALESTINIAN HOMES

Resolution 1544 (2004) Adopted by Vote Of 14 in Favour to None Against, with 1 Abstention (United States)

The Security Council called on Israel this afternoon to respect its obligations under international humanitarian law, particularly the obligation not to undertake home demolitions contrary to that law.

Adopting Council resolution 1544 (2004), by a vote of 14 in favour, none against and 1 abstention (United States), the Council also expressed grave concern regarding the humanitarian situation of Palestinians made homeless in the Rafah area.

Reaffirming its support for the Road Map, the Council called on both parties to immediately implement their obligations under that plan.

Speaking after the Council action, the Observer for Palestine said today's slaughter of innocent Palestinian children by the Israeli occupying forces in the Rafah camp was the most recent and most telling illustration of the vicious and barbaric actions of the occupying Power. Since the beginning of May, the Israeli occupying forces had killed at least 96 Palestinians, including 28 children.

During the past several days, the occupying Power had escalated its unlawful practices in the Rafah area, particularly the Rafah refugee camp, causing excessive and vast damage. The humanitarian impact had been overwhelming. Declarations that hundreds more Palestinian homes in Rafah were targeted for demolition made it more clear than ever that Israel's aim was the effective levelling of the Rafah camp and areas in the city of Rafah itself.

Israel's representative said that several Palestinians had been killed during a large procession of several hundred demonstrators, including many gunmen, of whom four to five were armed terrorists. The demonstration had been organized by none other than the Palestinian Authority, in violation of the established curfew. While Israel regretted any loss of civilian life, terrorists operated among civilians in Gaza, and tragedy could strike. Israel had done, and would continue to do, everything possible to prevent harm to innocent civilians.

The one-sided draft resolution rebuked Israel, but failed to expressly condemn the Palestinian terrorism that had necessitated Israeli action, he said. Meanwhile, the Council had never dealt with the dangers of arms smuggling through the tunnel of Rafah from Egypt. "Today, Israel stands at the gates of hell in the Gaza Strip", he said. The Rafah tunnels were typically dug inside residential homes to evade discovery, concealed under bathrooms, living rooms and kitchens; intentionally hidden under children's beds; and concealed by loose planks and rags. Since April, the Israeli Defence Forces had exposed eight underground tunnels used for smuggling weapons.

Following the vote, the representative of the United States said that his Government had urged the Israeli Government to exercise maximum restraint. However, Palestinian terrorists had been smuggling weapons through Gaza, and the Palestinian Authority had not taken sufficient action to halt those activities. The Government of Israel, as well as those of neighbouring States, must strive to provide the best conditions on the ground to halt the violence.

The representative of Algeria, one of the sponsors of the text, said the Council today had been united in rejecting the scandalous conduct of Israel and had decided to send it a strong signal. It could not continue to flout the Council's authority and the norms of international law with impunity.

Also addressing the Council this afternoon were the representatives of the Russian Federation, France, China, Romania, Spain and Pakistan.

The meeting began at 5:26 p.m. and adjourned at 6:38 p.m.

The Security Council met this afternoon to discuss the situation in the Middle East, including the Palestinian question.

The Council was meeting in response to the request contained in a letter dated 17 May from the Permanent Representative of Yemen (document S/20041393). Council members had before them a text of a draft resolution submitted by Algeria and Yemen (document S12004/400), as well as identical letters addressed to the Secretary-General and the Council President (document S/20041394).

Action on-Draft-Resolution

The draft resolution was adopted by a vote of 14 in favour to none against, with 1 abstention (United States).

Speaking after the vote, ABDALLAH BAALI (Algeria) said he welcomed the adoption by the Council of a resolution on the situation in the Palestinian territory. It unambiguously condemned the actions in Rafah, where tens of unarmed civilians, including many children, had fallen under the fire and missiles of the Israeli army in barbaric acts condemned throughout the world. He also welcomed the fact that the Council was expressing grave concern regarding the large-scale demolition of homes, in flagrant violation of international law and the Geneva Conventions.

He said he was particularly pleased that the Council today had been united in rejecting the scandalous conduct of Israel and had decided to send it a strong signal. It could not continue to flout the authority and norms of international law with impunity. The international community now was expecting that Israel should abide by its will and end the destruction and provocation against Palestinians and, in good faith, abide by its commitments as laid down in the Road Map, under which it had been called upon to take a series of steps.

Equally important was for Israel to immediately cease its military operations in Rafah and withdraw its troops without further delay, he said. After today's butchering, Israel would be well counselled to heed the voice of reason just this time. Today's action by the Council demonstrated its ability to meet its responsibilities and respond to the expectations of the international community.

JAMES CUNNINGHAM (United States) said that the Government of Israel had expressed its deep regret for the deaths. The United States had urged the Israeli Government to exercise maximum restraint. That Government, as well as those of neighbouring States, must strive to provide the best conditions on the ground to halt the violence.

He said that Palestinian terrorists had been smuggling weapons through Gaza and that the Palestinian Authority had not taken sufficient action to halt those activities.

ALEXANDER KONUZIN (Russian Federation) expressed support for the text, saying that his delegation was guided by fundamental principles. Russia was concerned by the latest upsurge of violence, which continued to kill innocent civilians, including women and children. Innocent victims were being subjected to collective punishment.

Lasting peace could be achieved only through negotiations based on the relevant Security Council resolutions, he said. Israel must bring its actions in line with the Road Map, which it had itself approved. While Israel had the right to security, it must adhere to the Geneva Conventions. There must be an immediate and mutual end to the violence, however difficult that might be.

MICHEL DUCLOS (France) said he voted in favour of the resolution because it seemed an appeal to reason and restraint, as had already been done by the European Union and the Secretary-General. France was dismayed by the recent violence and expressed its sympathy to the civilian population affected by the Israeli military operations.

He said his country and the European Union had condemned the large-scale demolition of Palestinian homes in Rafah, which was disproportionate and contrary to international law and the obligations of Israel under the Road Map. Similarly, France expected from the Palestinian Authority that it carry out more determined action for security, with particular regard to the campaign against terrorism. The destruction of homes and the military operations must cease immediately. A ceasefire was urgent, and that included all parties and groups. Also urgent, without delay, was for the Palestinians and the Israeli Government to implement their obligations under the Road Map.

CHENG JINGYE (China) had been surprised at the Israeli large-scale demolition of Palestinian homes. That practice violated international law. He also condemned the Israeli military actions, which had caused heavy civilian casualties in Gaza. Those actions taken by the Israelis would only aggravate the already worsening situation in the Middle East and in no way help the resumption of peace talks. He urged Israel to halt immediately such actions and return to the path of political settlement. Based on that position, China had supported the draft resolution.

He appealed, once again, to the Israelis and Palestinians to cease the vicious cycle of violence and resume contacts and dialogue as soon as possible, and implement the relevant obligations under the Road Map. The international community should intensify efforts to push through a speedy resumption of its implementation. The Chinese Government and people had deep sympathy for the sufferings of the Palestinian people and were ready to provide them with the appropriate humanitarian assistance.

MIHNEA MOTOC (Romania) said that the evolution of the situation had been marked and confirmed by the escalating violence. All actions to fight terror must be taken in accordance with international law. Romania encouraged both parties to declare a ceasefire and seek the way of negotiations.

YANEZ BARNUEVO (Spain) said that the vote on the resolution had been a speedy, united and balanced action on the part of the Security Council in light of the recent situation in Gaza, which imperilled the entire peace process.

Spain had followed the situation with deep alarm, he said. The actions carried out today had serious consequences, and the Spanish Government had no alternative but to condemn the demolition of Palestinian homes. At the same time, Spain recognized the right of the State of Israel to self-defence. However, the use of force would not speed the road to that security. Negotiations were the only way.

MUNIR AKRAM (Pakistan), Council President, speaking in his national capacity, said he voted for the resolution, which was the minimum necessary response to the Israeli military incursions in Rafah, which had left scores of Palestinian civilians dead or injured. Pakistan condemned those actions. The blatant attack on demonstrators today was the latest violation of international humanitarian law, especially Israel's obligations as an occupying Power under the Geneva Conventions. Silence at that critical juncture was not an option for the Council. It was, therefore, a matter of some satisfaction that it had at last been able to pronounce itself on the continued violations of international law and humanitarian norms in the occupied Palestinian territories.

Unfortunately, in Palestine, as in certain other parts of the world, the legitimate campaign to root out terrorism had been abused by the occupying Power to suppress the legitimate right of peoples to self-determination. Peace in the holy land, as elsewhere, could not be established merely by imposing a "fait accompli" on the weaker party. The Israeli actions were bound to cause further deterioration in the security situation, which was already volatile, due to the continued Israeli occupation of Arab territories. Those actions would already further aggravate the humanitarian situation there, particularly in Gaza.

The ability of the Security Council and the international community to bring durable peace to Palestine and the Middle East on the basis of the Council's resolutions and the Quartet's Road Map could produce positive results throughout the Arab and Islamic world. Failure to do so would further intensify the frustration and anger among Arab and Islamic peoples, increase insecurity and instability in the entire region, and escalate support for terrorism and extremism.

NASSER AL-KIDWA, Observer for Palestine, said that the slaughter today of innocent Palestinian children by the Israeli occupying forces in the Rafah camp was the most recent and most telling illustration of the vicious and barbaric actions of the occupying Power. Since the beginning of May, the Israeli occupying forces had killed at least 96 Palestinians, including 28 children. Palestinians and emergency rescue personnel, poorly equipped and in desperate need of supplies, had been unable to keep up with the rising number of casualties.

In addition to the human loss and devastation, Israel continued to pursue its illegal and inhumane practice of destroying Palestinian homes and properties, causing widespread destruction and material loss and compounding the grief, suffering and humanitarian hardships of the Palestinian people.

He said that during the past several days, the occupying Power had escalated those unlawful practices in the Rafah area, including particularly the Rafah refugee camp, causing excessive and vast damage. The humanitarian impact had been overwhelming.

With the ongoing military operation carried out by Israel, and the declarations that hundreds more Palestinian homes in Rafah were targeted for demolition, he said, it was more clear than ever that the aim of the Israeli actions was the effective levelling of the Rafah camp and areas in the city of Rafah itself. Indeed, some of the statements made by Israeli officials were starkly clear about that very intention.

DAN GILLERMAN (Israel) said the Council had convened at the urgent behest of the Palestinian Observer, under a barrage of information, misinformation and disinformation. The numbers distributed by the Palestinians were exaggerated and totally false. He was disappointed that some members of the international community, including in the statement attributed to the Secretary-General, had been misled by the Palestinian propaganda machine, resulting in false conclusions, which did not reflect the facts on the ground.

He said that, during a large procession of several hundred demonstrators, which included many gunmen, several Palestinians had been killed, of which four to five were armed terrorists. The incident had occurred as the crowd left central Rafah along the main road towards Israeli Defense Forces in Tel-Sultan. The demonstration had been organized by none other than the Palestinian Authority, in violation of the established curfew.

While Israel regretted any loss of civilian life, those numbers put into proportion today's incident, which itself had taken place under conditions of heavy fighting by Palestinian terrorists, he said. Under the incredibly difficult circumstances in which Israel had taken action against the terrorist infrastructure in the Gaza Strip, terrorists operated among civilians and tragedy could strike.

He said his country had done and would continue to do everything it could to prevent harm to innocent civilians. Even during times of war, the death of innocent civilians was regrettable, but "we cannot be deluded by false pretense and any ambiguity between the terrorists and those who fight this deplorable scourge", he stressed.

Regrettably, certain Council members had been galvanized to condemn Israel's response to the ongoing Palestinian terrorist campaign, and not those actions that had brought the region to despair and compelled Israel to take defensive measures, he said. The one-sided text rebuked Israel, but failed to expressly condemn the Palestinian terrorism that necessitated Israeli action.

Meanwhile, he said, the Council had never dealt with the dangers to peace and security of smuggling arms through the tunnel of Rafah from Egypt. It had not met to condemn the horrendous desecration of the bodies of Israeli soldiers - young men who had been killed during a defensive operation to dismantle those tunnels. Nor had it come together following the hijacking of a United Nations Relief and Works Agency for Palestine Refugees in the Near East (UNRWA) ambulance by armed elements in Gaza last week. Neither had it stood up against the murder of a mother and her four daughters in the Gaza Strip or the continuing cultivation of a culture of hate and destruction by the Palestinian leadership.

He said that the Council would not serve the cause of peace in the Middle East by condemning Israeli actions and ignoring the violence, terrorism, and incitement that continued to emanate from the Palestinian leadership. Such repeated rituals emboldened the terrorists and not those who sought to dismantle it.

"Today, Israel stands at the gates of hell in the Gaza Strip", he said. The southern city of Rafah served as the "Arms Smuggling Gateway" of the Palestinian Authority and the main pipeline for transporting weapons and ammunition into Gaza. Since September 2000, subterranean tunnels, constructed underneath the "Philadelphia Route", had been used by Iran and Hezbollah, as well as by Palestinian terrorist organizations like Hamas and the PFLP, for turning the Gaza Strip into a base for missile and rocket attacks against Israeli targets.

He said that those "tunnels of terror" provided the conduit for the smuggling of large amounts of diverse weapons, among them hundreds of kilograms of explosives, hundreds of rifles, tens of thousands of rounds of ammunition and dozens of RPG rockets and launchers, which were entirely incompatible with signed agreements and any plan to return to non-violent negotiations. The smuggling of massive arsenals and weapons was of epidemic proportions, and the cynical use of civilian areas to launch terrorist attacks, invariably led to the loss of innocent life and affected the basic right of people to lead their lives in peace.

Faced with the failure of the Palestinian leadership to comply with its obligations to fight terrorism, stop incitement and prevent weapons smuggling, Israel remained obligated to act in self defence against a threat that posed a clear and present danger to innocent lives, while upholding its obligations under international law, he said. The purpose of the Israeli Defence Forces action in Gaza was to terminate the transfer of all illegal weapons by underground tunnels to Gaza. One security measure employed in that regard was the demolition of structures that posed an operative security risk to Israeli forces.

He said that if Israel did not act today to fight against the weapons smuggled and manufactured in Gaza, next month Katyusha rockets would be aimed at the homes of its citizens.

The Rafah tunnels were typically dug inside residential homes to evade discovery by Israeli security personnel, he explained. Those were concealed under bathrooms, living rooms and kitchens, and were intentionally hidden under the children's beds, concealed by loose planks and rags. Since April, the Israeli Defence Forces had exposed eight underground tunnels used for smuggling weapons in the area of Rafah, in addition to 11 underground tunnels since the beginning of the year, and 90 underground tunnels since the beginning of the intifada in September 2000. Just this week, Israeli forces discovered a new tunnel in Rafah already activated for use in smuggling arms into Gaza. The tunnel was 150 metres long, five metres deep and had four openings that led directly into Palestinian homes in the area.

United Nations

S/PV.4972

SPECIAL RAPPORTEUR ON OCCUPIED TERRITORIES "HORRIFIED" AT ISRAELI ACTION IN GAZA

Thursday, May 20th, 2004 UNHCHR

The Special Rapporteur of the Commission on Human Rights on the situation of human rights in the Palestinian territory occupied by Israel since 1967, John Dugard, today made the following statement

"The Special Rapporteur of the Commission on Human Rights on the situation of human rights in the Palestinian territory occupied by Israel since 1967 wishes to add his voice to those who have expressed their horror and concern about Israeli military action in Gaza and in particular in Rafah. Conservative estimates show that 2,200 persons have lost their homes following the demolition of 191 homes in Gaza since the beginning of May. Over 30 Palestinians have been killed and hundreds injured. The refugees of Rafah are once more having to seek refuge in temporary structures. These actions constitute a violation of international humanitarian law and constitute war crimes under Article 147 of the Geneva Convention relative to the Protection of Civilian Persons in Time of War, of 12 August 1949 (Fourth Geneva Convention). They also amount to collective punishment which violates both humanitarian law and international human rights law. It is impossible to accept the Israeli argument that these actions are justified by military necessity. On the contrary, in the language of Article 147 of the Fourth Geneva Convention, they are "carried out unlawfully and wantonly".

In the first instance, the Special Rapporteur calls upon the Government of Israel to desist from such activity and to observe its international obligations. The Special Rapporteur also calls on the Security Council to take appropriate action to stop the violence, if necessary by the imposition of mandatory arms embargo on Israel of the kind that was imposed on South Africa in 1977.

The Special Rapporteur reminds Members of the Security Council in general and the Permanent Members of the Security Council in particular of their obligations to take action to restore international peace and security in the region. The Special Rapporteur sees no reason why an arms embargo should not be an appropriate measure. The Special Rapporteur is aware of the tendency of some Member States to use the veto in all action affecting Israel. In this respect, they repeat the behaviour of Permanent Members in respect of South Africa before 1977. The Special Rapporteur urgently calls on all Member States of the Security Council to behave responsibly, in accordance with their international obligations, and not to allow domestic political considerations to undermine their international obligations".

AI INDEX: MDE 15/054/2004 21 May 2004

AMNESTY INTERNATIONAL

Public Statement

AI

Israel/Occupied Territories: Call for independent investigation into Rafah killings

Amnesty International urges the Israeli authorities to promptly carry out a thorough and independent investigation into the killing of eight Palestinians, four of them children, and the injury of dozens of others by the Israeli army during a demonstration in the southern Gaza Strip town of Rafah, on 19 May 2004.

Amnesty International delegates were in the vicinity of the demonstration at the time of the incident. They saw Israeli army helicopters hovering over the area where the demonstration was taking place, dropping what appeared to be flares; shortly after they heard several rounds of heavy shelling.

Demonstrators and eyewitnesses claim that the loss of life and injuries were caused by shelling from Israeli army helicopters and tanks stationed nearby. According to Israeli army officials, tanks shelled an empty building in order to deter the demonstrators from proceeding towards Israeli army positions;they also state that Israeli helicopters fired a missile at a nearby open space.

The Israeli shelling hit a built-up area on Sea Street, the main east-west road in Rafah, where the Palestinian demonstrators were walking. An Israeli army aerial photograph published in the Israeli media shows that the building at which the tank shelling was aimed is located in a built-up area on the street where the demonstrators were marching.

Israeli officials have alleged that the demonstrators were led by gunmen. While Amnesty International cannot confirm or deny the presence of armed Palestinians among the demonstrators, the organization's delegates did not see any armed men when they passed the demonstration prior to the attack. In addition, they did not hear any Palestinian fire prior to or following the Israeli army shelling. Furthermore, the footage from television crews who filmed the demonstration prior to, during and after the shelling, reviewed by Amnesty International's delegates, does not show armed individuals in the demonstration.

Based on information available, Amnesty International is concerned that the means and methods used by the Israeli army during a non-violent demonstration in a built-up area, which resulted in the loss of life and injuries to Palestinians, were excessive and violated international law.

In light of a pattern of inadequate investigations or lack of investigations into unlawful killings and excessive use of force by the Israeli security forces resulting in death or injury to Palestinians, it is imperative that a thorough and independent investigation be promptly carried out by the Israeli judicial authorities. The scope, methods and findings of the investigation must be made public and those responsible for human rights violations must be brought to justice.

AMNESTY INTERNATIONAL

PRESS RELEASE

Israel and the Occupied Territories: Evictions and demolitions must stop.

Israel's unjustified destruction of thousands of Palestinian and Arab Israeli homes as well as vast areas of agricultural land has reached an unprecedented level and must stop immediately, Amnesty International said today.

Over the last three and a half years, Israeli armed forces have demolished more than 3,000 homes, leaving tens of thousands of men, women and children homeless or without a livelihood.

In a report released today — Israel and the Occupied Territories. Under the rubble: House demolition and destruction of land and property — Amnesty International said:

"The grounds invoked by Israel to justify the destruction are overly broad and based on discriminatory policies and practices."

"The authorities gave us different justifications for refusing us the building permit. .. Each time we succeeded to challenge or disprove the reason they had given us for the refusal, our application was rejected on different grounds. We spent thousands of dollars on this process. In the end we understood that it was hopeless and we built our home without a permit. "

The home of Salim and 'Arabia Shawamreh in the village of 'Anata has been demolished four times and is now again under threat.

According to the United Nations, more than 2,000 homes in Gaza have been destroyed in the last three years and 10 percent of the agricultural land. In the West Bank, almost 90% of Israel's fence/wall is being built on occupied territory and at least 600 homes have been destroyed.

- In the Occupied Territories, demolitions are often carried out as collective punishments for Palestinian attacks or to facilitate the expansion of illegal Israeli settlements. Both practices contravene international law and some of these acts are war crimes.

- Discriminatory planning and building policies make it practically impossible for Israeli Arabs and Palestinians to obtain building permits.

- In Israel, the demolition of homes for lack of building permits in the Arab sector is a recurrent phenomenon, whereas demolition of homes without building permission in the Jewish sector is almost unheard of.

- Forced evictions and house demolitions are usually carried out without warning with families given little or no time to leave their homes and salvage their possessions.

- Most cases of house demolition and destruction of land are not subject to legal supervision or appeal.

Amnesty International is calling on Israel to halt all unlawful destruction of homes and land, including for the expansion of Israeli settlements and/or for the building of the fence/wall in the Occupied Territories.

The Palestinian Authority is called upon to take measures to prevent attacks by Palestinian armed groups on Israeli civilians.

Amnesty International is also pressing for other States, particularly the US, to stop the sale or transfer of weaponry and equipment that are used to commit unlawful destruction of homes and other human rights violations..

Israel   and   the   Occupied   Territories
Under the rubble: House demolition and destruction of land and
property. Executive Summary

INTRODUCTION

More than 3,000 homes, vast areas of agricultural land and hundreds
of other properties have been destroyed by the Israeli army and security
forces in Israel and the Occupied Territories in the past three and a half
years. Tens of thousands of men, women and children have been made
homeless or have lost their livelihood. Thousands of other houses have been
damaged, and tens of thousands of others are under threat of demolition,
their occupants living in fear of homelessness. House demolitions are usually
carried out without warning, often at night, and the occupants are forcibly
evicted with no time to salvage their belongings. Often the only warning is
the rumbling of the Israeli army's US-made Caterpillar bulldozers beginning
to tear down the walls of their homes. The victims are often amongst the
poorest and most disadvantaged. In most cases the justification given by the
Israeli authorities for the destruction is "military/security needs", while in
other cases it is the lack of building permits. The result is the same: families
are left homeless and destitute, forced to rely on relatives, friends and
humanitarian organizations for shelter and subsistence.

House demolition has been a long-standing policy in the Occupied
Territories and in the Arab sector in Israel. However, in the past three and
a half years the scale of the destruction has reached an unprecedented
level. The destruction of Palestinian homes, agricultural land and other
property in the Occupied Territories, is inextricably linked to Israel's long-
standing policy of appropriating as much as possible of the land it occupies,
notably by establishing Israeli settlements in violation of international law.
In Israel it is essentially the homes of Palestinian citizens of Israel (Israeli
Arabs) which are targeted for demolition. The phenomenon is linked to
the state's policy of large-scale confiscation of land, restrictive planning
regulations and discriminatory policies in the allocation of state land which
makes it difficult or impossible for Israeli Arabs to obtain building permits.

This document summarizes a 65-page report: Israel and the
Occupied Territories: Under the rubble: House demolition and
destruction of land and property (Al Index: MDE/15/033/2004, May
2004), which analyses the main patterns and trends of forced eviction,
house demolition and destruction of property by the Israeli army and
security forces in Israel and the Occupied Territories in the light of
international human rights and humanitarian law

PATTERNS AND IMPACT OF PROPERTY DESTRUCTION

The destruction of houses, land and other properties falls into two categories: houses built without a permit and houses, land and other properties which the Israeli authorities contend are destroyed for "military/security needs":

1 - Unlicensed houses: In the Arab sector in Israel demolition of houses for lack of building permits is a recurrent phenomenon, whereas house demolition in the Jewish sector is virtually unheard of. In the Occupied Territories it is also invariably Palestinian homes which are destroyed, while illegal Jewish settlements continue to be expanded.

2 - "Military/security needs": Most of the destruction in the Occupied Territories falls under this category. The scale of the destruction is massive, including more than 3,000 homes, large areas of cultivated land, hundreds of shops, workshops, factories and public buildings. Tens of thousands of other homes and properties have been damaged, many beyond repair. The Israeli army's criteria to define "military/security needs" are extremely broad. This category can be divided into four, at times overlapping, sub-categories:

A. Punitive demolitions of houses belonging to families of Palestinians known or suspected of involvement in suicide bombings and other attacks against Israeli civilians and soldiers have become routine, frequently resulting in neighbouring houses also being destroyed or damaged.

B. Houses, land, and other properties which the Israeli authorities claim it is necessary to destroy for "security needs", notably to build or expand roads or other infrastructure for the benefit or protection of Israeli settlers or soldiers.

C. The destruction of houses, land and other properties which the Israeli authorities contend were used or could be used by Palestinian armed groups to shoot or launch attacks against Israelis. This category, which the authorities often refer to as "preventive", is extremely broad and such demolitions are often also manifestly carried out in retaliation for Palestinian attacks and as a form of collective punishment on the inhabitants of the area. In some cases the destruction also serves the purpose of removing Palestinians from areas where Israel has a particular interest in seizing or consolidating control of the land and/or benefit Israeli settlements.

D. Properties which the Israeli army contends were destroyed in the course of combat activities.

Impact on the economic situation: In addition to the demolition of thousands of homes, the extensive destruction of agricultural land will continue to have severe repercussion on the Palestinian economy for many years to come. Agriculture was a major sector of the Palestinian economy, especially since most Palestinians who used to work in Israel have no longer been permitted to do so in recent years. The land on which trees and crops stood is now mostly inaccessible to Palestinian farmers. Even if Palestinians were allowed to resume farming the land which has been destroyed in recent years, it would take a long time and considerable resources for it to become productive again.

Impact on women: Families whose homes have been demolished often cannot afford a new home and have to rely on relatives or friends for shelter. Most Palestinian women do not work outside the home, which is their primary responsibility and the space which they feel is their own. Hence, they are more affected by the discomfort of living in someone else's space, where they can no longer take responsibility for the administration of the family space and activities.

"Women suffer immensely from forced eviction ... Domestic violence is higher in the precarious and often stressful situation of inadequate housing, especially before and during a forced eviction." Centre on Housing Rights and Evictions to the UN Commission on Human Rights, March 2003

The loss of privacy and space often causes increased tensions between family members, including an increase in domestic violence. In these circumstances women are less inclined to complain and seek redress because in the face of the loss of the family home their grievances may not be seen as a priority, and because the additional practical and financial difficulties caused by the destruction of their home make it more difficult to find a solution to their individual problem.

DESTRUCTION FOR "MILITARY/SECURITY NEEDS"

Punitive house demolition: The Israeli army has destroyed close to 500 homes of families of Palestinians known or suspected of involvement in suicide bombings or other attacks against Israeli civilians or soldiers since 2001, when Israel officially resumed punitive demolitions.(1) These houses are usually blown up, whereas for other types of demolitions the army generally uses bulldozers. The powerful explosive charges used by the army frequently result in nearby houses also being destroyed or seriously damaged in the process.

Noha Maqadmeh, a mother of 10 and nine months pregnant, was killed in her bed by the collapsing walls of her home in central Gaza Strip when the Israeli army blew up an adjacent house. Her husband and most of her children were injured and six other nearby houses were destroyed by the blast, leaving some 90 people homeless. Her husband told Amnesty International: "We were in bed, the children were asleep; the bedroom was the most sheltered room, at the back of the house... There was an explosion and walls collapsed on top of us. I pulled myself from under the rubble... I started to dig in the rubble with my hands; first I found my two little boys and my three-year-old girl. ... one by one we found the other children but my wife remained trapped under the rubble with our youngest daughter, who is two; she was holding her when the wall fell on her... "

The Israeli authorities claim that these demolitions are not intended as punishment, but rather to "deter" Palestinians from getting involved in attacks. Israel has never destroyed the homes of Israeli Jews who committed serious attacks, such as the murder of Prime Minister Rabin, or bomb attacks against Palestinians or Israeli Arabs. These punitive forced evictions and house demolitions are a flagrant form of collective punishment and violate a fundamental principle of international law, which stipulates that collective punishment is never permissible under any circumstances.

"Preventive" and "security" destruction: House demolition has been most extensive in the Gaza Strip, one of the most densely populated areas in the world. Since October 2000, close to 3,000 homes have been destroyed, most of them homes of refugees. According to the United Nations Relief and Works Agency (UNRWA) between October 2000 and October 2003, more than 2,150 homes were destroyed and more than 16,000 were damaged in the Gaza Strip. In the same period 600 other homes were destroyed in the West Bank. Much of the destruction has targeted the refugee camp in Rafah, in southern Gaza, where close to 1,000 homes have been destroyed and hundreds of others partially destroyed or seriously damaged.

From 10 to 13 October 2003, the Israeli army destroyed some 130 houses and damaged scores of others in Rafah refugee camp and nearby areas, making more than 1,200 Palestinians homeless, mostly children. The army stated that it had uncovered three tunnels used by Palestinians to smuggle weapons from Egypt. Suha'Abdallah, whose house was partially destroyed, told Amnesty International: "There was no tunnel or anything in our home, anyone can come and see for themselves; part of the house is still standing but it is not safe anymore. ... now what are we to do? Destroy the rest of the house ourselves so that it does not fall on anyone".

In the preceding six weeks some 50 other houses were also demolished in Rafah, leaving hundreds more Palestinians homeless.

"You have a very striking picture of people fleeing. But fleeing to where? If you're in Rafah, you can't go south because there is a border, you can't go west because there is an ocean, and you can't go north and you can't go east because there is nowhere to go. You can't get out of Gaza." : Peter Hansen, UNRWA Commissioner-General in October 2003.

Until the autumn of 2000 the first rows of houses in the refugee camp stood only meters from the border with Egypt. **Row after row of houses have since been destroyed, up to 300 meters, contrary to claims by the Israeli authorities that only houses used by Palestinians in attacks were targeted.** Already from the end of 2000 Palestinians living in the refugee camp told Amnesty International that Israeli soldiers had told them that many rows of houses would be destroyed. Statements by Israeli officials indicate that this was indeed the intention. Major-General Yom Tov Samiah, the then Commander of Israeli army Southern Command, in the wake of the destruction of some 60 Palestinian homes in Rafah refugee camp on 9 and 10 January 2002, told Israeli Radio: "These houses should have been demolished and evacuated a long time ago... Three hundred meters of the Strip along the two sides of the border must be evacuated... Three hundred meters, no matter how many houses, period. "(2)

The Israeli army also destroyed hundreds of non-refugee homes and other properties and vast areas of cultivated land throughout the Gaza Strip. More than 10% of Gaza's agricultural land has been destroyed in the past three and a half years. According to the UN Office for the Coordinator of Humanitarian Affairs (OCHA) more than 1,800 acres of agricultural land were destroyed and more than 226,000 trees were uprooted in the Gaza Strip in 2002 and 2003 alone.(3) Agricultural infrastructure, including hundreds of wells and water storage pools and water pumps which provided water for drinking, irrigation and other needs for thousands of people, have been destroyed along with tens of kilometers of irrigation networks.

The case of the Bashir family illustrates many of the patterns of forced eviction, house demolition and destruction and expropriation of land described in this report. Khalil Bashir, a school principal, his wife Souad, their six children and his elderly mother, have long been under pressure from the Israeli army to leave their home and their land, in the village of

Deir al-Balah, in the Gaza Strip, near the Israeli settlement of Kfar Darom. Since October 2000 the Israeli army has destroyed the nearby houses of Bashir's brother and parents and most of their cultivated land around the house, and has taken over the top floor of the Bashirs' house and turned it into an army base, confining the family to the ground floor, frequently harassing and ill-treating the family and pressuring them to leave the house. Israeli soldiers shot and injured Khalil Bashir and two of his children in or around the house. In the last incident in February 2004, 15-year-old Yusuf Bashir was shot in the back and seriously injured by Israeli soldiers as he was outside his home with his father and UN staff members who had visited the house.

"... The home should be the safest place but for our family it is not; yet it is our home and we should not be forced to leave it. No one should be forced out of their home, and we won't leave our house.. ". (Khalil Bashir's daughter, Amira, to Amnesty International)

In the West Bank large scale destruction of houses and other properties began in early 2002, with a series of prolonged Israeli army incursions which left a trail of destruction in every refugee camp and town raided. Army tanks rolled over parked cars, broke down walls and house fronts and smashed electricity poles and water mains.

Forty-year-old Nabila al-Shu'bi, who was seven months pregnant, her three young children, her husband, two of her sisters-in-law and her father-in-law, were left to die under the rubble of their home, when it was demolished by Israeli army bulldozers on 6 April 2002 in Nablus. The Israeli army kept the area under strict curfew for days, denying access to rescue workers, and it was not until a week later that their bodies were found under the rubble of the house by relatives. Nabila's elderly aunt and uncle survived, trapped under the rubble for a whole week

The largest single wave of destruction carried out by the Israeli army was in Jenin refugee camp in April 2002. The army completely destroyed the al-Hawashin quarter and partially destroyed two additional quarters of the refugee camp, leaving more than 800 families, totaling some 4000 people, homeless.(4)

Aerial photographs and other evidence show that much of the house destruction was carried out after clashes between Israeli soldiers and Palestinian gunmen had ended and Palestinian gunmen had been arrested or had surrendered.(5) Since then Israeli army raids and destruction of homes and properties throughout the West Bank have continued.

On the morning of 5 September 2003 Israeli soldiers blew up a seven storey building in Nablus in which eight families lived, including 31 children. Ibtisam, a teacher and mother of four, told Amnesty International: At about 9-9.30 pm Israeli soldiers called on all of us living in the building to get out... we scrambled to get the children from their bed and get out. It was a panic; I didn't have time to take milk or anything for my baby.... The soldiers took us all to the school across the road, blew up the door to get it open and put us all inside... We were kept there all night, with no food, water, nothing... There was a lot of shooting... Then suddenly the soldiers blew up the building, without allowing us to go in to get anything. We were left with nothing, in our pajamas everything got buried in the rubble.

Five days later, on 10 September, an eight-storey apartment building was similarly blown up by the Israeli army in Hebron, making 68 people, 53 of them women and children, homeless.

Destruction of "temporarily" confiscated land: The Israeli army continues to seize and destroy land throughout the West Bank and Gaza Strip for "military/security needs".

In January 2004, the Israeli army issued 12 "temporary" seizure orders for tracts of land near Israeli settlements in the Gaza Strip. The order states: Notice is hereby given that on
- the Commander of the Israel Defense Forces in the Gaza region, in wake of the special circumstances which exist in the region, and for imperative military needs, has ordered that the land marked on the map appended to the order regarding seizure of land (2004-2) (Kfar Darom security fence) (Gaza region) shall be seized for the construction of security components

On paper the land is not confiscated but only "temporarily" seized by the Israeli army for unspecified "military/security needs" for a set period only. However, "temporary" land seizure orders can be extended indefinitely and in the overwhelming majority of cases the land has never been returned to its owners. Land "temporarily" seized has been routinely used to expand and build Israeli settlements, roads for settlers and related infrastructure and, more recently, to make way for the fence/wall which Israel is building through the West Bank.(6)

The fence/wall: According to the Israeli authorities the fence/wall is intended to prevent entry into Israel to Palestinian suicide bombers and other potential attackers. However, the fence/wall is not being built between Israel and the Occupied Territories but mostly (close to 90%) inside the West Bank, cutting off communities and families from each other, separating Palestinians from their land, work, education and health care facilities and other essential services. This, in order to facilitate passage between Israel and more than 50 illegal Israeli settlements located in the West Bank. The route of the fence/wall inside the West Bank is purportedly aimed at protecting unlawful Israeli settlements and results in unlawful destruction and appropriation of Palestinian property and other human rights violations. "Military/security needs" cannot be invoked to justify measures that benefit unlawful Israeli settlements at the expense of the occupied Palestinian population. In its present configuration, the fence/wall violates Israel's obligations under international law.

The failure of the Israeli Supreme Court: Most cases of house demolition and destruction of land and properties are not subject to legal supervision or appeal. In 2002 the Supreme Court ruled that in cases of demolitions for "military/security needs" those affected must be allowed to appeal unless doing so would "endanger the lives of Israelis or if there are combat activities in the vicinity." However, **theCourt subsequently ruled that advance notice did not need to be given if it would hinder the success of the demolition, a virtual green light for demolitions to be carried out without the possibility of appeal. This is what happens in most cases.**

In cases of advance notification of intended destruction where the owners of the targeted properties have appealed, the Israeli Supreme Court has usually accepted the Israeli army's assessment of what constitutes "military/security needs", and has permitted the demolitions. Amnesty International believes that the Israeli Supreme Court has too readily accepted the Israeli army's overly broad definition of "military necessity" and that by endorsing this interpretation, the Supreme Court has failed to protect Palestinians in the Occupied Territories from arbitrary destruction of their homes and property and from forced evictions.

DEMOLITIONS OF UNLICENSED HOUSES: DISCRIMINATION IN PLANNING POLICIES AND ENFORCEMENT MEASURES

"We have to begin to educate the Arab public to build high... There is no reason that everyone in the Arab sector should live in houses" Israeli Interior Minister Abraham Poraz, 21 January 2004.

At the root of the problem of demolition of unlicensed houses in the Arab sector in Israel and in parts of the Occupied Territories lie Israel's land and planning policies and the manner in which they are enforced. These policies have been characterized by discrimination against Israeli Arabs and Palestinians both in the use of state land, including land previously expropriated from Palestinians, and in the manner in which plans are drawn up for the use of privately owned land, as well as in the enforcement of planning and building regulations.

The expropriation/confiscation of large areas of Palestinian land has significantly diminished the reserves of available land on which Palestinians and Israeli Arabs can build to accommodate the natural growth of their communities. Planning and building regulations in these areas further restrict the amount of privately owned land on which Israeli Arabs and Palestinians can build.

The home of Salim and 'Arabia Shawamreh has been demolished four times between July 1998 and April 2003. The house has since been rebuilt with the help of volunteers as a peace centre but is again under threat of demolition. Salim, 'Arabia and their seven children lived in the overcrowded Shu'fat refugee camp in Jerusalem. They eventually bought a plot of land in the nearby village of 'Anata. After having spent more than four years and a lot of money trying to obtain a permit, they lost hope and built their home without a permit. They told Amnesty International: The authorities gave us different justifications for refusing us the building permit. ... Each time we succeeded to challenge or disprove the reason they had given us for the refusal, our application was rejected on different grounds. We spent thousands of dollars on this process. In the end we understood that it was hopeless and we built our home without a permit".

The Occupied Territories: Palestinians in the West Bank and Gaza Strip are barred from leasing or building on land which has been declared state land because state land is not for leasing or building on by "alien persons", and the entire Palestinian population of the Occupied Territories are defined as aliens by Israeli law. After it occupied the West Bank and Gaza Strip, Israel froze planning in Palestinian towns and villages. Planning schemes dating back several decades and no longer suitable to cater for the needs of a growing population were used as the basis for refusing building permits to Palestinians. At the same time, however, Israel developed comprehensive planning schemes for more than 150 Jewish settlements it established throughout the Occupied Territories in violation of international law.

Building restrictions in the Occupied Territories since the Oslo Accords

"Our policy is not to approve building in Area C" Israeli Army spokesperson to Amnesty International delegates in 1999.

"There are no more construction permits for Palestinians". Israeli army Legal Advisor Colonel Shlomo Politus, to the Israeli Parliament on 13 July 2003.

Under the Oslo Accords 60% of the West Bank was classified as Area C, where Israel retained responsibility for civil affairs. As a result Palestinians have continued to be prevented from building in most of the West Bank. In the past three years the Israeli army has demolished some 500 Palestinian houses in Area C on the grounds that they were built without permit. At the same time Israel dramatically accelerated the establishment and expansion of illegal settlements in Area C and around East Jerusalem and has built an extensive network of roads throughout the Occupied Territories to connect these settlements to each other and to Israel. In the seven years of the Oslo peace process, from 1993 to 2000, the number of Israeli settlers in the West Bank and Gaza Strip increased by more than 50%. The expansion of Israeli settlements in these areas continues. According to the Israeli Central Bureau of Statistics, in 2003 housing construction increased by 35% in the settlements in the Occupied Territories.

On 21 August 2003, on the morning of his wedding, As'ad Mu'yin had his house demolished; the house of his cousin Ziad As'ad, who had married a week earlier, was demolished at the same time. The two adjacent houses were in the West Bank town of Nazla'Issa. As'ad Mu'yin had been living on the ground floor of the house with his parents and three brothers and had furnished and prepared the second floor to move in with his wife. The house was demolished before he could do so. The new furniture and the wedding gifts disappeared under the rubble, along with the content of the family home on the ground floor. He told Amnesty International: "The army came early in the morning, at about 1am. I was getting ready for the wedding, for a very happy day. They had bulldozers ... they gave us 15 minutes to leave the house. We had no time to salvage anything. They said that we did not have building permits.... But everyone knows that Israel does not give building permits to Palestinians in Area C. "

Israel: Since the establishment of the state of Israel more than 700 Jewish towns and villages have been established but not a single Arab one. Dozens of Arab villages which existed prior to the establishment of the state were subsequently re-classified as non-residential areas. Some 93% of the land in Israel is state land, but some of it is administered through the Jewish National Fund, the Jewish Agency or other bodies which do not lease land to non Jews. These concerns have been recognized by the Or Commission, an official body, in 2003.(7)

Excerpts from the Or Commission report (September 2003) 36) In the first 50 years of the state's existence the Arab population has grown seven fold but the amount of land allocated for housing construction has remained almost unchanged. Thus the population density in the Arab sector grew considerably ... new localities were not established ..land was not usually allocated for building in the Arab sector. Residents of the Arab sector who wish to build on land which they own but which is under the jurisdiction of neighbouring Jewish local authorities were blocked by the regulation of these authorities. 37) A major obstacle facing construction for housing purposes in the Arab sector has been the lack of outline and master plans. ... in the Arab sector there were unreasonable delays. Added to that was the problem of the lack of effective representation of the Arab sector in planning and building committees....local commissions were not established in Arab localities and these localities were placed under the jurisdiction of commissions managed by Jews.... the decisions regarding the developments of the Arab sector have not been sensitive enough to the needs of the Arab population.... by the end of the century half of the Arab localities still did not have approved master plans ... in large parts of the areas of jurisdiction (of the Arab localities) private land owners could not build houses legally. A widespread phenomenon of unlicensed buildings ... partly stems from the inability to obtain building permits Demolition orders were issued for houses of Arabs... It has been claimed that behind the legal situation ... a situation of double standards has been created towards the Arab citizens.

The unrecognized Bedouin villages in the Negev region: Some 60,000-70,000 Bedouins live in some 45 "unrecognized villages" in the Negev, Israel's southern region. Although the Bedouins have lived in the Negev for generations their villages have never been recognized by the authorities and the inhabitants are not allowed to build houses or to farm the land, and live in constant fear of forcible eviction and house demolition. In the past two years alone the security forces have demolished scores of homes in these villages and have destroyed the Bedouins' crops by helicopter spraying on several occasions. No warning was given before spraying the area and several people were taken ill as a result.

Since more permanent constructions in the unrecognized Bedouin villages are more likely to be destroyed, many Bedouins are forced to live in shed-like homes, which offer little protection against the extreme desert climate. Even so, most of their homes and animal sheds are under the threat of demolition. The ILA puts the number of unlicensed (and thus liable to demolition) structures in these villages at 60,000, of which 25,000 are houses, and the Israeli Interior Ministry gives a figure of 30,000.

(8)

On 4 August 2003 Israeli security forces demolished 10 homes in Sa'wa, one of the unrecognized Bedouin villages, including the home of 'Ali and Sara Abu Sbeit and their six young children. 'Ali Abu Sbeit told Amnesty International: "The police and border guards came at about 1am. We were still asleep.. they had bulldozers. They tied my hands behind my back and took me, my wife and the children out. They did not allow us time to take anything out of the house. ... Since our home was destroyed we have been staying with our relatives, but not all together because there are a lot of us. ... This is the second time that my home has been demolished. The first time was in 1997 and I had to demolish the house myself, or else the authorities were going to make me pay the cost of the demolition ... after I lived with my mother for three years, but now there isn't space for all of us there. Then in 1999 I built this home, and now we are homeless again".

The authorities have been putting pressure on the Bedouins living in the unrecognized villages to sign agreements renouncing their claims to this land and move to urbanized townships planned for them by the authorities. In past decades about half of the Bedouin population has given in to government pressures and moved to five townships lacking in infrastructure and job opportunities, which were set up by the Israeli authorities especially for the Bedouins. These Bedouin townships remain amongst the poorest localities in the country and have high rates of unemployment and crime. The 60-70,000 Bedouins who still live in the unrecognized villages have resisted the government's pressures to give up their land and traditional lifestyle of farming and animal-grazing and to move to such townships. While stepping up efforts to concentrate the Bedouin population into small townships with little or no employment or development prospects, the authorities have encouraged and sponsored the establishment of new Jewish villages and single family farms in the region.

APPLICABLE INTERNATIONAL LEGAL STANDARDS

Both in Israel and in the Occupied Territories, Israel is bound by international human rights law, including the international human rights treaties to which Israel is a State Party, including the International Covenant on Economic, Social and Cultural Rights (ICESCR), the International Covenant on Civil and Political Rights (ICCPR) and the International Convention on the Elimination of All Forms of Racial Discrimination (ICERD). In the Occupied Territories, in addition to international human rights law, Israel's conduct as the occupying power must also comply with the provisions of international humanitarian law applicable to belligerent occupation, including the Fourth Geneva Convention relative to the Protection of Civilian Persons in Time of War of 12 August 1949 (Fourth Geneva Convention).

Israel has consistently denied its obligation to apply the UN human rights treaties which it has ratified in the West Bank and Gaza Strip and has consistently rejected the applicability of the Fourth Geneva Convention. However, Israel stands alone in its contention. The applicability of both the Fourth Geneva Convention and international human rights treaties has been repeatedly reaffirmed by the relevant bodies and by the international community.

International human rights law

The right to housing: The right to housing is a basic right, which is a fundamental component of the right to an adequate standard of living and central to the enjoyment of other human rights, guaranteed by Article 11(1) of the ICESCR.

The right to housing encompasses the right to live somewhere in peace, security and dignity, as well as the right to adequate housing. The right to adequate housing not only includes adequate privacy, space, security, protection from the elements and threats to health, ventilation at a reasonable cost, but also, among other things, legal security of tenure - including protection against forced eviction, harassment and threats.

In May 2003 the UN Committee on Economic, Social and Cultural Rights (CESCR) expressed serious concerns about Israel's practices which violate the right to housing of Israeli Arabs, including Bedouins in Israel, and of Palestinians in the Occupied Territories.(9)

Discrimination: The fundamental duty of a State to guarantee rights without discrimination is enshrined in the international human rights treaties, including the ICCPR (Article 2(1) and Article 26) and the ICESCR (Article 2(2)).

Article 5(e)(iii) of the ICERD forbids any discrimination in the exercise of the various rights, including the right to housing.

Israel's housing and land policies violate the right to non-discrimination of Israeli Arabs and of Palestinians. In March 1998 the UN

Committee on the Elimination of Racial Discrimination (CERD) called "... for a halt to the demolition of Arab properties in East Jerusalem and for respect for property rights irrespective of the ethnic origin of the owner. " and expressed concern "... about ethnic inequalities, particularly those centring upon what are known as "unrecognized"Arab villages [in Israel]. " (10)

Forced eviction: Through forced eviction and the mass demolition of homes in the Occupied Territories and, to a lesser extent, Israel, the Israeli authorities have deliberately made tens of thousands of Palestinians and thousands of Israeli Arabs homeless just in the past few years.

Whether it justifies such action on grounds of "military/security needs" or whether such action is imposed as a form of collective punishment, or is carried out in enforcement of planning regulations, large-scale forced evictions are inconsistent with the realization of the right to adequate housing. The obligation of the state under international law is that it must refrain from forced evictions. The CESCR "... considers that instances of forced eviction are prima facie incompatible with the requirements of the

Covenant and can only be justified in the most exceptional circumstances, and in accordance with the relevant principles of international law."(11)

International humanitarian law

Prohibition on destruction of property and disproportionate use of force: According to Article 53 of the Fourth Geneva Convention and Article 23(g) of the 1907 Hague Regulations Israel, as the Occupying Power, is forbidden from destroying the property of Palestinians in the West Bank and Gaza Strip, unless it is militarily necessary to do so. According to Article 147 of the Fourth Geneva Convention, "extensive destruction and appropriation of property, not justified by military necessity and carried out unlawfully and wantonly" is a grave breach, and hence, a war crime.

Military necessity should not be interpreted in a broad and vague manner, which would undermine the fundamental norms of international human rights and humanitarian law. Measures intended to have long term preventative effects are thus not justifiable on the grounds of absolute military necessity. In the case of long-held occupied territory over which the occupying power exercises effective control, military necessity must be read extremely narrowly - in light of the concept of proportionality inherent in policing standards, rather than conduct of hostilities standards which should only apply in the course of actual armed conflict. Demolitions and evictions should never be anything but a last resort. In the past three and half years the Israeli army has carried out extensive destruction of homes and properties throughout the West Bank and Gaza which is not justified by military necessity. Some of these acts of destruction amount to grave breaches of the Fourth Geneva Convention and are war crimes.

Prohibition on collective punishment: The Fourth Geneva Convention specifically prohibits collective punishment. Its Article 33 stipulates: "No protected person may be punished for an offence he or she has not personally committed. Collective penalties and likewise all measures of intimidation or of terrorism are prohibited. "

The prohibition on collective punishment is also a cardinal rule of human rights law. The recently accelerated Israeli practice of demolishing houses owned by relatives of suicide bombers or other Palestinian armed attackers is a blatant form of collective punishment. Collective penalties also include such measures as attacking an entire community in retaliation for acts committed by members of that community, or arbitrarily restricting the movement of an entire population.

MAIN RECOMMENDATIONS

TO THE ISRAELI AUTHORITIES:

•	Punitive demolitions and the destruction of houses, land, and other properties without absolute military necessity as prescribed by international humanitarian law should stop immediately.

•	The law must be amended in a manner so as to require that, except during the actual conduct of military operations or armed confrontations which make the destruction absolutely necessary, no demolition should be carried out without prior notification to the concerned parties, who should be given adequate time and opportunity to challenge before an independent and impartial court of law any demolition order.

• The creation and expansion of Israeli civilian settlements in the Occupied Territories and infrastructure to support them, including roads, must stop and Israel must cease and prohibit the destruction of houses, land or other properties for these purposes.

•	Israel must stop construction of the wall/fence within the Occupied Territories, remove what has already been constructed within the Occupied Territories, restore seized property, and ensure reparation for land and property seized, confiscated or destroyed.

• A judicial commission of inquiry should be established to investigate all the cases of destruction, confiscation and damage to property carried out by the Israeli army in the Occupied Territories since October 2000, in order to establish the extent of the damage caused and the necessary reparation.

• Israel should invite the international community to deploy qualified and experienced observers in the Occupied Territories to monitor the conduct of the Israeli army, Palestinian armed groups and Palestinian security forces. Such independent, expert observers should report publicly on the conduct of all parties in light of international law, including in relation to destruction of and damage to property.

• All outstanding orders for forced evictions and demolitions of unlicensed houses should be cancelled and a moratorium should be placed on future forced evictions and demolitions until such time as the law is amended in a manner that complies with international standards.

• Laws and policies governing the zoning and allocation of land in Israel must be reviewed and provisions which are discriminatory must be repealed or amended.

• Legal recognition/status should be granted immediately to the unrecognized villages. Legal security of tenure should be afforded to the residents of these unrecognized villages and efforts to forcibly remove their inhabitants should be immediately halted.

• Effective redress and reparation should be granted to those whose homes have been demolished. TO THE PALESTINIAN AUTHORITY (PA):

• The PA should take all possible measures to prevent attacks by Palestinian armed groups and individuals against Israeli civilians in the Occupied Territories and inside Israel.

•   The PA should take all possible measures to ensure that Palestinian armed groups and individuals do not initiate armed confrontations from residential civilian areas.

•   The PA should support the call on the international community to deploy qualified and experienced observers in the Occupied Territories to monitor the conduct of the Israeli army, Palestinian armed groups and Palestinian security forces.

TO THE INTERNATIONAL COMMUNITY:

•   The International community and states parties to international human rights and humanitarian law treaties to which Israel is a party must take steps to ensure Israel's compliance with its obligations under

international law.

•   States, particularly the US, should stop the sale or transfer of weaponry and equipment that are used to commit unlawful destruction of homes and other serious violations of international human rights and humanitarian law, until they secure guarantees that Israeli forces will not use the equipment to commit

violations.

TO CATERPILLAR Inc.

•   Caterpillar Inc., the US company which produces the bulldozers used by the Israeli army, should take measures - within the company sphere of influence - to guarantee that its bulldozers are not used to commit human rights violations, including the destruction of homes, land and other properties.

BACKROUND

The human rights situation in Israel and the Occupied Territories has seriously deteriorated since October 2000. Since then violence and human right abuses have reached unprecedented levels. More than 2,500 Palestinians, including some 450 children have been killed by the Israeli army. More than 900 Israelis, most of them civilians, including some 100 children have been killed by Palestinian armed groups in suicide bombings and other attacks. Tens of thousands of Palestinians and thousands of Israeli civilians have been injured, many seriously.

In addition, the Israeli army has carried out large-scale destruction of Palestinian houses, land and other properties and has imposed increasingly stringent restrictions on the movement of Palestinians in the Occupied Territories. As a result the Palestinian economy has virtually collapsed, and unemployment and poverty have increased dramatically in the West Bank and Gaza. Two thirds of the Palestinian population now live below the poverty line and malnutrition and other medical conditions are spreading.

These and other concerns about the human rights situation in Israel and the Occupied Territories have been addressed by Amnesty International in numerous reports and other material (available on www.amnesty.org)

****

(1) This practice was used in previous decades but was suspended from 1997 to 2001. (2) Voice of Israel, 16 January 2002.

(3) Consolidated Appeal Process 2004 (CAP) on: http:'%ochadms.unog.ch

(4) Information supplied to Amnesty International by UNRWA on 13 June 2002.

(5) See: Amnesty International's report Israel and the Occupied Territories: Shielded from scrutiny: IDF violations in Jenin and Nablus, 4 November 2002 (AI Index: MDE 15/143/2002).

(6) See Amnesty International's report Israel and the Occupied Territories: The place of the fence/wall in international law, 19 February 2004 (AI Index: MDE 15/016/2004).

(7) The Or Commission was set up by the Israeli authorities to investigate events surrounding the killing by Israeli police of 13 Israel Arabs in protest demonstrations in October 2000.

(8) State Comptroller report 52B of 2000 (The Bedouin Diaspora in the Negev, page 111, paragraph 2).

(9) Concluding Observations of the CESCR: Israel, 23/05/2003; UN Doc: E/C.12/1/Add.9, paras 16, 26 and 27.

(10) CERD/C/304/Add.45, paras.I I and 19. (11) CESCR, General Comment 4, para 18.

— V —

SUING TO RECOVER FOR THE SETTLEMENTS

While the chances for redress in the US Courts are greatest for extrajudicial killings, those who lost their land to the settlements in the West Bank have almost as strong a case. Unfortunately, they do not have the express cause of action granted by Congress in 1991 for extrajudicial killings under the Torture Victims Protection Act (TVPA) discussed previously. Instead these claimants will have to rely on the Alien Tort Claims Act (ATCA) of 1789, an Act which is currently under fierce attack from the Big Business community, aided and abetted by the Bush Administration.

This 1789 Act had been long dormant, but was picked up by Holocaust and other human rights victims to go after multinational corporations and banks, as well as former government and military officials, for violations of internationally recognized human rights, wherever committed. In a recent case before the US Supreme Court, the business community and the Bush Administration have argued that this is an archaic law, never intended to be used for the purposes now being employed and needs to be sharply curtailed. Justice Scalia signaled another revolutionary jump by the Supreme Court when he asked rhetorically: "What is the 'law of nations'?" This is like the sketch by Jimmy Durante who would stand in front of a huge elephant in a goofy attempt to hide it, and ask indignantly, "What Elephant?"

American Companies in Israel

Having established that the settlements are against the law of nations, what causes of action would exist for anyone who was damaged by the settlement policy in Israel. This would include the Palestinians whose land was confiscated, whose homes were demolished, the businesses that were ruined by the various Israeli closures of villages and towns in the West Bank and myriad others.

Would the dozens of American companies doing business in Israel and in any of the settlements be subject to suit under the Alien Tort Act? Certainly executives of Coca Cola, Burger King, Microsoft, Ford Motor, Boeing, Caterpillar, Mac Donald's, etc., if they are doing business in the settlements, have to be aware of the universal condemnation of the Israeli settlement policy. We would think that each of these companies, to the extent that they aid and assist in the settlements, would be subject to suit in the United States.

Another interesting category of defendant would be the US Government agency, the National Space and Aeronautics Agency. The literature of the Judea and Samaria College in the West Bank settlement of Ariel claims that through the Israeli Space Agency it is working with NASA on a robotics and mechanical engineering project. Would NASA be subject to suit? While interesting, in all probability the suit would be dismissed on the basis of sovereign immunity, a legal protection which Mac Donalds, Microsoft and Coca Cola do not have.

The Settlements

After Israel was granted part of the old Palestine as an independent state by the United Nations in 1948, its borders have bounced around somewhat due to various wars and incursions, all of which were lost by the inept armies of its Arab neighbors who vainly tried to push Israel into the Sea. Nevertheless, the borders that have gained wide international support are those that became the armistice lines after the 1967 war. Israel had quickly beaten the combined armies of its neighbors and occupied, among other places, the Gaza Strip (taken from Egypt) and the West Bank (taken from Jordan). Since then, the Israel Army has in effect occupied these territories and, together with East Jerusalem and the Golan Heights, are referred to as the "Occupied Territories."

Since 1967 Israel has changed the borders of Jerusalem and annexed large parts of it. Likewise, it has financed and encouraged Israelis to move into the West Bank and Gaza to set up settlements. The motivation expressed publicly has been varied, from extending a security perimeter, to retaking the land of Judea and Samaria that God had given to the Chosen People. Some of the settlements have taken on the characteristics of cities, though surrounded by fences, guarded by troops and connected to Israel with exclusive roads that the natives are not allowed to use. Much of the best parcels in the West Bank have been so confiscated, as has the vital and scarce resource of water.

Since 1967 the international community has been vainly asking Israel to withdraw its troops from the Occupied Territories. While countries like Korea and Vietnam, and to a lesser extent, Iraq, have been devastated by UN Armies for defiance of UN Security Council Resolutions, the anomaly is that Israel has been able not only to ignore the Resolutions, but continuously to effectively annex pieces of these territories for itself. The pieces and the arrangements for their connection to Israel and their security have created confined areas or ghettos for the natives, or the Arab population. As a result of this isolation these communities have become stagnant, uneconomic ghettos much dependent on the charity of the world for their daily bread.

What remedies are available for the Arabs in the West Bank, Gaza, the Golan Heights and in East Jerusalem who claimed to have been wronged by the Israelis? There are various categories of wrongs, and the damages would be varied as well. Some of the obvious groups would be:

1.   Land taken without compensation.

2. Land taken with inadequate compensation.
3. Jobs lost because of an inability to travel from one Arab village to the next.
4. Jobs lost because of exclusion from Israel.
5. Deaths caused by Israeli checkpoints in the occupied territories preventing people from reaching hospitals or other aid in a timely manner.
6. Poverty caused by the ghettozation of their land into uneconomic sections.
7. Death and malnutrition caused by the above.
8. Wrongs to the culture of the Palestinians caused by the disruption of education and normal social activities.
9. The damage done cumulatively by the daily humiliations of living as a despised race under the guns of a regional superpower.

The Alien Tort Law

In 1789 Congress enacted the First Judiciary Act which in part provided as follows:

> *The district courts shall have original jurisdiction of any civil action by an alien for a tort only, committed in violation of the law of nations or a treaty of the United States.*

This has become known as the Alien Tort Law.

Congress in 1789 apparently had no difficulty in defining an area of law in which the District Court had jurisdiction as being torts (that is, wrongful acts) committed in violation of the "law of nations." (Unlike Justice Scalia 216 years later doing the Jimmy Durante sketch: "What Elephant?") The members of the first Congress must have had a clear understanding of the "law of nations" in order to give the district courts jurisdiction over acts that were against it. Likewise, it was no mystery to these founding members of the US that some court had to have jurisdiction over violations of those agreements the country had made with foreign countries, that is, treaties. Treaties and the law of nations became part of the federal law the moment this country came into existence, and they were the highest law of the land – defeating contrary enactments of municipalities, cities, states and even Congress itself.

The Constitution further expressly provided that treaties were to be considered as the law of the land, meaning the highest law in the US against which local regulations, state laws and regulatory enactments had to bow.

Such is the nature of our constitutional form of government and the principles that have guided the country for over 200 years. It would not be until the arrival of the Second Bush Administration and Justice Scalia of the US Supreme Court that the very notion of the "law of nations" would be questioned, as noted above. But until this point, numerous lawsuits have attested to the viability of the Alien Tort Law and its usefulness in redressing wrongs to aliens.

Until now the Federal Courts have had no difficulty in determining what the "law of nations" in this statute meant. In Filartiga v. Pena-Irala 630 F 2d 876(CA 2d Cir. 1980), the court found that the "law of nations" mentioned in the Alien Tort Act has always been part of the federal common law of the United States. Consequently, if a tort which is recognized by international law were committed against an alien anywhere in the world, and that alien could bring the perpetrator within the jurisdiction of the Federal Courts (usually by personal service in the US), the perpetrator could be sued and monetary damages recovered. The courts had no difficulty in determining in any particular case what the law of nations was. Certain wrongful conduct which offends norms that have become well-established and universally recognized, said the court in Tachinoa v. Mugabe, 234 F. Supp. 2d 401 (S.D. N.Y. 2002), repeating a common refrain of the courts, violates the law of nations and gives rise to a right to sue cognizable by exercise of federal jurisdiction under the Alien Tort Claims Act.

What is "well established and universally recognized," in another formula adopted by the courts, can be determined by consulting the works of jurists, the general usage and practice of nations, or by prior judicial decisions recognizing and enforcing that law. Flores v. Southern Peru Copper Corp., 253 F. Supp. 2d 510 (S.D.N.Y. 2002). Not every wrong is recognized as a universal wrong that can be remedied under the Alien Tort Law. It has to be such that it is *universally* abhorred and that its prohibition commands the "general assent of civilized nations." Jafari v. Islamic Republic of Iran, 539 F Supp 209 (N.D. Ill. 1982,) .

For our purposes, an important measure of the law of nations is the Geneva Conventions of 1949. Numerous courts have held that those Conventions embody the universally recognized law of civilized nations. "The alleged acts . . . are clearly in violation of international law as it stands today. Common Article 3 of the Geneva Conventions, which has been ratified by over 180 states . . . protects civilians not participating in the conflict by requiring that they be 'treated humanely.' . . . It prohibits, among other things, 'murder of all kinds, mutilation, cruel treatment and torture,' kidnapping, and summary executions." Doe v. Islamic Salvation Front, 993 F. Supp. 3 (D.D.C. 1998).

Likewise, international treaties ratified by most of the world and Resolutions of the United Nations General Assembly, the Security Council and various recognized and official UN bodies have been held to enunciate universally recognized rights. What have they said about the Israeli settlements in the Occupied Territories?

Article 46 of the Law and Customs of War on Land (Hague IV, 1909) states:

> *Private property cannot be confiscated.*

Article 49 of the Fourth Geneva Convention Relative to the Protection of Civilian Persons in Time of War (1949) states:

> *The Occupying Power shall not deport or transfer part of its own civilian population into the territory it occupies.*

The United Nation Security Council **Resolution 242**, is repeatedly recited by all the parties involved (even ironically in the Bush-Sharon Agreement ceding parts of the West Bank to Israel in flagrant contravention of **Resolution 242**) and by outsiders as the cornerstone for a solution in the Middle East, was passed on November 22, 1967 with the strong support of the United States. The substance of 242 has today become a ghost to the policymakers in Washington, as it always was to Israel, though Israel, like Washington, signed on to it and has mumbled "242" like a prayer ever since. But what did 242 actually say? Part of the Resolution reads as follows:

Emphasizing the inadmissibility of the
acquisition of territory by war . . . .

Yet Israel in effect claims parts of Gaza, the Golan Heights, East Jerusalem and the West Bank as part of the spoils of war, though calling it annexation only in the case of East Jerusalem.

Once, perhaps, that may have been acceptable to the international community. But it is not today. The world has tried to become more civilized and peaceful, coming to a consensus on rules that would help mankind live in peace. Today one of those inviolable rules is set forth in the United Nations Charter created after the devastation of World War II in an attempt to avoid such devastation again. That is why the Security Council repeated that inviolable rule at the beginning of its **Resolution 242**:

Emphasizing the inadmissibility of the
acquisition of territory by war . . . .

Quite simply, then, the Israeli Settlements in the Occupied Territories are in flagrant violation of that rule.

The 1967 Security Council Resolution 242 continues:

Affirms that . . . a just and lasting peace . . . should
include . . . both:

Withdrawal of Israel armed forces from territories
occupied in the recent conflict;

Termination of all claims or states of belligerency
and respect for and acknowledgement of the
sovereignty, territorial integrity and political
independence of every State in the area and their
right to live in peace within secure and recognized
boundaries free from threats or acts of force; . . . .

The Security Council further called for "achieving a just settlement of the refugee problem."

Thirty seven years later, what have we?

- Israel has not withdrawn from the Occupied Territories.
- The refugees have not been compensated.
- Israel surrounds all the Palestinian territories and engages daily in "threats or acts of force."

The dichotomy between how the Palestinians have been treated and how the Israelis expect to be treated is so great as to be humorous. Fifty six years after the granting of their land and homes to the Israelis, the hundreds of thousands of Palestinian refugees have not been compensated. Yet even *before* the 7,500 Israeli settlers in Gaza leave the property previously stolen from the Palestinians, the Israelis insist that those settlers be compensated for the assets they leave behind – or they will burn everything down.

Thus, while Sharon was meeting with Bush and being called a hero for establishing the new "Prison of Gaza" on the Mediterranean Sea, his National Security Adviser, Giora Eiland, was meeting with senior World Bank officials, seeking some form of compensation for the settlers. As if orchestrated, a few days later Mark A. Heller, an associate at the Jaffee Center for Strategic Studies at Tel Aviv University, in an Op Ed article in the <u>New York Times</u> thought that this was a magnificent opportunity for Europe finally to do something useful about achieving peace in the Middle East – by *buying* the settlements. ("Settlements for Sale," April 19, 2004.)

By coincidence, Walter Russell Mead, a senior fellow at the Council on Foreign Relations almost at the same time commented in his own <u>Times</u> Op Ed article that this glaringly disproportionate failure to provide the Palestinian refugees with compensation since 1948 has festered and fed deep resentment. ("Why They Hate Us, Really" April 21, 2004.)

We have to assume that this resentment will grow even greater when and if the 7,500 Gaza settlers, perhaps after burning down their homes, their stolen orchards and after poisoning the water wells, leave the 1 million 500 thousand impoverished Palestinians behind in Gaza. The Arabs will then see those settlers being comfortably ensconced in American-financed suburban homes with running water, green gardens, crowded barns and all the security the Israeli Defense Forces have to offer. Perhaps it will be somewhere in an erstwhile barren desert in Israel or perhaps it will be on newly confiscated hilltops with pretty views in the West Bank.

On July 20, 1979 the Security Council in **Resolution 452**, again with the strong support of the UnitedStates, roundly condemned the establishment of settlements in the occupied territories and insisted that Israel not only cease development, but withdraw from all the settlements (*"the policy of Israel in establishing settlements in the occupied Arab territories has no legal validity and constitutes a violation of the Fourth Geneva Convention"*). In 1987 and 1988 in yet more **Resolutions, 605 and 607,** the Security Council reminded Israel that the international community considered Israel bound by the terms of the Fourth Geneva Convention of 1949 and condemned the policies of Israel, this time shooting unarmed civilian demonstrators, in the occupied territories "which violate the human rights of the Palestinian people" and further demanded that Israel stop deporting Palestinians from Jerusalem and the other occupied territories.

The United Nations Commission on Human Rights in 1999 confirmed by a unanimous resolution that the Fourth Geneva Convention applied to the occupied territories. In 2000 it further expressed its grave concern about:

> *"the continuing Israeli settlement activities, . . . including the expansion of the settlements, the installation of settlers in the occupied territories, the expropriation of land, the demolition of houses, the confiscation of property, the expulsion of local residents and the construction of bypass roads, **which change the physical character and demographic composition of the occupied territories**, including East Jerusalem, **since all these actions are illegal** . . . ."* [Emphasis added.]

The International community for decades has insisted that Israel leave the Occupied Territories unmolested. It was feared that Israel would "change the physical character and demographic composition of the occupied territories." This was assumed to be an evil and a wrong. Not, however, to the Administration of George Bush. In his April 15, 2004 letter to Sharon, after repeating the mantra that the parties must fashion a solution in accordance with Resolution 242, he stated a new principle:

*"In light of **new realities on the ground**, including already existing major Israeli populations centers, it is unrealistic to expect . . . return to the armistice lines . . . ."*

"New realities on the ground." These words will in the future become perhaps the most terrible legacy of the Bush Administration. Like Munich, it sanctions criminal and outlaw behavior. How many generations will it take to erase this shame?

<u>Remedies under the Alien Tort Law</u>

Can the refugees themselves seek redress under the Alien Tort Law? If they can deliver a summons on people or entities in the United States, it would seem that there would be good causes of action for compensation. A review of the types of claims which the Federal Courts have recognized suggests what some industrious litigant for the Palestinians could do in the United States.

In <u>Doe v. Unocal Corp</u>., 963 F. Supp. 880 (C.D. Cal. 1997) the court held that a good cause of action was asserted against the oil company for participating with the Burmese government in forced labor and slave trading on gas pipeline projects in Burma.

In <u>Sinaltrainal v. Coca-Cola Co</u>,, 256 F. Supp. 2d 1345 (S.D. Fla. 2003) it was held that the Federal district court had jurisdiction over a Colombian soft drink bottler, in a suit claiming that defendants were liable for death of plant workers at hands of a paramilitary unit, even though the bottler was a corporation.

An automobile manufacturer was considered a state actor subject to a private cause of action under the Alien Tort Claim Act where it used forced labor provided by the German government during World War II. <u>Iwanowa v. Ford Motor Co</u>., 67 F. Supp. 2d 424 (D.N.J. 1999).

Then there are the various suits against banks in the US which are related to the international banks that profited from confiscations during the Holocaust. Likewise, subsidiaries of banks in the US who do business in the Settlements, should be subject to suit under the Alien Tort Claim Act. See, for example, <u>Bodner v. Banque Paribas</u>, 114 F. Supp. 2d 117 (E.D.N.Y. 2000).

— VI —

THE AMERICAN WEAPONS INDUSTRY

What culpability do the companies in the United States that supply Israel with its weapons have for the illegal extrajudicial killings?

Can they be sued in the United States by the representatives of those victims?

<u>The Companies</u>

A myriad of companies have contracts either directly with Israel, or with the US Defense Department, to supply Israel with weapons – from night vision equipment to fighter planes. In addition, many other US companies, not directly involved in the business of producing weapons, have relationships with companies that do produce such weapons or have contracts with Israeli companies who produce the weapons. Another list of potential defendants are all the ancillary companies that are needed in the United States, including foreign international companies that have subsidiaries in the US, to gather together and transport the weapons, their parts and the related services, like training pilots, to Israel.

The legal teams for the Palestinians are going to have to do their homework and select, as early cases, the most prominent companies and those that are most directly involved, like the manufacturers. Then the teams can work down to the ancillary players, like transportation and banking. In addition, the investigation will need to gather the evidence necessary to clearly and conclusively tie the weapons used in extrajudicial killings to these companies – the trail will have to be laid out to the judges in the Federal Courts and every chain in the link must be based on solid information.

The Boeing Company

The most obvious potential defendants would be the manufacturers of the weapons used to assassinate the targets selected by the Israeli Defense Forces. Prominent among them would be The Boeing Company (Apache Helicopters and Hellfire Missiles) and Lockheed Martin (F-16 Fighters). Indeed Boeing has developed a particularly close relationship with Israeli companies. In a Press Release by Boeing on November 18, 1998, Boeing executive Tom Schick is quoted as stressing the importance and mutual benefits of the relationship between The Boeing Company and Israel. He was in Israel to represent Boeing at the annual international aerospace industry conference in Jerusalem, where he also met with clients and business partners. Schick emphasized that Israel was a very important region for Boeing, citing Boeing relationships with more than 30 industrial partners in Israel.

On February 11, 2003 Boeing announced that it and the Israel Aircraft Industries had signed an agreement to establish the production infrastructure to manufacture components of the Arrow Missile in the United States. James Evatt, senior vice president of Boeing Missile Defense Systems was at the Israeli facility at Beer Yaakov, Israel to sign the agreement. The deal was a co-production agreement wherein Boeing would be responsible for production of approximately 50 per cent of the Arrow missile components in the US, while the Israel Aircraft company would be responsible for integration and final assembly of the Arrow missile in Israel.

According to the Arms Trade Resource Center, as of 2002, Israel had 50 F-4F Phantom Fighter Planes, 98 F-15 Eagles, 42 AH-64 Apache Attack Helicopters and numerous AGM 114 Hellfire and Harpoon Missiles – all produced by Boeing. It is safe to say that the Israeli Air Force depends heavily upon Boeing.

In the newspaper reports on the Yassin and Rantisi assassinations, various commentaries and Palestinian witnesses referred to the use of Apache helicopters and Hellfire missiles in the killings. These, however, were only newspaper reports and the legal team for the Palestinians will have to establish that Boeing equipment was used in fact used in the assassinations.

The Causes of Action

Most of the legal precedents would suggest that actions can be brought under the Alien Tort Law. The usefulness of that statute, however, is now up to a test in the United States Supreme Court and that will have to be followed (Sosa v. Alvarez-Machain). But the Torture Victims Protection Act could also be used as a basis, even though that Act is limited to individuals. The individual officers of Boeing could be sued. In addition, there is at least one case holding that a corporation could be sued under the TVPA under the principles of agency and conspiracy (Sinaltrainal v. Coca-Cola Co,, 256 F. Supp. 2d 1345 (S.D. Fla. 2003)). Finally, as the most well-established principles of international law are part of the federal law of the United States, jurisdiction would also exist under the general "federal question" statute (28 U.S.C. 1331: "The district courts shall have original jurisdiction of all civil actions arising under the Constitution, laws, or treaties of the United States.").

Military Assistance and Sales

Congress has put certain restrictions in the legislation authorizing the sale of weapons, as well as in the legislation providing for the giving of weapons free of charge to foreign nations. At first glance these restrictions should prohibit use by Israel of American weapons in such illegal activities as extrajudicial killings or indiscriminate bombardments in the occupied territories. However, Presidents and Congress have all but ignored those restrictions over the years. Periodically a warning to Israel would be issued; the President under the relevant statute would send a public or secret letter to Congress detailing violation of the restrictions by Israel (as in the Israeli invasion of Lebanon), but usually nothing of any significance followed these warnings – which of course have been repeatedly ignored.

However, private litigants with standing, as the Palestinian representatives of those assassinated by Israel would definitely have, could make use of the statutes described below for two purposes: 1) in a suit for damages under the Torture Victims Protection Act or under the Alien Tort Law; and 2) in a suit by such litigants seeking an injunction against the various federal agencies and private weapons companies that aid or abet in the violation of these restrictions.

Congress, in its Statement of Policy for Military Assistance to Foreign Nations, reaffirmed the "policy of the United States to achieve international peace and security through the United Nations so that armed force shall not be used except for individual or collective self-defense" (22 USC § 2301). Thus in § 2302 it is stated: "Defense articles and defense services to any country shall be furnished solely for internal security, for legitimate self-defense, ..." Further, in § 2304 (1) Congress recognized its international obligations as set forth in the Charter of the United Nations to promote respect for human rights: "Accordingly, a principal goal of the foreign policy of the United States shall be to promote the increased observance of internationally recognized human rights by all countries."

Thus Congress provided that "no security assistance may be provided to any country the government of which engages in a consistent pattern of gross violations of internationally recognized human rights. Security assistance may not be provided to the police, domestic intelligence, or similar law enforcement forces of a country, and license may not be issued under the Export Administration Act of 1979 . . . to a country, the government of which engages in a consistent pattern of gross violations of internationally recognized human rights . . . ." (22 USC § 2304 (2)).

As part of the administration of foreign military assistance, Congress set up a procedure which required the Secretary of State to issue annually a Human Rights Report "with respect to practices regarding the observance of and respect for internationally recognized human rights in each country proposed as a recipient." As a basis for such a Report, Congress instructed that "consideration shall be given to (1) the relevant findings of appropriate international organizations, including nongovernmental organizations, such as the International Committee of the Red Cross; and (2) the extent of cooperation by such government in permitting an unimpeded investigation by any such organization of alleged violations of internationally recognized human rights" (22 USC § 2304 (2) (b)).

These restrictions and prohibitions have worked well in the cases of a number of countries, but have been invisible with respect to Israel. There is no will or desire in the Executive branch or in Congress to enforce these laws against Israel. The Secretary of State dutifully reports each year on the egregious violations of human rights by Israel, including extrajudicial killings, disproportionate use of force in retaliation, illegal collective punishment in the demolishing of homes, businesses, sewer systems and other infrastructure in the occupied territories, the setting up of innumerable checkpoints in the occupied territories which restrict movement of Palestinians in their own areas, etc., etc. The Secretary of State also virtuously cites such nongovernmental organizations as the International Red Cross, which was specifically mentioned as a source by Congress, and other independent human rights watch groups, as Amnesty International, Peace Now and B'Tselem about the continuous violations of international law and UN Resolutions by Israel. (See The State Department Reports and excerts from them at the end of Chapter IX below.) *But then nothing happens.* There is no recommendation to cease aid to Israel. There is no recommendation to limit use of US weapons by Israel. And Congress does not respond to these Annual Reports disclosing repeated and gross violations of human rights by Israel with any demand that something be done about them. In the hands of the President and Congress, this lofty sounding law with all its good intentions to prevent use of American weapons for evil -- is a dead law.

However, for private litigants, the evidence is all there in the US Secretary of State Annual Reports on Human Rights; in the reports by Amnesty International; the declarations, resolutions and reports of the United Nations Commission on Human Rights, and a dozen other human rights groups. The representatives of the victims of Israel's extrajudicial killings would have causes of action not only for damages in violation of this statute, but to obtain injunctions.

Injunctions prohibiting the issuing of licenses by the Army to Boeing for the shipment of Apache Helicopters would be entirely appropriate under this law. And that would be only the beginning. Separate suits could be brought against US weapons manufacturers for knowingly shipping weapons to Israel for use by Israel in extrajudicial killings and other violations of human rights as recognized by the civilized nations of the world. Mandamus would also lie against the Department of Defense in shipping excess military equipment to Israel; against the CIA in cooperating with Israeli intelligence; against the other military and atomic agencies that license doing business with Israel or Israeli companies involved in weapon manufacturing or the gathering of intelligence.

In <u>McCartin v. Norton</u> the 9th Circuit held that 28 USC § 1331 provided federal courts with jurisdiction to review the actions of federal agencies since such were federal questions (674 F. 2d 1317 (9th Cir. 1982)). Likewise, if the action of the agency is not specifically made non-reviewable by law, any federal agency action is reviewable by the federal courts (<u>Parkview Corp. v. Department of the Army</u>, 490 F. Supp. 1278 (D.C. Wis. 1980)).

Under § 1331 federal courts can review agency actions provided the matter is an actual case or controversy and is ripe for review and the claimant has sufficient interest or standing. <u>TM Systems, Inc. v. United States</u>, 473 F. Supp. 481 (D.C. Conn. 1979). Mandatory injunction was found to be available in a suit brought under either § 1331 or § 1361 as an injunction essentially in the nature of mandamus. <u>Carpet, Linoleum and Resilient Tile Layers, Local Union No. 419, Brotherhood of Painters and Allied Trades, AFL-CIO v. Brown</u>, 656 F. 2d 564 (10th Cir. 1981).

In federal courts, mandamus is an ancillary remedy available after a right has ripened into a demand. <u>Dwyer v. LeFlore County</u>, 97 F. 2d 823 (C.C.A.Okl. 1938). Despite traditional judicial reluctance to interfere with the military, United States district court was found to have the power and duty to determine whether the Armed Services were following applicable regulations and statutes. <u>Spencer v. Laird</u>, 442 F. 2d 904 (2nd Cir. 1971). Another court has held that although federal courts lack jurisdiction to review discretional judgments of military officers acting within scope of their authority, this rule is not absolute and courts can review military orders which allegedly violate Acts of Congress. <u>Blameuser v. Andres</u>, 473 F. Supp. 767, (D.C. Wis.) affirmed 630 F. 2d 538 (1979).

The legal representatives of Yassin and Rantisi, for example, would certainly have a ripe cause of action under the Torture Victims Protection Act and therein also an ancillary remedy could seek to enjoin the Army from licensing sales of Apaches by Boeing to Israel. One of many routes these actions could take.

CATERPILLAR INC.

The vital importance of Caterpillar Inc. to the Israeli program of demolition of Palestinian homes, farms, orchards, roads, sewer systems, etc., was highlighted on March 16, 2003 when an American was killed in Gaza by a Caterpillar tractor.

Rachel Corrie was a peace activist from Olympia, Washington and was staying, with other volunteers of the International Solidarity Movement, in Palestinian homes being threatened with demolition by the Israeli Army in Rafah, the Gaza strip . She and other volunteers had been sparring with two Israeli specially modified D9 Caterpillar Bulldozers and an Israeli tank for two hours that day. The bulldozers were tearing apart orchards and plowing down houses of Palestinians for some vague "security" reasons. While Rachel and the other voluteers were trying to prevent the bulldozers from tearing down one house, she was killed when the military driver of a Caterpillar bulldozer just ran over her.

She had been clearly marked with bright clothes and everyone, including the bulldozer driver, could see her. Nevertheless, the soldier buried her under a pile of rubber, breaking numerous bones and causing her death.

Following that incident a movement was started in the United States to convince Caterpillar to stop doing business with Israel. The response from Caterpillar was that there was nothing it could do about how buyers used their equipment -- it was both practically and legally impossible to regulate the use of its products. Ironically, at the shareholder's meeting of Caterpillar in April, 2004, just before the scandalous Israeli incursion in Rafah and the destruction of dozens more homes, a Shareholder Proposal to require the company to stop doing business with Israel was soundly defeated.

A coalition of groups, headed by Jewish Voice for Peace (www.jewishvoiceforpeace.org) succeeded in putting before the shareholders of Caterpillar a Proposal which read in part:

WHEREAS:

> *It is a matter of public record that since 1967, the Israeli government has used Caterpillarequipment, including specially modified D9 and D10 bulldozers to destroy over 7,000 buildings in the West Bank and Gaza Strip, leaving 50,000 men, women and children homeless;*

> *It is a matter of public record that the Israel Defense Forces (IDF) have used Caterpillar equipment to uproot hundreds of thousands of olive trees as well as orchards of dates, prunes, lemons and organges causing widespread economic hardship and environmental degradation in rural area of Palestine.*

James W. Owens, Chairman of Caterpillar, has stood by the company's formula response as set forth in its comment on this Proposal:

"Caterpillar shares the world's concern over unrest in the Middle East. . . . . However, . . . we have neither the legal right nor the means to police indiviudal use of that equipment. . . ."

Coincidentally, or perhaps not so coincidentally, the Bush Administration just a month earlier had awarded Caterpillar Financial, a subsidiary of Caterpillar Inc., with the prestigious Malcolm Baldrige National Quality Award. Here are two images of the award ceremony that is on the Caterpillar Financial Press Kit web cite. Therein Caterpillar states that "Media personnel can use the images on this page for Cat Financial related story purposes only." This of course is Cat Financial related and here are the images.

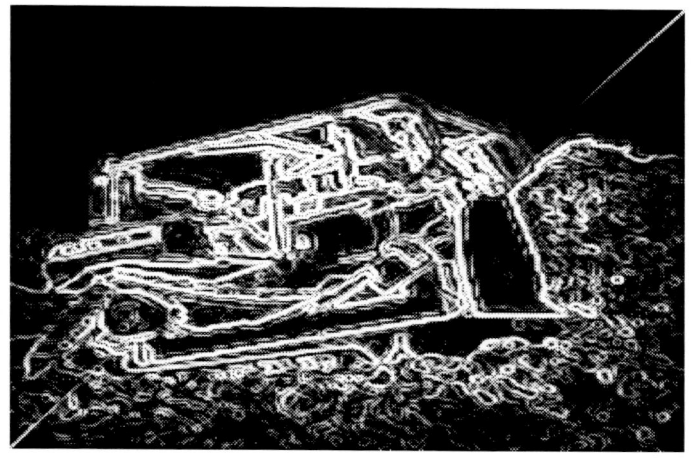

D10R   145,507 lb.

D11R CD   248,600 lb

"U.S. President Bush Congratulates Cat Financial President Jim Beard, March 9, 2004.

"Jim Beard enthusiastically concludes his acceptance speech at the Malcolm Baldrige National Quality Award Ceremony . . . in Arlington, Virginia."

Photos by Ron Sachs

The following series of three photos depicting Rachel Corrie's killing were take by Joseph Smith and Richard Purssell. They are included in a handout for the International Solidarity Movement and appear on the Stop Caterpillar website (www.catdestrpushomes.org). They were taken over the time period of 3 pm and 4:47 pm on March, 16, 2003.

In any lawsuits by the Palestinians against Caterpillar, it would have to be shown that Caterpillar knew that its equipment was being used illegally. The worldwide publicity of Ms. Corrie's death and the work done by organizations like Jewish Voice for Peace and Stop Caterpillar firmly establish knowledge on the part of Caterpillar's management of such illegal use.

If that were not enough, Amnesty International took note of Caterpillar's pivotal role in the illegal demolitions in its Annual Report on Israel and the Occupied Territoris, dated May 18, 2004.

The Report noted that in the past three and a half years the Israeli Army had destroyed more than 10% of Gaza's agricultural land. In 2202 and 2003 alone in the Gaza Strip 1,800 acres of farmland and 226,000 trees were bulldozed. "Agricultural infrastructure, including hundreds of wells and water storage pools and water pumps . . . have been destroysed along with tens of kilometers of irrigation networks."

At the end of its report, Amnesty International listed a number of appeals it was making to the Israeli Government, to the Palestinian Authority, to the International Community and then, extraordinarily, to a private American organization: Caterpillar Inc. To the management of Caterpillar it addressed these words:

> *Caterpillar Inc., the US company which produces the bulldozers used by the Israeli army, should take measures -- within the company sphere of influence --to guarantee that its bulldozers are not used to commit human rights violations, including the destruction of homes, land and other properties.*

With such international notoriety, even without extensive discovery into the files of Caterpillar in Tennessee or in Israel, the Palestinian plaintiffs can establish that Caterpillar knew that its equipment was being used illegally.

The response by Mr. Owens and the rest of Caterpillar management is woefully inadequate, and legally unsupportable. There are dozens of laws in the United States and court cases which would not only support Caterpillar's cessation of business relations with Israel, and with any company using its equipment in Israel or selling or leasing its equipment to Israel, but would in fact *require* it. The task of the Palestinian litigators is to get a Federal Court to enjoin Caterpillar to stop doing business with Israel. This might actually be the easiest case for the Palestinians and they should consider initiating this lawsuit first.

In any such lawsuit, the requested injunction should be very broad in order to cover the myriad ways businesses have learned to get around embargoes and other prohibitions. Not only must the company be enjoined from selling or leasing directly to Israel, but also to any other entity that would send the equipment or use the equipment in Israel or the Occupied Territories, including any US agencies. Caterpiller must also be enjoined from furnishing any spare parts or manuals or any other training or support material to Israel, directly or indirectly. Any operations on the ground in Israel owned or leased by Caterpillar must be closed. These are just some examples of the route that the Palestinian litigants must take.

None of these injunctions will be effective unless individuals are held liable. Then all the loopholes and other games that

executives wink at in order to avoid taxes and other laws will be more closely watched by them. Thus in any lawsuit by the Palestinians, the individual managers of Caterpillar must be held personally responsible if the court's injunction is bypassed. As in the financial statements to the SEC, the Chief Executive should be required each year to submit an affidavit as to compliance with the injunction and what steps have been taken to actively enforce the injunction. Visits to Israel and inspections of equipment there by the company or by agents should also be required to assure that notwithsatnding every other precaution, the equipment is still winding up in Israel.

(These two images, as those of Rachel Corrie, are taken from the website of "Stop Caterpillar" www.catdestroyshomes.org.)

(Except as noted Neither the logo nor the name nor the photos of Caterpillar were authorized by Caterpillar for this publication.)

— VII —

COMING TO AMERICA
Part II

There is a constant stream of Israelis coming to America, either as visitors, officials, students or immigrants. As any other alien, the Israeli must qualify under various American laws to be allowed into the US. Then, later there are further restrictions for longer stays, for Green Cards and finally for naturalization. This Chapter examines the threshold requirements for entry into the United States. In addition, it also examines what the Palestinians could do about the constant stream of Israelis in and out of the US.

The Immigration and Nationality Act has a section describing those aliens who would be <u>inadmissible</u> to the US (8 U.S.C. § 1182). In addition to the usual exclusions based on mental and physical diseases, the law makes inadmissible to the US "any alien convicted of, or who admits having committed, or who admits committing acts which constitute the essential elements of . . . a crime involving moral turpitude . . . or an attempt or conspiracy to commit such a crime.. . . " (8 U.S.C. § 1182 (2)(A)(i)(I)).

Murder easily qualifies as a crime involving moral turpitude. The assassination of Yassin, Rantisi and the hundreds of other Palestinians targeted for summary execution by the Israeli Governmentthe would involve, then, crimes of moral turpitude. On the face of the statute, then, *everyone* involved in the assassinations -- from Ministers in the Cabinet to the controllers in the radar room who tracked these victims, to the person pulling the trigger or firing the missile -- would be inadmissible to the US. .

Israelis are fully knowledgeable about the international community's condemnation of these assassinations in the occupied territories, the instances of collective punishment, and all the other crimes attendant upon the occupation. A number of Israeli soldiers and pilots have honorably refused to participate in any activities involving the occupied territories — and were accordingly punished by the Israeli Government. But the point is that Israelis are highly educated and they have read, over the years, the Resolutions of the United Nations, the Reports of the UN Commission on Human Rights, the International Red Cross, Amnesty International and numerous other human rights watch groups. They **know** that the world considers these targeted killings as crimes against humanity, as reprehensible to the laws of civilized nations.

Consequently, upon application to visit or otherwise enter the United States, and certainly before being naturalized, every Israeli should be examined to determine if she or he has had a part in these crimes of moral turpitude. For instance, were they members of any forces used in the occupied territories, like the Givati Brigade? If so, they must be excluded. Willfully shooting and injuring another is a crime involving moral

110

turpitude, requiring denial of an immigration visa. 1937, 39 Op. Atty. Gen. 95.

Under a Section entitled "Terrorist Activities," Congress, in the Immigration and Nationality Act, has also declared inadmissible any alien who "has engaged in a terrorist activity" or who "has, under circumstances indicating an intention to cause death or serious bodily harm, incited terrorist activity."

The Act leaves little to mystery or room for interpretation, as it carefully defines "terrorist activity." Among the various actions considered to be a terrorist activity are the following:

> *(III) A violent attack upon an internationally protected person . . . or upon the liberty of such a person* [e.g., residents of the Occupied Territories].
> *(IV) An assassination. . . .*
> *(VI) A threat, attempt, or conspiracy to do any of t*
> *the foregoing."*
>
> 8 U.S.C. § 1182 (a) (3) (B) (ii).

Those clauses alone would seem sufficient to cover anyone at all involved in the assassination of those 200 plus Palestinians that were targeted by the Israeli Government from 2001 to the beginning of 2004 and the many others targeted and killed by Israel since then, almost on a daily basis. The American law on conspiracy would also bring in many incidental players to these murders. However, Congress wanted to make sure that *every single culprit* in these assassinations was included, even those who would claim that they "saw no evil, heard no evil and spoke no evil." The term "engage in terrorist activities," therefore, is carefully and quite broadly defined. Congress says that the term

> *"means to commit, in an individual capacity or as a member of an organization, an act of terrorist activity or an act which the actor knows, or reasonably should know, affords material support to any individual, organization, or*

> government in conducting a terrorist activity at any time,
> including any of the following acts:
> (I)   The preparation or planning of a terrorist activity.
> (II)   The gathering of information on potential targets
>   for terrorist activity.
> (III)   The providing of any type of material support,
>   including a safe house, transportation,
>   communications, funds, false documentation or
>   identification, weapons, explosives, or training, to
>   any individual the actor knows or has reason to
>   believe has committed or plans to commit a terrorist
>   activity."

Congress' broad net to include every possible player in an assassination is further evidence of the strong Congressional intent to condemn this form of terrorism. Thus any alien even *remotely* connected, directly or indirectly, with the 200 plus assassinations of the Palestinians is absolutely inadmissible for entry into the US.

As noted elsewhere, the fact that the Israel Government has made assassination a state policy does not exclude assassination from coming within this definition of terrorism. Targeted killing is so abhorrent to the laws of civilized nations that no state sanction, however open and defiant of the international community, can exclude if from this definition. Congress made this clear in the Committee Reports accompanying the Torture Victims Protection Act in 1991: "*A state that practices torture and summary execution is not one that adheres to the rules of law.*" This statement, unfortunately, now fits Israel like a glove, and it seems proud of it. A visit to the Israel Defense Forces website on almost any day finds the IDF bragging about another successful target killing.

A federal case which explicitly rejects the Act of State defense in extrajudicial killings is <u>Letelier v. Republic of Chile</u>, 488 F. Supp. 665 D.C. Col., 1980). Heirs of the former ambassador and foreign minister of Chile and of a United States citizen who claimed that those two had been assassinated under orders from the Government of Chile were able to maintain an action against the Government of Chile.

The court held that the defendant foreign state could not claim sovereign immunity by calling the killings open and public political assassinations. The rule of immunity of a foreign government to civil suit in the US does not apply, the court held, where the action involves conduct designed to result in the assassination of an individual. The fact that the American Administration under Nixon and Kissinger turned a blind eye to these killings, or perhaps encouraged them, did not affect the ruling. Likewise, the Bush Administration's ignoring the extrajudicial killings by Israel would not affect a court's decision.

The alien from Israel, therefore, seeking entry into the United States, must be asked, and he or she must disclose, any possible connection with these 200-plus assassinations.

The various INS forms and applications for immigration visas, work permits and naturalization all contain questions which should elicit from the alien whether he or she had been involved in any of the above activities. The failure of an alien to truthfully answer these questions would become additional grounds for exclusion (8 U.S.C. § 1182 (a) (6) (C) – "misrepresentation").

Nevetheless, we recommend that the Paslestinians bring suit in a Federal Court to require the INS to make its forms more effective in screening out Israeli participants in crimes against them. For instance, the question which comes closest to forcing disclosure of participation in these assasinations and other human rights crimes in the current Application for Immigration Visa and Alien Registration (DS-230, 05-2001) is No. B of the Sworn Statement:

> *Do any of the Following classes apply to you?*
> *. . . . who admits having committed a crime*
> *involving moral turpitude."*

However, since the IDF and the Israeli Government are so proud of their extrajudicial killings and summary executions, it might not occur to a former Israeli soldier that assasinations on the orders of his Government could be "crimes of moral turpitude." The questions, then, related to assasinations in Israel and the Occupied Teritories should be more as what the INS does when questioning aliens from Haiti.

In stark contrast to the general question of crimes of "moral turpitude," stands Question No. L on the same form:

> *[Are you one] "who has ordered, carried out or materially assisted in extrajudicial and political killings and other acts of violence against the Haitian people. . .*
> *."*

Getting the INS to add the words *"or against the Palestinian people"* to this clause would be a logical move for Palestinian litigants. In addition, the INS should require that the military records of any Israeli who attempts to enter the US be made part of the necessary documentation for application. The records should be detailed enough to indicate whether the applicant ever served in the Occupied Territories or in any of the Border Police or intelligence services of Israel -- raising a presumption that he or she might have been involved in a summary execution or some other crime of moral turpitude (e.g., collective punishment; torture).

If the questions on the forms fail to elicit from Israeli aliens participation in the assassinations, torture or collective punishment of Palestinians, then oral questioning by immigration officials on entry should focus on that.

The current Application for Naturalization Form is not much better in disclosing these crimes (Form N-400 (Rev. 07/23/02). Question 9 (c), for example, asks whether the applicant has every been associated with "a terrorist organization." It may not occur to an alien who served in an Israeli military unit in the Occupied Territories that he or she had been part of a terrorist organization.

Question No. 11 on the Naturalization Form is only slightly more helpful in eliciting whether the alien participated in extrajudicial killings or collective punishment:

> *"Have you ever persecuted (either directly or indirectly) any person because of race, religion, national origin, membership in a particular social group, or political opinion?"*

Anyone who served with the Israeli Military, intelligence services or border police in the Occupied Territories, or had anything to do with any Israeli agency relating to the Occupied Territories (like the Housing agency funding the settlements, building roads, building the Barrier), would be required to answer: "yes" to that question if answered honestly. It is doubtful, however, that at this point the INS would consider failing to disclose membership in the Israeli Military as a misrepresentation. Palestinian litigants in the US will need to have a court order the INS to dig deeper into the military record of Israeli applicants.

Mandamus from a Federal Court would be available to Palestinian litigants to force the State Department and the INS to modify and clarify their forms, to improve their questioning of Israeli applicants and to deny admission to anyone who was directly or indirectly, as described above, involved in targeted killings, torture, collective punishment, and the like.

An alien who "assisted" or "otherwise participated" in persecution under a Nazi regime, was deportable , notwithstanding the government's failure to show that he was personally involved in any specific atrocities, where he served as armed SS guard at Auschwitz and Sachsenhausen and on prisoner transports during World War II. Hammer v. I.N.S. 195 F. 3d 836 (6th Cir.), cert. denied 120 S. Ct. 1247 (1999).

A District Court has subject matter jurisdiction to review agency action if the action is not otherwise made unreviewable. Merrill Ditch-

_____, 670 F. 2d 139 (9th Cir. 1982). Judges regularly find that District Courts have jurisdiction under the Declaratory Judgment Act, the Administrative Procedure Act, and the federal question statute, 28 U.S.C. § 1331, to review the validity of Immigration and Naturalization Service policy. See, e.g., Louis v. Nelson, 544 F. Supp.973 (D.C. Fla. 1982).

In addition to the military groups and names listed in the section dealing with the catastrophe in Rafah in May, 2004 (see page 311), as an assist to the INS we are listing here the photos and names of some of the military people in Israel responsible for these murders and demolitions. They should be posted in INS offices across the world as a WANTED list to make sure that none of these war criminals gets into the USA.

No. 1 to 10 are Members of the General Staff, as of May, 2004:

1. Gen. MOSHE "BOOGIE" YA'ALON
2. Gen. GABI ASHKENZAI
3. Gen. GIL REGEV
4. Gen. UDI SHANI
5. Gen. BENNY GANTZ
6. Gen. EYAL BEN REUVEN
7. Gen. MENAHEM FINKELSTEIN
8. Gen. YOSEF MISHLAV
9. Gen. ELYEZER SHKEDY
10. Gen. YITAH RON TAL

Other General Staff Members:

Generals:	Dan Halutz	Moshe Kaplinski
	Yedidia Ya'ari	Itzhak Harel
	Aharon Ze'evi (Farkash)	Udi Adam
	Udi Shani	Ruth Yaron
	Amos Yaron	Meir Dagan	(Mr.) Avi Dichter

Wanted: No. 1

Wanted: No. 2

Wanted: No. 4

Wanted: No. 3

Wanted: No. 5

Wanted: No. 6

Wanted: No. 8

Wanted: No. 7

118

Wanted: No. 9   Wanted: No. 10

Other war criminals recently active and who should be on an INS watch list to assure that they are not allowed to enter the USA:

Maj. General Dan Harel
Maj. General Yair Naveh
Maj. General Yedidia Ya'ari
Maj. General Yisrael Ziv
Maj. General Yishai Bar
Maj. General Yoav Gallant
Brig. General Shmuel Ben-ziv

Maj. General Amos Yaron
Maj. General Shmuel Keren
Maj. General Yossi Beinhorn
Maj. General Meir Dagan
Silvan Shalom
Gideon Meir
Shaul Mofaz
Avi Pazner
Uzi Landau
Captain Jacob Dallal
Zeev Boim
Brig Gen. Shmuel Zakai
Maj. Sharon Feingold
Lt. Col. Grisha Yakobowits
Col. Pinchas ("Pinki") Zoaretz

Members of the: GIVATI BRIGADE
                  GOLANI BRIGADE
                  BEDUIN DESERT PATROL
                  BORDER POLICE
                  NAHAL BRIGADE

                  SHIN BET

-- VIII --

ISRAELI BANKS IN THE UNITED STATES

Introduction

This Chapter examines how Palestinians victimized by
Israel's settlement policy could force Israeli banks out of the U.S. and
perhaps prohibit U.S. Banks from dealing with Israeli Banks.

As in most lawsuits, these lawsuits, primarily in Federal
Court to compel the Federal Reserve to take certain action, will need
to be brought by persons who can claim to have been injured by the
defendants. One primary example would be a Palestinian family

who lost its home or farmland to Israelis for the establishment of an Israeli colony or settlement in the Occupied Territories, or for the roads, water, electric and sewer lines burrowed through Palestinian lands for the exclusive use of the Israeli settlers. Or it could be the Palestinians whose families lived in Jerusalem for hundreds of years and then suddenly found themselves classified as unwanted aliens with restrictive rights in their own land by Israel's forced annexation of East Jerusalem. Such would be classic plaintiffs who could bring suits in U.S. Federal Courts to compel US and state regulatory agencies to disapprove any applications made by Israeli banks to do business in the United States, and to terminate those approvals that have previously been given.

A) The Regulatory Process

    1) *The Board of Governors of the Federal Reserve*

As of June, 2000, foreign banking organizations in the U.S. held over $923 billion in assets, approximately 19 percent of the total commercial banking assets in the U.S. . According to the Federal Reserve Bank of New York, they therefore "play an integral role in the U.S. financial system" (foreign control of various forms of banking organizations as of 2000: 348 branches, 111 agencies, 79 U.S. commercial banks and 18 Edge or Agreement corporations). In the United States, since enactment of the Foreign Bank Supervision Enhancement Act of 1991, the Board of Governors of the Federal Reserve (the "Board" or the "Federal Reserve") has the primary authority to approve or disapprove applications by foreign banks to do business in the U.S.. The subsequent supervision of these foreign banks is shared by various agencies, depending on the type of entity approved, including the Comptroller and the Federal Deposit Insurance Corporation, with the primary rule making and examination authority being the Federal Reserve.

Foreign banks wishing to set up shop in the U.S. need to obtain approval from the Federal Reserve pursuant to an application process. US law sets minimum standards for such approval. Aside from financial requirements, which are obviously the first concern of the Federal Reserve, the Board may take into account

> *Whether the foreign bank and the United States affiliates of the bank are in compliance with applicable United States law.* (12 USC § 3105 (d) (3) (D)).

A foreign bank branch, agency or representative office has the same rights and privileges as domestic entities in similar categories *"and shall be subject to all the same duties, restrictions, penalties, liabilities, conditions, and limitations that would apply under the National Bank Act to a national bank doing business at the same location. . . ."* Thus the foreign bank's branch, agency or representative office

> *shall conduct its operations in the United States in full compliance with provisions of any law of the United States or any State thereof which —*
>
> *(A) impose requirements that protect the rights of consumers in financial transactions . . .*
>
> *(B) prohibit discrimination against any individual or other person on the basis of the race, color, religion, sex, marital status, age, or national origin of (i) such individual or other person or (ii) any officer, director, employee, or creditor of, or any owner of any interest in, such individual or other person.(12 USC §3106a (1).)*

No application from any foreign bank can be approved

> *unless the entity making the application has agreed to conduct all of its operations in the United States in full*

> *compliance with provisions of any law of the United States or any State thereof which—*
>
> *(A) impose requirements that protect the rights of consumers in financial transactions, ...*
>
> *(B) prohibit discrimination against individuals or other persons on the basis of . . . race, color, religion, sex, marital status, age, or national origin . . . (* 12 USC §3106a (2).)

Among the consumer protection statutes that apply to foreign banks in the U.S.are the Equal Credit Opportunity Act and the Fair Housing Act. In addition, as to its own employees, all the state and federal laws against discrimination in employment apply.

The Board has promulgated rules intended to implement these statutory requirements. According to such rules the Board, in reviewing an application by a foreign bank to do business in the United States, may utilize certain discretionary standards, including

> *Whether the foreign bank and its U.S. affiliates are in compliance with applicable U.S. law, and whether the applicant has established adequate controls and procedures in each of its offices to ensure continuing compliance with U.S. law.* (12 C.F.R. § 211.24 (c)(2)(vi).)

The Board, in reviewing the application, may also take into consideration

> *the history of operation of the foreign bank . . . in its home country . . . .*
>
> (12 C.F.R. § 211.24 (c)(3).)

The Board can order a foreign bank to terminate its activities in the U.S. if it finds that:

There is reasonable cause to believe that the foreign bank or any of its affiliates has committed a violation of law . . . in the United States; and as a result of such violation . . . the continued operation of the foreign bank's [operations] would not be consistent with the public interest. . . . (12 C.F.R. §211.25 (a).)

In making its determination to terminate, the Board may

take into account the . . . the history of operation of the foreign bank . . . in its home country. . . . (12 C.F.R. § 211.25 (b).)

In the Bank Holding Company Supervision Manual issued by the Federal Reserve for guidance in the examination of banks, the Board provides a "Policy Statement" on the supervision and regulation of foreign banking organizations. Part of that statement reads as follows:

The Board believes that in general, foreign banks seeking to establish banks or other banking operations in the United States should meet the same general standards of strength, experience and reputation as required for domestic organizers of banks and bank holding companies.

In that same statement, however, the Board did recognize that foreign banks operate outside the US in accordance with different legal and social environments so that

the general policy of the Board [is] not to extend U.S. bank supervisory standards extra-territorially to foreign bank holding companies. The Board will give due regard to these factors in applying the principle of national treatment. (BHC Supervision Manual 2100.1.1, December 1992;)

Since the main interest of the supervisory agencies, such as the Comptroller, the FDIC, and the Board, is directed at the "safety and soundness" of the operations of the foreign banks in the U.S., these regulatory agencies are instructed by the Board to "place primary emphasis on assessing the financial well-being of the U.S. offices." Nevertheless the Board at the same time enjoins the supervisory agencies that

> *They are also concerned with adherence to U.S. law and regulation by these offices.*

While examining compliance by these offices to U.S. law and regulations, the Board cautions the supervisory agencies not to ignore the operations of the foreign banks in their home country because "ultimate responsibility for branch and agency activities resides in head offices overseas." Therefore the agencies must

> *collect information on the consolidated operations of the foreign banks and expand their contacts with senior management of the banks.* (BHC Supervision Manual, 2100.1.2, December 1992.)

THE QUESTION OF COMPLIANCE WITH THE LAWS AGAINST DISCRIMINATION BY ISRAELI BANKS.

The Federal Reserve therefore has indicated its interest in the reputation and behavior of the foreign banks in their home countries, as that will obviously indicate what the behavior of the U.S. entities they control will be in the U.S. A significant aspect of the behavior of

128

the U.S. branches of these foreign banks is their adherence to U.S. law, and in particular laws relating to finance, including the laws prohibiting discrimination "on the basis of . . . race, color, religion, . . . or national origin . . . ."

The question then is twofold: 1) Does the history and behavior of Israeli banks in their home country indicate whether they have the institutional ability or corporate desire to adhere to fundamental U.S. laws prohibiting discrimination based on race, religion or national origin; and 2) What can be determined of the "character and reputation" of Israeli banks from their activities in their home countries, particularly with respect to discrimination based on race, religion and ancestry?

A strong argument can be made, therefore, that Israeli banks who practice institutionalized and routine discrimination in their own country based on race, religion and ancestry, can not be expected to faithfully and honestly abide by fundamental American values and laws which find such discrimination invidious, destructive to our social fabric and unlawful. This alone may be sufficient to disallow Israeli banks from doing business in the U.S.

2) *New York State Banking Department*

Foreign banks wishing to set up any operations in New York State must also obtain approval from the Superintendent of Banks. The review process relies heavily on the information and format supplied in the application made to the Federal Reserve. However greater emphasis is placed in the New York's approval regime on character and fitness.

An application to obtain a license will be approved by the NY Superintendent only if he or she finds

> *that the financial responsibility, experience, character, and general fitness of the foreign banking corporations . . . are such as to*

command the confidence of the community and to warrant belief
that the representative will operate honestly, fairly, and efficiently . .
. . (Article V-B, New York Banking Law, § 221-d.)

As part of the NY approval process, all applicants are to sign two separate agreements relating to commitments not to discriminate on the basis of any illegal category. One form is the same as the agreement required by Section 9(b) of the International Banking Act of 1978, as added by Section 311 of Public Law 95-630. In the package for a foreign bank application for a NY license is the NY form required by Section 9(b) of the IBA, <u>FB 102, Annex H</u>. In that form the foreign banks agree to

> *Conduct all operations in the United States in full*
> *compliance with provisions of any law of the United States or any*
> *State thereof which –*
> *(A) prohibit discrimination against individuals or other*
> *persons on the basis of race, color, religion, sex, marital status, age,*
> *or national origins . . . .*

New York State, however, apparently is not satisfied with just that one agreement to abide by non-discrimination laws. It also requires the applicant to execute a "Certificate of Compliance With Section 296-a Of the Executive Law Of the State of New York" (<u>FB 102, Annex I</u>). This Certificate of Compliance requires the foreign organization to agree and certify that it *"will comply in all respects with Section 296-a of the Executive Law of the State of New York."*

Section 296-a is a very detailed series of provisions intended to prohibit various forms of unlawful discrimination, directly or indirectly, in the granting of credit and loans. Prohibited is any form of discrimination based *on "race, creed, color, national origin, sexual*

130

orientation, military status, age, sex, marital status, disability, or familial status . . . ."

AMERICAN FUNDAMENTAL PROHIBITION AGAINST INVIDIOUS DISCRIMINATION

These repetitive non-discrimination agreements under both the Federal Reserve procedure and the New York State procedure for approval of foreign bank applications underscore this very core American value: non-discrimination based on an invidious basis: including race, color, creed and ancestry.

Can an Israeli bank pass the character and reputation test which includes this fundamental American principle of non-discrimination? Can Israeli banks that by Israeli law and practice are relied upon by their government to routinely discriminate in the granting of credit against Arabs, Muslims and Palestinians possibly "warrant belief that the representative [in NY] will operate honestly, fairly and efficiently . . . ." We think the answer is that it obviously cannot, and we believe a Federal Judge would agree with us.

3)   *Federal Reserve Approval Controversies*

That the issues of character, fitness, reputation and the operation of the foreign bank in its own country are essential to the approval process for foreign banks applying to do business in the US was highlighted in several applications made to the Federal Reserve in recent years.

Swiss Bank Corporation

When the Union Bank of Switzerland and the Swiss Bank Corporation sought approval from the Federal Reserve Board to merge (since they had some banking operations in the US), the merger approval was vehemently opposed by various groups and individuals based on allegations of Swiss Bank participation in the atrocities of the Holocaust overseas. At the heart of the objections was the alleged connivance of the Swiss Bank during WWII in hiding tainted property, including massive amounts of gold, stolen from the Jews by the Nazis. In addition, complaints were made that the Swiss Bank was not vigorously seeking to find the heirs of Jewish depositors who had perished in the Holocaust, the issue of the "dormant" accounts.

Among those objecting to the merger's approval was U.S. Senator Alfonse D'Amato of New York and Governor George E. Pataki of New York. Governor Pataki issued a press release (March 24, 1998) stating:

> Before these two institutions are given the chance to launch a new era in their respective histories, they must convince New York's bank regulators and the Federal Reserve's Board of Governors that they're doing everything in their power to rectify a great injustice from the past. . . . ."

The Acting Superintendent of the New York State Banking Department, Elizabeth McCaul, wrote a letter to Federal Reserve Chairman Alan Greenspan outlining New York State's objection to the approval:

> The home office's [of the Swiss Bank] seemingly inattentive regard for the depositors who fell victim to the Holocaust, or their heirs . . . raises regulatory questions about the character and fitness of these banks' privilege to maintain operations in the United States.

The Swiss Bank application was eventually approved by the Federal Reserve and a license to do business in New York was granted by the NY Banking Department. This was accomplished, however, only after exhaustive and complex investigations and agreements by the Swiss Bank to leave no stone unturned to locate the heirs of dormant accounts and to compensate any possible claimant for any wrong participated in by Swiss Bank during the WWII period. American commissions and Swiss commissions were set up to follow through on these agreements.

The Federal Reserve in its decision approving the merger reviewed the extensive efforts being made by Swiss Bank to remedy the sins of the past, including cooperation with the Volcker Commission and the Claims Resolution Tribunal. It also noted that independent bodies had been set up by the Swiss Government for the same purpose, among them the Bergier Commission, with which the Swiss Bank was able to show the Board that it was fully cooperating. Finally, the Board was able to list as favorable to the Swiss Bank the fact that the Bank had entered into a special agreement on Holocaust issues with the New York State Banking authorities during the proceedings, resulting in the withdrawal of objections from New York. The Board therefore concluded:

> To the extent that the matters raised by commenters [on the Holocaust issues] relate to the factors that the Board is authorized to consider, the Board concludes, based on all the facts of record and for the reasons discussed above and in this order, including the cooperation of UBS and Swiss Bank with the appropriate investigating and supervisory authorities, that such matters do not warrant denial of the proposal.

The Deutsch Bank

A similar scenario was played out when the Deutsche Bank of Germany proposed to acquire the U.S. bank, Bankers Trust Corporation. Objections were raised about the activities of Deutsch Bank during the Holocaust, including direct funding of a concentration camp. Among the objectors was New York City

Comptroller Alan G. Hevesi (now the Comptroller of New York State). Again the Board's decision describes a long list of remedial steps undertaken by Deutsch Bank to rectify the past and to compensate Holocaust victims and their heirs. The Board decided:

> To the extent that the matters raised by commenters relate to the factors that the Board is authorized to consider, the Board has considered, in particular, the past efforts of Deutsche Bank to investigate and address its Holocaust involvement, and the forthcoming and ongoing efforts of current management to resolve these matters. . . . For these reasons, and based on all the facts of record, the Board concludes that the Holocaust-related matters presented by commenters do not warrant denial of the proposal.

Similarly the NYC Comptroller withdrew his objections (Press Release, May 5, 1999) in light of the progress made by the applicants in addressing their Holocaust activities.

For our purposes it is important to note that the Federal Reserve, in reviewing these applications, had examined the activities of a foreign bank in its own country, not just in the U.S.. Secondly those activities were measured by the rules of international law. German law at the time, the WWII period, did not prohibit the confiscation of the property and the taking of the lives of its Jewish citizens. The degradation and attempted annihilation of the Jews of Europe that became the war crimes outlined and prosecuted by American officials during the historic Nuremberg trials, were sanctioned by the German Government at the time and were performed in full accordance with German law. It was a "State Policy" and an "Act of State". Yet these acts committed in accordance with German law were determined by the Nuremberg Tribunal to have been crimes against humanity and in violation of customary law of nations. These principles that guided the Nuremberg Judges were later enshrined in the Four Geneva Conventions of 1949. These Conventions have been accepted by all the civilized nationals of the world. Both the U.S. and Israel have signed and pledged adherence to the Geneva Conventions.

The Board at the same time, however, attempted to narrow the effect of these decisions by carefully mentioning, in both cases, that it was limited by its statutory authority to consider only certain, specified factors in deciding whether to approve applications by foreign banks. It thereupon found that *some* of the issues raised by the Holocaust matter came within *certain* of those factors, and some of them did not. The Board, however, did not specify either which of the Holocaust issues were relevant or which of the authorized factors had covered them. Yet it spent substantial portions of its time and its decision in dealing with the allegations made against the Banks based on their participation in the Holocaust. The Board therefore agreed, though reluctantly, that sufficient issues in the Holocaust matter raised by the objectors were relevant to the statutory factors it had to consider in reviewing applications by foreign banks. Put another way, it is evident that had the Swiss Bank and the Deutsch Bank stonewalled the Board on these objections, they would never have received approvals. The Board therefore proceeded on the assumption that *some* of the standards and factors it was obligated to consider by statute did apply in these cases.

These decisions in the Swiss Bank and Deutsche Bank cases establish two important points as precedents: 1) the character and reputation of a foreign bank as shown by its activities abroad are relevant considerations for the Board in reviewing an application; and 2) the standards of customary international law are to be applied to measure such character and reputation.

The authors feel, however, that the Board was being unnecessarily ambiguous and coy with respect to its authority. For example, the Board could have stated quite simply that it was basing its authority to review such matters on whether these entities were in compliance with applicable U.S. law (12 U.S.C. § 3105 (d) (3) (D)), recognizing expressly as it did impliedly that the customary law of nations were part of the applicable U.S. law. Two other simple and clear statutory bases for considering the Holocaust crimes as relevant in examining the applications were Congress' directives 1) that the Board take into consideration the views of the State authorities (12 U.S.C. § 3105 (d) (6) (C)), and 2) that the Board could impose on its approval *any* other conditions "it deems necessary" (12 U.S.C. § 3105 (d) (5)). As New York had raised the Holocaust matter in questioning the character and fitness of the banks, so the Board *had* to consider that issue in determining the character and fitness of the banks. On a more discretionary tack, the Board, in attempting to determine what "other conditions" it wished to impose on its approval, could have made inquiries of the Banks as to what remedies they were offering to the victims of the Holocaust and their heirs. There are even more statutory provisions that it may have cited as authority to look at these past illegal acts, but instead it chose to be somewhat ambiguous, hoping perhaps to avoid complicating its work in the future by not encouraging non-financial objections to bank applications by "outsiders."

Conclusion

In lawsuits by Palestinians seeking injunctions that would require the Federal Reserve to terminate the activities of the Israeli Banks in the U.S., therefore, it is relevant to examine the way the Israeli Banks operate in their own country and also test this operation by the standards of customary international law, particularly the principles enunciated at Nuremberg and embodied in the Four Geneva Conventions of 1949.

B) Israeli Banks in the United States

The Federal Reserve Board of Governors has approved applications to do business in the U.S. from five of the six largest Israeli Banks. The information below was obtained from D&B, records of the Bank of Israel and filings with the Federal Reserve Board.

1)   *The Israeli Banks*

Bank Hapoalim B.M.

Bank Hapoalim is the largest bank in Israel with $59 Billion in assets, 12, 464 employees and 325 full-service branches in Israel, including the settlements in the Occupied Territories. It has three branches in New York City; a branch in Chicago; an agency in Miami; a representative office in San Francisco and a wholly-owned subsidiary, Signature Bank, in New York which itself has 10 branches. According to its 3/31/04 Quarterly Report on file with the Bank of Israel (Banking Supervision Division) it accounts for 32.4% ($42 Billion) of the credit extended to the public in Israel and 51.1% of the banking system's credit extended to the Government of Israel.

Bank Leumi le-Israel B.M.

Bank Leumi is the second largest bank in Israel, with assets of $56.3 Billion, 10,888 employees, 244 branches in Israel (including the Occupied Territories). Leumi has five branches or agencies in New York, four in California, one in Illinois and two in Florida. According to its 3/31/04 Quarterly Report is provides 29.8% ($38.6 Billion) of the Israeli Banking system's credit to the public in Israel and 19.8% to the Government of Israel.

Israel Discount Bank Ltd.

Israel Discount is the third largest bank in Israel with assets of $31.9 Billion, 8,551 employees and 200 branches. In the U.S. it has branches in New York, Florida and California. It provides 13.4%

($17.4 Billion) of the Israeli banking system's credit to the public and 6.4% of the system's credit to the Israeli Government.

United Mizrahi Bank Ltd.

United Mizrahi, Israel's fourth largest bank, has assets of $18 Billion, 80 branches in Israel and 3,408 employees. It also owns the Tefahot Israel Mortgage Bank which is Israel's largest mortgage bank with 35 branches and outlets also in Mizrahi branches. (Mizrahi has just purchased the rest of Tefahot's shares which it did not own and is merging Tefahot into Mizrahi, resulting in a combined 90 branches). Mizrahi was approved by the Board to do business in the U.S. and has a branch in Los Angeles. Mizrahi accounts for 10.5% ($13.5 Billion) of the banking system's credit to the public in Israel and 1.9% to the Government.

Union Bank of Israel Ltd.

Union Bank is Israel's sixth largest bank with assets of $4.6 Billion, 1,054 employees and 23 branches. In the United States it has a branch in New York. In Israel it provides 2.6% ($3.4 Billion) of the banking system's credit to the public and 1.0% to the government.

2)   *The Argument for Termination of Federal Reserve Approvals*

A number of arguments could be made for revoking the approvals already given to Israeli banks and for denying any further applications from Israel. Discrimination against the Arabs and Muslims in Israel is so institutionalized that it is impossible for any Israeli Bank to pass the character test on this issue. (For example, through a cacophony of laws, regulations, history and practices, Arabs cannot own or lease land in about 80% of Israel. See www.adalah.org.)Also, how can a bank that lends money to a Government whose official policy sanctions murder (extrajudicial killings) and collective punishment (home demolitions) possibly pass the character and fitness tests? For this Chapter, however, we will focus on the activities of the Israeli banks in the Occupied Territories.

As discussed in Chapter III, the settlements are illegal. On the bases of the Geneva Conventions and the UN Charter, all civilized countries have agreed that land could not be confiscated by force; that an occupying power could not legally colonize the occupied territory; that the citizens of the occupied territory could not be displaced or have their homes or farms taken from them by force of any kind. All of such actions have been taken by the Israeli Government, with no apologies, and they are continuing to this day in defiance of the international community. Yet these are violations of fundamental and customary international law and this refrain has been repeated constantly from 1967 in numerous UN Security Council Resolutions, all of which were agreed to by the U.S..

Can an Israeli Bank which does business in these illegal colonies, and thus sustains them, qualify in character and fitness and obtain approval from the Federal Reserve to do business in the U.S.? We believe the answer clearly is that they cannot, on various grounds. First of all they are committing crimes against humanity by participating in the unlawful settlement of occupied territories. As such they have violated, and they continue to violate the laws of the United States which has by treaties and its own statutes made crimes against humanity part of the law of the U.S.

We do not have sufficient concrete information to describe in detail how the Israeli banks do business in the settlements. The Palestinian plaintiffs will have to develop these facts. However, for the reasons described below we believe it is fair to conclude that these banks participate in the settlements and provide essential and extensive banking services to the illegal settlers. This makes them, by well established legal principles, accomplices to crimes against humanity.

To induce immigration to Israel the Government provides substantial cash grants to immigrants, called the "Absorption Basket" payments. An immigrant, however, cannot receive these grants unless he or she has opened up a bank account in Israel upon arrival. The Israel Government's <u>Guide for The New Immigrant,</u> at page 42 states the following:

> In order to receive the monthly Absorption Basket payments, it is necessary to open an account at the bank of your choice, and to provide the Ministry of Immigrant Absorption with the account number. It is recommended to do this with a few days of your arrival.

Every immigrant, therefore, opens a bank account upon arrival, choosing any one of the Israeli banks he or she desires.

It is no secret that many of these immigrants are encouraged to move on and live in the illegal settlements by the Government and the various groups that give advice and assistance to them. The Ministry of Immigrants Absorption advertises that immigrants who choose go to the settlements, rather than settle in Israel itself, would receive special additional benefits, from extra cash grants to more favorable mortgage. During this process the Government utilizes the Israeli banking system in various ways as an integral part of colonizing the settlements in the Occupied Territories.

For example the Ministry advises immigrants that these additional benefits available to people willing to live in the settlements are more fully described by the lenders at the mortgage banks. "List of Settlements according to Nationally Preferred Areas may be obtained at the mortgage banks." (Ministry of Immigration website, 8/14/04). In addition, the Ministry advises immigrants in its welcoming literature that purchasing apartments in certain designated settlements would entitle the prospective settler to even additional payments and points in the complicated system for allocating residences, mortgages and jobs:

> *This addition is given to immigrants purchasing apartments in the following settlements:*
>
> - *Kfar Daron*
> - *Morag*
> - *Ma'ale Efraim*
> - *Netzarem*
> - *Kiryat Arba*
> - *Kiryat Shmona*

(Ministry of Immigrants Absorption, http://www.moia.gov.il/english/housing/housing6.htm, 9/2/04).

Since the Ministry requires immigrants to open a bank account upon arrival, and each immigrant is told that the choice of bank is up to him or her, we think it is fair to conclude that the banks described above (Hapoalim, Leumi, Discount, Mizrahi, Union Bank) are chosen by the immigrants in approximately the same proportion as the Banks' portion of their outstanding credit to the public. Thus nearly 90% of the immigrants who move into the illegal colonies of the Occupied Territories get their Absorption Basket payments from the same banks who have received approval to do business in the U.S..

These banks therefore play a vital and pivotal role in settling immigrants into the illegally confiscated lands of Palestine. That should be more than enough to convince a Federal Judge to order the Federal Reserve to terminate the approvals for these Israeli banks on the basis of failures in character and fitness, currently engaged as they are in assisting violations of fundamental and customary international law.

American Banks in Israel

It appears that the only U.S. bank that has an official branch in Israel is Citigroup. It calls itself "Citigroup Israel," has its offices in the Platinum Building in Tel-Aviv and offers a wide array of financial services, primarily to companies in Israel.

We leave it to the law firms hired by the Palestinians to determine if there are grounds for pursuing Citigroup because it has chosen to do business with an *hostis humani generis*. Does Citigroup's activities assist in any way the outlawed policies of the Israeli Government (i.e., extrajudicial killings, land confiscations, collective punishment, torture) or does Citigroup Israel participate in the financing of the illegal settlements (e.g., does it finance or otherwise assist companies with factories or offices in the illegal settlements)?

— IX —

U.S.

TAX EXEMPTION

Introduction

Israel receives a large amount of dollars from tax exempt U.S. organizations. This privileged "501 (c) (3)" status, granted by the Internal Revenue Service, frees these organization from taxes and also grants tax deductibility for contributions to them. In this manner many millions of dollars of tax obligations each year are shifted from one group of taxpayers to the rest of the taxpayers.

Here we examine whether Palestinians can stem the flow of these tax-free dollars to Israel by contesting, on a case by case basis, the tax exempt status of some of these groups.

A)   The Purpose of Tax Exemption

To allow any group the ability to avoid taxes on its own income and also grant tax deductions to taxpayers contributing to that group requires substantial justification in any society, but particularly more so in the U.S., with its tradition of equal treatment before the law. After all, it is shifting part of the burdens and obligations of maintaining our government, the armed forces, our infrastructure and our social programs from these donors to the rest of the U.S. taxpayers. People of course can do what they want with their money, but when it results in adding to the tax burdens of others, it becomes of interest to everyone.

The concept of a "charity" in common law lies at the basis of such justification. The various meanings of "charity" as defined in Webster's Collegiate Dictionary are:

1. *benevolent goodwill toward or love of humanity.*

2. *a: generosity and helpfulness, esp. toward the needy or suffering; also: aid given to those in need;*

   b: an institution engaged in relief of the poor;

   c: public provision for the relief of the needy;

3. *a: a gift for public benevolent purposes;*

   b: an institution (as a hospital) funded by such a gift.

The IRS and the courts have applied the principles of common law charitable trusts to organizations seeking tax exempt status. In the IRS website it has a "FAQs" for 501 c(3) status, a shorthand for the Internal Revenue Code section providing for such

144

exemption, 26 USC § 501 (c)(3). In Question No. 1 the IRS describes a
tax exempt organization:

> *"Charitable" Organization.*
>
> *A. The term "charitable" is used in the generally
> accepted legal sense . . . . The term includes relief of the poor
> and distressed, or of the underprivileged; advancement of
> religion; advancement of education or science; erection or
> maintenance of public buildings, monuments or works;
> lessening of the burdens of Government; and promotion of
> social welfare by organizations designed to accomplish any
> of the above purposes, or (i) to lessen neighborhood tensions;
> (ii) to eliminate prejudice and discrimination; (iii) to defend
> human and civil rights; or (iv) to combat community
> deterioration and juvenile delinquency. Regs. § 1.501 (c)(3)-
> 1.*

A tax exempt group's articles of organization must require
that it be operated exclusively for one or more exempt purposes. It
will be considered by the IRS to do so

> *only if it engages primarily in activities which accomplish
> one or more § 501 (c)(3) purposes. An organization will not
> be so regarded if more than an insubstantial part of its
> activities is not in furtherance of an exempt purpose.*
> FAQ I. (A) (3).

In the "Application for Recognition of Exemption Under
Section 501(c)(3) of the Internal Revenue Code" (IRS Form 1023), the
IRS requires the applicant in Part II, Line 1, to provide

a detailed narrative description of all of the activities of the organization – past, present, and planned. Do not merely refer to or repeat the language in the organizational document. List each activity separately in the order of importance based on the relative time and other resources devoted to the activity. Indicate the percentage of time for each activity. Each description should include, as a minimum, the following: (a) a detailed description of the activity, including its purpose and how each activity furthers your exempt purpose; (b) when the activity was or will be initiated; and (c) where and by whom the activity will be conducted.

These disclosures are considered particularly important by the IRS. In its accompanying instructions for this Line, the IRS advises the applicant:

> *It is important that you report all activities carried on by the organization to enable the IRS to make a proper determination of the organization's exempt status.*

B)   <u>Illegal or Violates Fundamental Public Policy</u>

Tax exempt status may not be granted to an organization or, if granted, may be

revoked for any of the following reasons:

1.   More than an insubstantial part of the resources of the organization is used for other that the activities it listed in its Application;

2.   Any of its actual activities are illegal.

3. A substantial part (perhaps over 5%) of its activities are contrary to "fundamental public policy."

These principles have been spelled out and applied over the years in a number of

IRS Rulings and court cases. The most significant court cases are <u>Bob Jones University v. United States</u>, 461 U.S. 574 (1983) – activities contrary to fundamental public policy (racial discrimination) and <u>Church of Scientology of California v. Commissioner</u>, 83 T.C. 506 (1984) – illegal activities (tax fraud).

If an activity is illegal, the IRS does not need to make any determination

as to whether the illegal act is a substantial part of the organization's activities. One illegal act, if done at the direction of the organization, or ratified by it, would be sufficient grounds to revoke tax exemption status.

However, if the activity is contrary to fundamental public policy, a one

time incident would not be enough to warrant revocation. The IRS must make an additional finding, namely, that a substantial portion of the organization's activities are involved. The IRS has never specified what it considers "substantial;" but a good rule of thumb would be anything over 5%, as that is the guideline for the amount of lobbying a 501 (c)(3) charity can engage in without jeopardizing its status.(See Rev Rul. 71-447, 1971 – 2 C.B. 230; Rev. Rul. 75-231, 1975 – 1 C.B. 158; Rev. Rul. 80 – 278, 1980 – 2 C.B. 175. See also <u>Illegality and Public Policy Considerations</u> by Jean Wright and Jay H. Rotz. "The Exempt Organization Continuing Professional Education Technical

Instruction Program For Fiscal Year 1994" appearing on the IRS
website.)

C)   U.S. Tax Exempt Groups and Israel

Jewish charitable organizations in the U.S. have had a long and
honorable history. They have been truly "charitable" organizations
by the tests of both Webster's definition and common law
precedents. Their work was particularly sanctified during the mass
migration to America from Eastern Europe, Russia and the
Mediterranean around 1900 — in providing the necessities of life to
the immigrants; and then again during the Thirties and WWII — in
rescuing and giving succor to the holy host of innocents being
pursued for annihilation across the entire continent of Europe.

Since the United Nations validated the State of Israel in 1948,
however, many traditional Jewish charities in America have been
turning more and more of their time and resources to the State of
Israel. In addition, numerous groups have sprung up solely for the
purpose of supporting programs in Israel.

The authors are of the opinion that the tax-free status of a
significant portion of the millions of dollars each year that are not
going to the U.S. Treasury but instead are going to projects in Israel
is not justified under our tax law. These millions are being used to
further violations of law and for activities contrary to fundamental
American public policy. What, for example, is "charitable" about
buying binoculars, bullet-proof vests, armored vehicles and the like,
for Jewish fundamentalists who are knowingly risking their and
their families lives in an attempt to undo a thousand years of history
by forcibly settling in Arab towns and villages. Whatever can be said
about their courage and faith, it cannot be said that these people are

involved in acts of benevolence toward mankind or the lessening of neighborhood tensions or the advancement of human and civil rights or nondiscrimination and harmony among the races. That being the case, their supporters in the U.S. cannot shift tax burdens from one group of Americans who favor such activities to those who do not or are indifferent to such. <u>The Church of Scientology</u> case reaffirmed the important U.S. legal principle that religious beliefs cannot justify violations of the law. There are no excerptions to this fundamental American idea.

The courageous pioneers in the Israeli settlement of Elon Moreh – Shechem need a number of things for their survival in the now-hostile environment of the Arab West Bank. We will put aside for the moment the fact that these settlements are illegal under international law so that *any* support of them is also illegal. Nevertheless, one has to ask what is benevolent about buying military equipment and armored vehicles for these settlers? This is the equipment made necessary only because of the hostility created by these very settlers who are now engaged in a civil war with their Arab neighbors of their own making. By now everyone knows that the ultimate goal of these settlers is to push all the Arabs out of "Greater Israel" (which includes the West Bank, Gaza and some undetermined additional real estate). So when a single Jew moves into an Arab village or town and takes even one house or an apartment in one building, either by force with the Army's help under some pretense of military necessity, or by buying out the Arab owner, the rest of the neighborhood fully understands that this is just the beginning of an attempt to exile them. Anger, hostility and resistance are the inevitable offspring

.

The 501 (c)(3) charity, *Friends of Elon Moreh* (P.O. Box 5435, Passaic Park, N.J. 07055), on their website ask for donations, which they expressly advertise as tax deductible, to purchase a number of things, among them being 20 "shoulder rests" at $400 each for a total of $8,000. What are these "shoulder rests"? The Friends of Elon Moreh tell us:

> *Today all of the team members* [individuals on the "Rapid Response Team" for the settlement] *carry long M-16 rifles with them at all times. These are clumsy and often are difficult to maneuver in close quarters inside a building. Shorter shoulder rests are available to alleviate their problem.*

Their website also provides us with a picture of the members of the Rapid Response Team:

The *Friends of Elon Moreh* do not tell us who paid for the M-16s. However, they also ask for $9,000 for two $4,500 telescope lenses; $8,000 for four $2,000 infra-red binoculars; $3,000 for walkie-talkies and $1,000 for a relay antennae for use by the settlements Rapid Response Team. This is a group of individuals who want to expand Israel to what they consider are its historic boundaries – notwithstanding the United Nations delineation of its borers in 1948 that gave it legitimacy among the nations of the world. Their ambitions may be admirable to many, butt they inevitably invite violent conflict with the millions of people who already inhabit the land and naturally resist moving out. Pursue this Quixotic dreams if they wish, but the issue here is whether they can further burden the U.S. taxpayer with these dreams.

Could this be what Congress intended when it provided for the special and privileged status of tax exempt "charitable" organizations? It is clear to us that a Federal Court Judge would think not.

Then there is the 501 (c)(3) group called *"American Friends of Alteret Cohanim"* (Three – West 16th Street, 5th Floor, New York, NY 10011) raising $1,075,000 tax deductible dollars in 2003 to develop, among other projects, a "Pre-Military Mechina Program" at its Yeshiva in Arab, or East, Jerusalem. The program prepares Yeshiva students "for combat unit service in the IDF" (http://www.ateret.org.il/new/project.php?id=205 , August 31, 2004). Again, the American Friends offer us a photo of what the donations will presumably be used for:

Among its other projects are the unwelcome and illegal moving into and renovation of yet more buildings in Arab East Jerusalem, thus continuing to provoke deep unrest with their neighbors, the very opposite of what a charitable group would be expected to support. Palestinian litigants can question the IRS in a Federal Court as to what the IRS considers benevolent about this group's projects.

A handful of extreme fundamentalists are also generating anger and turmoil in the Palestinian town of Jericho. Even in opposition to their Government, which has its own scheme and program for settling the West Bank and cleansing it of Arabs, these individuals persist in trying to push Palestinians out of Jericho and make Jericho a Jewish town once again — after two thousand years. The *American Friends of New Communities in Israel, Inc.* (6 Timber Trail, Suffern, NY 18901) on their website ask for tax deductible dollars to send to these fundamentalists so they can continue to stir up havoc in this Palestinian town.

The controversial right wing Rabbi Haim Meir Druckman was recently appointed by Sharon to supervise the new conversion court system. Druckman was quoted by the <u>Jerusalem Post</u> (July 12, 2004) as saying that the Prime Minister had "decided to bring the courts under his authority because he sees conversion as a national priority." The major task of the conversion courts is to convert the hundreds of thousands of immigrants from the former Soviet Union who, though Jews, are not officially considered "halachicly Jewish."

Druckman is a fervent Zionist demanding that Israelis annex permanently all the West Bank, Gaza, the Golan Heights and East Jerusalem – namely, the Occupied Territories for the creation of the Greater Israel. He also is famous for sponsoring laws and policies to discriminate against Israeli Arabs in the purchase or renting of homes. In 2002 he obtained the support of the Sharon Government when as a legislator he introduced a bill that would enable state land to be apportioned for Jewish use only, thus excluding any Arab Israelis based only on their religion or race.(<u>Haaretz Daily</u>, July 8, 2002.)

On September 8, 2004, Rabbi Druckman, as head of the Bnei Akiva network, together with other right-wing settler rabbis, published a letter they had sent to the government urging it not to worry about killing Palestinian civilians if it would interfere with the war on terrorism. The letter read in part:

> *There is no need to avoid hitting or even killing*
> *Palestinians who are not involved in terrorism when this*
> *will harm the efforts to defend Israeli lives. . . . Jewish Law*
> *provides that during war time, such as that which we are*
> *now experiencing, there is no difference between the*
> *populace and the army. If a danger arises to Israeli soldiers*
> *or to civilians, Jewish ethics teach that our lives take*
> *precedence over others.*

Arutz Sheva Israel National News, September 7, 2004; Haaretz Daily, September 7, 2004; Jerusalem Post, September 7, 2004.

Rabbi Druckman, therefore, clearly promotes at least two policies that are contrary to fundamental American public policy: invidious discrimination and the deliberate killing of non-combatant civilians. Yet this same Rabbi Druckman heads the international organization of *Bnei Akiva* and is on the board of directors of something called the *Terror Victims Association*. In the United States taxpayers can make tax deductible donations to Rabbi Druckman by contributing to the 501 (c)(3) organization *"American Friends of Yeshivot Bnei Akiva"* (11 Broadway, Suite 901, New York, NY 10004) and the "Central Fund of Israel" (980 – 6th Avenue, 3rd Fl., New York, NY 10018).

With these facts, Palestinian litigants should have no difficulty in convincing a Federal Judge that American taxpayers should not be further burdened by tax deductible contributions made by others to these groups.

154

Our favorite, however, for outlandish abuse of the tax system is the *"Friends of the Israel Defense Forces,"* a 501 (c)(3) organization that shifts the burden of supporting our Government to others for the purpose of doing just what their title suggests, supporting the Israel military forces. Again, where is the benevolence and goodwill toward mankind that the whole concept of "Charitable Trusts" is based on? These Friends of the Israeli military raised $15,100,000 in tax deductible contributions in 2003 (and thereby shifted an additional $5,000,000 in taxes to the rest of Americans — American who could just not see their way to sending money to assist the Israeli military).

The *Friends of the Israel Defense Forces* tell us that with this $15,000,000 each year it can continue to provide fitness and entertainment centers for the Israel military, including in such "outposts" as "Judea, Samaria [that is, the Palestinian West Bank] and Gaza" (http:///www/israelsoldiers.org/program.efm). The soldiers who are manning the checkpoints in the Occupied Territories, enforcing the curfews, bulldozing the Palestinian houses, chasing and gunning down "militants" (and bystanders) whose names show up on a continually growing list of men slated for summary execution by the Government, destroying orchards and farmland as punishments of the Arab community for this or that wrong committed by an Arab — apparently need a break from all this stress. So their American Friends, thanks to American tax deductible donations, are providing them with "social and recreational clubs, so that in their limited free time the soldiers can choose to exercise or relax. These activities are critical to soldier morale and well being" (id.).

These sentences bring back memories of those old movies where SS troops, weary from their torturing and killing of concentration camp inmates, indulged themselves in raucous orgies among themselves or with women forcibly recruited from those who were about to die; or relaxed at genteel soirées, drenching themselves in the intellectual and beautiful sounds of Wagner and Mozart.

We are of the opinion that a Federal Judge should have no difficulty in putting an end to the tax exemption of these friends of the military.

Nefesh B'Nefesh has raised $4,2000,000 so far in 2004, according to newspaper reports. Since its inception in 2002 by an orthodox rabbi in Florida and a wealthy colleague, it has provided financing and other support to convince and then transport 3,000 American Jews from the U.S. to Israel, many of them to live in the settlements of the Palestinian West Bank (Asbury Park Press, August 25, 2004, p.1; New York Times, July 15, 2004).

Is this what Congress intended when it established special tax rules for "charities" – that tax deductions be allowed to a group luring Americans to abandon the U.S., much less to settle in internationally outlawed communities? We have not yet examined Nefesh's Application for tax exemption filed with the IRS, but we would guess that in Part II, Line 1, it did not list among any of its activities its primary activity, namely, to cause a mass migration of Americans out of this country.

The 501 (c)(3) tax exempt organization *Kumah, Inc.* states in its Certificate of Organization (http://www.allyahrevolution.com/legal/incorp1.png) that its purpose is "to foster, advance and promote the practices of Judaism; to study and read the Torah, . . ." and similar laudatory goals. We assume this is the same language it used in its Application to the IRS for tax exemption (again, we have not yet seen the actual Application). Yet when it is raising tax deductible dollars from the public it is not so vague. It describes itself as "dedicated to encouraging and facilitating mass Aliyah [immigration] to Israel by all Jews in exile." Presumably all people of the Jewish faith in the U.S. are considered by this tax exempt group to be in "exile."

The Palestinian litigants and their attorneys need only to point out that promoting mass emigration from the U.S. to Israel is *not* the same activity as studying the Torah. In the organizers' minds they probably can rationalize this sleight of hand because of their particular vision of Judaism. But in fact it would be clearly deceptive to fail to disclose to the IRS what they really meant to do. To an IRS employee reviewing Nefesh's Application for tax exemption, it would not occur to him or her that promoting "the practices of Judaism; to study and read the Torah. . . ." meant inducing mass migration out of the U.S.

There appears to be many such tax exempt organizations in the U.S. illegally shifting tax burdens to taxpayers who do not share their faith in a Greater Israel – meaning the cleansing of the West Bank, Gaza, the Golan Heights and East Jerusalem of Arabs. A good number of these will be easy pickings for the Palestinian litigants and their attorneys. Pointing out the failure of these groups to honestly state their intended activities in their tax Exempt

Applications should be enough to have their status revoked. Then the records of the new groups set up in recent years solely for the purpose of supporting projects in Israel will have to be examined to determine if any of the projects they support are illegal, by U.S. law or by the fundamental laws of civilized nations accepted by the U.S.. In addition, what activities which may not be illegal per se may need to be examined to determine if they are contrary to fundamental public policy, such as the American policy against racial and national original discrimination. There are numerous groups that we feel would have their tax exemption status revoked in the face of a proper challenge along these lines of examination.

The examples of 501 (c)(3) tax exempt organizations that we have discussed above are admittedly extreme and account for only a tiny portion of the money raised by Jewish charities in the U.S. But their very continued existence makes it obvious that the IRS is not paying much attention to how tax exempt groups actually operate. Therefore, the more difficult and perhaps more troublesome task for both the Palestinian litigants and the Federal Judges hearing the cases will be to examine the more mainstream, venerable and traditional Jewish charities.

For example, *The Jewish Federation of Metropolitan Chicago* received $96,210,446 in tax deductible donations in 2003 and had assets of $333,030,621 (figures from the Charity Navigator). The Federation states that it allocated 43.4% of its income in 2003 to "Jews in need in Israel and other countries." This is clearly a significant portion of the Federation's resources. The question is: what portion of this 43.4% was used to support the illegal settlements, directly or indirectly. That some of it was used for such can fairly be concluded

158

from the fact that these funds are ultimately channeled through the Israel organizations that have actively encouraged and supported the illegal settlements, namely, the *Jewish Agency for Israel* and the *American Jewish Joint Distribution Committee.*

So the Palestinian litigants and their attorneys must determine if a significant portion of the $222,289,000 tax deductible donations raised in 2003 by *United Jewish Appeal – Federation of New York* (net assets: $601,787,000), for example, were used for illegal purposes in Israel or for programs that are against fundamental American public policy. Similar examinations will need to be conducted of the scores of other Jewish charities listed in the IRS Publication 78. For example, was any part of the $74,191,140 tax deductible donations raised in 2003 by the *Combined Jewish Philanthropies of Greater Boston* (net assets: $216,095,837) used to support in any way the illegal settlements; the $9,591,812 raised in 2003 by the *Jewish Federation of Greater Dallas*; the $38,309,657 of the *Jewish Federation of Greater Philadelphia*; the $103,090,547 of *Hadassah* (net assets: $537,439,466); the $7,412,265 of *Emunah of America*; the $4,680,570 of the *One Israel Fund*; the $31,907,136 of the *Jewish National Fund*; the $8,337,075 of *The Jerusalem Foundation*; the $76,576,650 of the *Jewish Federation Council of Greater Los Angeles*; the $68,166,803 pf the *Jewish Community Federation of San Francisco,* and so forth. (Figures obtained from website of "Charity Navigator" as of September 2, 2004).

The laws on tax exemption should be fairly administered for the benefit of all Americans. While the Palestinians will be attempting to slow down the Israeli onslaught, they will at the same time be doing a favor for all of us by these lawsuits to compel the IRS to enforce the law and thereby make the tax system more equitable.

D) STATE OF ISRAEL BONDS

Israel's external debt at the end of 2003 was $29.522 Billion, of which $13.730 Billion was owed under bonds guaranteed by the U.S. Government and $9.942 Billion was State of Israel bonds (*source*: Bank of Israel). In the United States the Government of Israel sells its bonds through the Development Corporation for Israel, a NASD-registered broker/dealer headquartered at 575 Lexington Avenue, New York, New York 10022-6195.

Palestinian litigants may attempt to shut down these sales because the dollars being raised in the U.S. are being used to fund an outlaw state, *hostis humani generis*. This outlaw status can be justified on just one of Israel's many violations of customary international law – summary execution (targeted killing or extrajudicial killing).The Government of Israel's official policy of extrajudicial killings is in violation of customary international law and U.S. law. As the U.S. House Committee that sent the Torture Victims Protection Act of 1991 to the House floor stated in its Report:

> "*A state that practices torture and summary execution is not one that adheres to the rule of law*" (House Report 102-367, Part 1, page 3; 102nd Congress, 1st Session, November 25, 1991).

International bodies have also found the settlements in the Occupied Territories illegal; the use of collective punishment and torture illegal; the Wall being built on Palestinian land as illegal.

While the United States, because of domestic political considerations, has shielded Israel from the effects of its unlawful activities, curiously it still recognizes that many of Israel's state policies are illegal. The U.S. did this when it joined in voting for numerous U.N. Resolutions on these subjects since 1967. In addition, though not specifically calling them illegal as such, the U.S. State Department in its Annual Reports on Human Rights in the Occupied Territories each year dutifully delineates each of these criminal acts. The Palestinian litigants need only submit the following items from the Report covering the year 2003 as evidence in a Federal Court to get a Federal Judge seriously to consider putting an end to the sale of Israel Bonds in the U.S..

> **United States State Department, Human Rights Report**: 2203 [Released February, 2004, covering the year 2003]:
>
> **Israel and the Occupied Territories**
>
> . . . .
>
> *Israel's overall human rights record in the occupied territories remained poor and worsened in the treatment of foreign human rights activists as it continued to commit numerous, serious human rights abuses.*
>
> *Security forces killed at least 573 Palestinians and 1 foreign national and injured 2, 992 Palestinians and other persons during the year, some of whom were innocent bystanders. Israel security forces targeted and killed at least 33 Palestinians, many of whom were terrorists or suspected terrorists. Israel forces undertook many of these targeted killings in area where civilian casualties were like, killing 47 bystanders in the process, including children. . . . .*

Israeli security units often used excessive force when confronting Palestinian demonstration, while on patrol, pursuing suspects, and enforcing checkpoints and curfews, which resulted in numerous deaths. In response to Palestinian attacks on Israeli targets, Palestinian civilian area suffered extensive damage as a result of IDF retaliation, which included shelling, bombing, and raiding.

Israeli soldiers placed Palestinian civilians in danger by ordering them to facilitate military operation, which exposed them to live fire between armed Palestinians and Israeli soldiers. . . .

Israeli forces sometimes arbitrarily destroyed, damaged, or looted Palestinian property during these operations. Israeli security forces often impeded the provision of medical assistance to Palestinian civilians by strict enforcement of internal closures that preventing passage of ambulances, . . .

Israeli security forces harassed and abused Palestinian pedestrian and drivers who attempted to pass through the approximately 430 Israeli-controlled checkpoints in the occupied territories. Israel conducted mass, arbitrary arrests in the West Bank during military operations, summoning and detaining males between the ages of 14 and 45.

Israel provided poor conditions for Palestinians in its prisons. Facilities were overcrowded. Sanitation was poor, and food and clothing at times were insufficient. Israel security forces and police officers beat and tortured detainees. Prolonged detention, limits on due process, and infringements on privacy rights remained problems.

Israel carried out policies of demolitions, strict curfews, and closures that directly punished innocent civilians. Israel demolished the homes of families and relatives of suspect terrorists as well as buildings it suspected terrorists used as hideouts. Israel's demolitions left hundreds of Palestinians not involved in terror attacks homeless.

Israel often demolished homes after suspects had already been killed or arrested. Israel maintained that such punishment of innocents would serve as a deterrent against future terrorist attacks.

The IDF destroyed numerous orchards, olive and date groves, and irrigation system on Palestinian-controlled agricultural land. Israel constructed parts of a large security barrier on land inside the West Bank isolating residents and limiting access to hospitals, schools, social services, and agricultural property. . . .

In several instances, Israel killed, injured, and obstructed human rights monitors and NGO workers through the use of excessive deadly force and the impositions of strict closures.

Israel censored Palestinian publications in East Jerusalem, raided and closed media outlets in the territories, blocked publications and broadcasts, and periodically detained or harassed members of the media and clergy. . . .

Israel security forces failed to prevent Israelis from entering Palestinian-controlled areas in the West Bank who injured or killed several Palestinians. In some cases, Israeli soldiers escorted Israeli civilians who beat Palestinians and damaged Palestinian property. . . .

IDF soldiers shot and killed suspects who were avoiding arrest, but in a number of cases who posed no apparent threat to IDF soldiers at the time of the incident. . . .

IDF soldiers fired without warning on unarmed Palestinian trespasses in or near restricted areas, on several occasions killing Palestinians. For example, on March 5, an IDF soldier shot and killed 75-year-old Abdallah Shehadeh al-Ash'hab as he rode a donkey collecting firewood on his property . . . .

During the year, IDF targeted for killing at least 44 Palestinians suspected of involvement in terrorism. In the process, IDF forces killed more bystanders, including children. IDF forces killed at least 47 bystanders of those targeted and injured a number of others, including bystanders, relatives, or associates. . . .

Israel employs physical pressure and degrading treatment and interrogation methods against arrested Palestinians in the occupied territories. . . . Interviews and studies by human rights groups during the year claim that torture is employed. The Public Committee Against Torture in Israel assessed that in the beginning of this year hundreds of Palestinians were subjected to torture or other cruel, inhuman or degrading treatment by Israel security agencies. . . .

The Israeli Government did not allow representatives of the International Committee of the Red Cross (ICRC) access to detainees until the end of their legal period of isolated detention. Detainees sometimes stated in court that their confessions were coerced, but judges rarely excluded such confessions. . . .

Israeli forces demolished the homes of the families and relatives of those convicted of or suspected of committing terror attacks, effectively punishing innocent Palestinians not implicated in the attacks. . . .

Israel's extensive curfews on Palestinian towns punished entire innocent populations.

[The authors will continue to look into other U.S. tax issues,   including:
• Payments of benefits by U.S. government agencies, primarily by the IRS and Social Security, to residents of the illegal settlements.]

POSTSCRIPT

As of September 10, 2004

There have been several important developments since <u>SO SUE ME!</u> went to the printers in May, 2004 which should be noted, most of them positive for the litigation chances of the Palestinians.

1.   The United States Supreme Court confirmed, 6 to 3, that aliens can bring causes of action for certain limited violations of international law against defendants in the US under the 1789 Alien Tort Law (<u>Sosa v. Alvarez</u>, 542 US − −(2004) [available on the Supreme Court's internet website]. (See our discussion of causes of action outlined in Chapter V, pages 81 et seq.) As expected Judge Scalia led the three- man posse (JJ. Thomas and Rehnquist) doing the Jimmy Durante sketch, "What law of nations?".

It is our opinion that the types of actions which the Supreme Court would   eventually recognize under the Alien Tort Law as violations of "specific, universal and obligatory" norms of behavior would include, at least, a) *collective punishment* (e.g., demolitions of homes of families of suicide bombers; vindictive demolition of Palestinian homes, farms and orchards after the killing of an Israeli; endless curfews and closures in the Occupied Territories); and b) *confiscation of property by conquest* (e.g., the settlements in the West Bank, Jerusalem and Gaza; the building of the Wall in Occupied Territories). Such activities, like piracy and slave trading, have today made the Israelis *hostis humani generis*, the enemies of all mankind. That the civilized world now considers

Israel *hostis humani generis* was epitomized in the nearly unanimous vote in the United Nations General Assembly on July 20, 2004 (150 to 6 with 10 abstentions) demanding that Israel comply with the United Nation's World Court's order to dismantle the Wall and encourage member nations of the UN to comply with their obligations under the Charter to enforce compliance by Israel.

2.   As a result of the **Abu Ghraib** prisoner abuse scandal and revelations of the dubious legal opinions (now being repudiated by the Bush Administration under the glare of public scrutiny) that had been given to the President by the Justice Department on his power to ignore the Geneva Conventions, there were very strong reaffirmations by Congress (e.g., a unanimous Senate Resolution reaffirming American adherence to the Geneva Conventions and particularly their prohibitions against torture), the Supreme Court (in side remarks made by the Court at pages 34 and 44 of its <u>Sosa</u> decision) and eventually by a prodded President, of the universal application and viability of the Geneva Conventions, particularly the convention against torture. This strengthens the causes of action outlined in our Chapters I and II under the Torture Victims Protection Act of 1991, virtually eliminating any possible use by nervous judges of the "political issue" device to avoid causes brought for *extrajudicial killing* and *torture*.

3.   On July 9, 2004 the International Court of Justice, the principle judicial body of the United Nations, in an Advisory Opinion to the UN General Assembly found that the wall being built by Israel to be illegal and must be

dismantled. The ruling had the unusual concurrence of 14 of the 15 judges, with the only dissent being the American judge, Thomas Buergenthal. But even Judge Buergenthal did not argue that the wall being built on confiscated land was legal, and he implied that after a full investigation it may very well be found illegal. But he thought the Court should study the issue further. On July 20, 2004, the UN General Assembly, by a vote of 150 for, 6 against (Israel, the United States, the Marshall Islands, Micronesia and Palau) and 10 abstentions, called on Israel to abide by the ruling and for the nations of the world to persuade Israel to do so. Rarely has the world community been so united on a subject. But the magnitude of its unity is matched by the depth of its impotency because one of the 6 contrary votes was the only superpower left, the United States.

The basis of the Court's decision was essentially that building the wall with its wide stretches of lateral roads and ditches on territory being temporarily occupied by Israel as a conquering state violates one of the most fundamental principles of modern international law agreed to in writing by nearly every nation of the world, namely, the inadmissibility of the acquisition of territory by force. This principle is set forth in the Hague Convention Respecting the Law and Customs of War on Land of 1907, the Fourth Geneva Convention of 1949, the UN Charter and in various Security Council Resolutions and prior rulings of the International Court of Justice.

Israel conquered these territories by war and has been an Occupying Power since 1967. The nations of the world have set up rules for an Occupying Power as part of the modern world's attempt to establish peace and harmony among nations. One of those basic rules is that the conquering nation cannot take for itself any of the conquered territory. Quite simply, if the Israelis have determined that a barrier was necessary to protect themselves against Palestinian suicide bombers, they could have built anything they wanted — on *their* land. Instead, even where the barrier closely follows the Armistice boundary of 1949 (the Green Line) the Israelis have confiscated wide stretches of Palestinian land and built the barrier and its ancillary roads and ditches on the other side of the Line — in the process destroying hundreds of homes, and numerous acres of farms, orchards and businesses belonging to the Palestinians. Any American homeowner would understand that this is wrong. If you decide to build a fence between yourself and your neighbor, provided the zoning laws allow it, you would not dream of erecting the fence over across on your neighbor's property. The fence goes up on the boundary line or on your own property.

For much of the route, however, the Israelis have directed the wall not only into Palestinian territory but deep inside the West Bank to coincidentally encircle or include on the Israeli side the settlements in the West Bank — themselves violations of the same basic prohibition against the taking of land by force. As a consequence the Court found that 237,000 Palestinians suddenly discovered that their homes now were on the Israeli side — but as they were not entitled to any Israeli citizenship rights, they now became yet another category of refugees and could anticipate being required by the Occupying Power to be photographed, fingerprinted and issued restrictive identity cards and passes to just to be able to move around their own villages. Many of these Palestinians also now found themselves cut off from their villages and farms, relatives, schools and jobs. The Court found that if the route is completed as planned it would similarly imprison another 160,000 Palestinians — new card carrying stateless people. On the other hand, the route would put 320,000 illegal Israeli settlers (including 178,000 in East Jerusalem) in the area between the Green Line and the Wall. Israel would have *de facto* annexed 975 square kilometers or 16.6 percent of the West Bank.

As the Court pointed out, this ruling was no surprise to anyone as it follows a long line of UN Security Council and General Assembly Resolutions declaring illegal the taking of land by conquest — as the Israelis have been doing since 1967, and continue to do each and every day. In addition to declaring the wall illegal and stating that Israel was obligated to dismantle it, the Court also declared that the legal obligations violated by Israel included certain obligations *erga omnes*. That is, they were of such a basic nature and so essential in the relations of nations and for establishing peace and harmony in the world that their violation was now the "concern of all States." The Court called upon the UN and all the States of the world to fulfill their own obligations under international law and bring about Israel's compliance with this ruling.

This is unlikely to occur. The world community can take action effectively only through the UN and with the concurrence of the United States. That will never happen. The Americans treated the decision with as much disdain as the Israelis. While having no direct influence on the causes of action described in SO SUE ME!, much of the arguments and legal reasoning as well as the factual background outlined in the Decision could be helpful in causes of action brought under the Alien Tort Law for *collective punishment* and *confiscation by conquest.*

4.   Meanwhile the Israeli Supreme Court, in an attempt to pre-empt the World Court's expected decision, a week earlier had issued a ruling of its own on the barrier, fence or wall. Not surprisingly it reached the *opposite* conclusion, though claiming to be interpreting the same principles of international law, including the Geneva Conventions. It ruled that Israel had the legal right to build the wall on Palestinian property, though it said the Government should make more efforts to lessen the pain to the Palestinians. The Sharon Government quickly embraced the ruling, saying that it would tinker with some of the boundary lines to soften the impact on the affected Palestinians, but still, of course, inside the Occupied Territories. Like its previous rulings on the sprawling settlements themselves in the West Bank, Gaza and Jerusalem; the connecting roads gouged through Palestinian farmland and orchards; the arbitrary curfews and closures; the extrajudicial killings; the arbitrary arrests and detentions; the deportations; the endless demolitions of homes, farmlands and orchards – the Israeli Supreme Court again managed to take the opposite position from the international community. It accomplished this legal feat not by any clever parsing of international law, but by the brutish, though simple, maneuver of driving a D10 Caterpillar bulldozer, called "military necessity," through the rules of civilized nations.

5. A Federal District Judge rendered judgment for the plaintiff in a lawsuit by a relative of Salvadoran Archbishop Oscar Romero against a participant in the assassination of the

Archbishop. Judge Oliver W. Wanger of the Federal District Court for the Eastern District of California awarded Romero's relative $2.5 million in compensatory damages and $7.5 million in punitive damages (J. Doe v. Alvaro Rafael Saravia, E.D. Ca., September 3, 2004). The defendant had been a former air force Captain and was operating as part of the para-military death squads supported by the Government of El Salvador. The Complaint filed by the Center for Justice & Accountability based its claims on the Torture Victim Protection Act (extrajudicial killing) and the Alien Tort Claims Act (crimes against humanity). See Chapters I and III. Judge Wanger found jurisdiction under both Acts and awarded damages based on those statutes.

This case is consistent with the decision cited in Chapter VII, Letelier v. Republic of Chile, (488 F. Supp. 665 D.C. Col., 1980) and is the first Federal decision since the Supreme Court confirmed the viability of the Alien Tort Claims Act in Sosa v. Alvarez.

The Palestinian litigants who come to the US to sue will have the initial procedural burden of showing to the US Courts that they have exhausted their remedies in the Israeli Courts. This decision by the Israeli Supreme Court which found justification for confiscation by conquest – a very basic and fundamental violation of international law – should alone stand as sufficient proof that it would be a waste of time and effort to seek redress first in the Israeli Courts. Those Courts, like the government, may pay passionate tribute to all the customary principles of democracy, fairness, justice, international humanitarian law, etc., but in the end they give their blessings to the murders, land grabs and the subjugation of a people that have been the hallmarks of Israeli Occupation since 1967.

Continuing extrajudicial killings and demolitions — the liquidation of two generations of Palestinian leaders:

The Israelis are continuing their daily incursions into the Occupied Territories, killing targeted "militants" and bystanders. All the Palestinians oppose the brutal Occupation, and many of the young men with extra courage and determination have become resistance fighters — in the long line of resistance partisans made famous by the subjugated Europeans under the Nazis. These are the future leaders of a Palestine — and the Israelis are carefully identifying these 20 and 25 year-olds, branding them as "militants" and simply killing them. The resulting chaos in the Occupied Territories is a state policy of Israel and like much of what it is doing will, in the authors' opinion, be counterproductive in the long run.

The Israelis are also continuing to bulldoze, with American Caterpillar tractors, dozens of Palestinian homes, farms and orchards in the name of security and with the repeated blessings of the Israeli Supreme Court. The process has been continuing daily and has been relentless. The condemnation by the international community has been brushed aside as the Israelis have nothing to fear from the civilized world — so long as the Americans continue to back them up.

And the Americans have not disappointed them. In the US the politicians continue to shamelessly pander to the Israeli Lobby — feverishly climbing over each other to demonstrate their even greater loyalty to Israel – no matter what the Israeli government does. This whole syndrome of pandering to the feared and respected pro-Israel powers in the US has even corroded the judgments of some American politicians. One disturbing example was the declaration by a US Senator that torture, for the right reasons, was entirely OK.

During the questioning of Attorney General John Ashcroft on June 8, 2004 by members of the Senate Judiciary Committee concerning the torture of Iraqi prisoners, Senator Charles E. Schumer of NY, reflecting the Israeli view of torture, reprimanded his fellow Senators for being so outraged by the tales of torture of the Iraqi prisoners. Sounding like an Israeli, he commended that there were few people in America or in that Senate room who would not agree to torture someone if it would save lives. Torture of Palestinians is routine in Israel and accepted by the Israeli public. Now a US Senator has adopted that posture — all in flat violation of US and International law and his own oaths as an attorney and as a Senator. After the International Court of Justice issued its ruling declaring the wall illegal and calling for its dismantling, both of the Senators from New York, Charles Schumer and Hilary Clinton, scurried to a podium before the UN in New York with the Israeli Ambassador to denounce the ruling.

In Presidential politics it was the same – no difference between either major candidate. Kerry had found himself momentarily silenced by Bush's grandiose "OK" to Sharon in April, 2004 to kill whomever he wished and to take whatever Palestinian land he wanted. It was difficult to surpass that stamp of approval. But just before the anticipated negative ruling of the International Court in July, Kerry sent his brother, Cameron, over to Israel to assure one and all that the candidate John Kerry was just as staunchly pro-Israel, no matter what, as anyone else. Cameron had conveniently, for this mission anyway, converted back to Judaism after marrying a Jewish lady.

IT IS STILL THE SAME — THE ONLY POSSIBLE REMEDY: SUE

Therefore the basic premise of <u>SO SUE ME!</u> remains the same. Israel will not be made to abide by the law of nations by any international body or by any political leader in the United States. Yet it is only the United States that can rein in the Israelis and all the American companies that give it the ability to take land by conquest, subjugate a people and kill them at will. It is from the United States that much of the money, weapons and bulldozers come that enable the Israelis to carry out their programs. If the Americans do not make the Israelis deal with the Palestinians in the Occupied Territories at least within the constraints of the laws recognized by all nations for the treatment of occupied people, then no one will. And the only American entity that has the independence to make Israel, the American Government and American and international companies and banks accountable for these atrocities, is the US Federal Courts.

So come Palestinians, and sue. Sue often and everywhere.

THE REPORTS

US STATE DEPARTMENT ANNUAL REPORTS ON HUMAN RIGHTS

Various US laws relating to military and economic assistance to foreign countries contain a routine provision that such aid must be terminated when it is found that the recipient government habitually violates human rights. For example, the Military Assistance and Sales Act contains this provision:

> *"No security assistance may be provided to any country the government of which engages in a consistent pattern of gross violations of internally recognized human rights."*

22 USC § 2304 (2).

Part of the process to determine if any aid recipient is such a violator – so that aid should be terminated – is a requirement Congress has imposed on the State Department to issue, each year by the end of February, a Human Rights Report for each recipient country.

The State Department does issue such Human Rights Reports each year to Congress. But it is not self activating. Regardless of what the report may disclose, nothing happens as a result unless there is also a finding by the President that the country involved is such a gross violator of human rights that under the statute it cannot receive any military or economic aid.

In the case of Israel, however, even though the Reports clearly indicate that Israel "engges in a consistent pattern of gross violationas of internationally recognized human rights," the President makes no such finding.

As a result we have each year the strange spectacle of the State Department routinely reporting in great detail on Israel's gross violations of international law in the Occupied Territories, enough to make Attila the Hun look like a Boy Scout, followed by utter silence from the President and Congress -- the Reports seem to have fallen into a Black Hole. These Reports to Congress have become merely an exercise in beauracratic self-abuse.

For one thing, the Report on Israel, a **country** recipient of aid, is obfuscated by the device of reporting at the same time on human rights abuses by organizations or groups -- not countries, such as Hamas and a number of other fringe Palestinian groups -- though these are NOT recipients of US Military Aid.

The juxtaposition of facts of human rights abuses by Israel with human rights abuses by Hamas or even by the PLO only obscures the issue. The law requires a Human Rights Report on the RECIPIENT country, so as to make a determination about continuing aid. Burying the activities of the Israeli Government, as the Reports do, under the parallel despicable activities of Hamas or the incompetency of the PLO only distorts and deflects the purpose of the Report. One comes away with the feeling that these are all bad guys, but our firend is not as bad as the others. That is not the purpose of the Report. It is to determine if our friend is misbehaving in such a gross way that it does not deserve our help any longer -- less we become a participant in its crimes.

Israel gets 3 Billion dollars a year in military and economic aid, plus uncounted assistance in various other forms, often disguised as joint projects or loan guarantees.

Hamas gets nothing. Why is a required report on Israeli violations of human rights then obscured with details of Hamas atrocities?

We do not ship Apache Helicopters or even cap pistols to the the Palestinian Authority. Why the PLO is reported on in the same breadth as Israel, must be only to confuse things and bury the atrocious facts being revealed about Israel's behavior.

Instead of a clear report on Israel that might get even the pro-Israeli crowd in Congress to start wondering, we have a profusion of abuses by a whole lot of squabbling groups, Hamas and Israel being just two of them. The focus, then is lost -- as apparently is the intent of the drafters. The pupose of the Report is gutted. It is easy then for neither the Executive nor Congress to pull the trigger on sending aid to an Attila the Hun type of government. The barbarities being committed by Israel do not look so terrible when compared with those of Hamas. Forgetten is the fact that we are not shipping any weapons to Hamas, and the law involved does not relate to Hamas, but to country recipients like our friend Israel. Israel's compliance with the law is lost in a quagmire of competing details . This conspiracy goes on year after year. .

Our contribution here is to alert the Palestinians to a slam dunk cause of action they have as revealed by the State Department Reports on Human Rights. Using these Reports themselves, they can go to a Federal Court and get a variety of orders terminating aid to Israel for violations of a host of Congressional restrictions.

[In the 2nd Printing, only the Report covering the year 2003 is given and the portions of the Report relating to the PA and Hamas have been deleted as irrelvant for the reasons stated above.]

United States State Department Human Rights Report 2003

[Issued February, 2004]

· · · · · · · ·

Israel and the Occupied Territories

The occupied territories (Including Areas Subject to the Jurisdiction of the Palestinian Authority):

Israel occupied the West Bank, Gaza Strip, Golan Heights, and East Jerusalem during the 1967 War. Pursuant to the May 1994 Gaza-Jericho Agreement and the September 1995 Interim Agreement, Israel transferred most responsibilities for civil government in the Gaza Strip and parts of the West Bank to the newly created Palestinian Authority (PA). The 1995 Interim Agreement divided the territories into Areas A, B, and C, denoting different levels of Palestinian and Israeli control. The PA controls security and civil affairs in Area A, civil affairs and shared responsibilities with Israel in Area B, and Israel controls certain civil functions and all security in Area C. In parts of the West Bank and Gaza, Israel exercised civil authority through the Israeli Ministry of Defense's Office of Coordination and Liaison (MATAK). The approximately 193,170 Israeli settlers (a decrease of approximately 15,000 since 2002) living in Area C of the West Bank and in the Gaza Strip were subject to Israeli law and, as citizens, received preferential treatment from Israeli authorities compared to Palestinians in the protection of their personal and property rights.

These distinctions were not in force during the year following Israel's reassertion of security control over most PA-controlled areas in 2002, which Israel carried out citing the PA's failure to abide by its security responsibilities. **The international community considered Israel's authority in the occupied territories to be subject to the Hague Regulations of 1907 and the 1949 Geneva Convention relating to the Protection of Civilians in Time of War**. The Israeli Government considered the Hague Regulations applicable and maintained that it largely observed the Geneva Convention's humanitarian provisions. Palestinians and **international human rights groups maintained**

that Israel consistently violated these provisions. (This annex on the occupied territories should be read in conjunction with the report on Israel).

. . . .

The "Intifada," or Palestinian uprising, began in September 2000. Since 2000, the security situation has deteriorated both within Israel and within the occupied territories. Israeli and Palestinian violence associated with the Intifada has claimed 2,369 Palestinian lives, 856 Israeli lives, and the lives of 48 foreign nationals, including 41 American citizens. Israeli military operations and armed attacks and terrorism by Palestinians against Israeli targets—including civilians within Israel, settlers, and soldiers in the occupied territories and Israel marked the conflict. On October 15, three American security personnel were killed and one wounded when a bomb detonated under their car as they drove in Gaza as part of a diplomatic motorcade. At year's end, the PA continued to investigate the incident. The attacks by Palestinians also included suicide bombings, roadside bombings, military actions against Palestinians included violence and abuse at checkpoints, incursions into Palestinian-controlled towns and villages, targeted killings, demolitions of homes, property, and public buildings, firing toward civilian areas with tanks and fighter aircraft, and intense gun battles with Palestinian gunmen. **By year's end, Israel asserted military control over all major West Bank cities except Jericho and Bethlehem, demolished homes, including those of suicide bombers and wanted men, conducted mass arrests, and forcibly relocated some suspects.** In response to the ongoing terrorist threat originating in the West Bank, Israel began construction of a security barrier to be built along parts of the Green Line and in the West Bank.

. . . .

Israeli security forces in the West Bank and Gaza Strip consisted of the IDF, the Israel Security Agency (the ISA-formerly the General Security Service, or GSS), the Israeli National Police (INP), and the paramilitary border police. Israeli military courts tried Palestinians accused of committing acts of violence and terror in Israeli-controlled areas. **Members of the Israeli security forces committed numerous, serious human rights abuses.**

. . . .

The occupied territories comprise the Gaza Strip, the West Bank, and East Jerusalem. The population of the Gaza Strip was approximately 1,397,011, not including some 7,781 Israeli settlers. In the Gaza Strip, 62 percent of the land consists of Area A; 6 percent of Area B; and 32 percent of Area C. In the West Bank, 18.1 percent of the land consists of Area A; 21.6 of Area B; and 60.3

184

percent of Area C. The population of the West Bank (excluding East Jerusalem) was approximately 2,237,194 not including some 187,854 Israeli settlers. In the West Bank, Area A includes 55 percent of the Palestinian population; 41 percent of the Palestinian population is in Area B; and 4 percent is in Area C (which also contains Israeli settlements). The population of East Jerusalem, within the municipal boundaries established by Israel in 1967 was approximately 385,600, including 177,333 Israeli settlers.

The economy of the West Bank and Gaza Strip is small, underdeveloped, and highly dependent on Israel and international assistance. Israeli curfews and closures, as well as the continuing conflict, severely impacted the economy. The economy relied primarily on agriculture, services, and small manufacturing. Before the beginning of the Intifada, up to 146,000 workers from the West Bank and Gaza (approximately 25 percent of the Palestinian work force) were employed in Israel. During heightened terrorist activity in Israel or periods of unrest in the West Bank or Gaza, Israeli-imposed closures on Palestinian cities, curfews, and strict limitations on movement within the West Bank and Gaza impeded Palestinians from reaching jobs or markets and disrupted internal and external trade.

In addition, the IDF and settlers destroyed sections of Palestinian-owned agricultural land and economic infrastructure.

The Government of Israel stated that some of these actions, such as the destruction of groves alongside roadways and security fences by the IDF, were necessary for security reasons.

Unemployment in the West Bank and Gaza was estimated at 30 percent, and approximately 63 percent of Palestinian households were living below the poverty line (54 percent of families in the West Bank and 84 percent of families in Gaza). These circumstances effectively prevented any amelioration of worker rights in the occupied territories.

During the year, the US Agency for International Development (USAID) and Johns Hopkins University reported that 7.8 percent of Palestinian children under 5 suffered from acute malnutrition, 11.7 percent suffered chronic malnutrition, and 44 percent were anemic.

Israel required Palestinians to obtain Israeli permits for themselves and their vehicles to cross from the West Bank or Gaza into Israel and Jerusalem.

Citing security concerns, Israel applied partial "external closure," or enhanced restrictions, on the movement of persons and products, often for lengthy periods. During times of violent protest in the West Bank or Gaza, or when it believed that there was an increased likelihood of such unrest or of terrorist attacks in Israel, Israel imposed a tightened, comprehensive version of external closure, generally referred to as "total external closure." Total external closures also were instituted regularly during all major Israeli holidays and during some Muslim holidays. During such closures, Israel prevented Palestinians from leaving the occupied territories.

Israel also placed Palestinians in the West Bank under strict "internal closure" for the entire year, allowing only Palestinians with special permits for work or health services to leave cities and pass through checkpoints on main roads. Most Palestinians were unable to leave their towns or were forced to travel without authorization on secondary roads. Israeli forces further restricted freedom of movement of Palestinians by imposing extended curfews on Palestinian towns or neighborhoods. These curfews did not apply to Israeli settlers in the same areas.

Israel's overall human rights record in the occupied territories remained poor and worsened in the treatment of foreign human rights activists as it continued to commit numerous, serious human rights abuses.

Security forces killed at least 573 Palestinians and 1 foreign national and injured 2,992 Palestinians and other persons during the year, some of whom were innocent bystanders. Israeli security forces targeted and killed at least 44 Palestinians, many of whom were terrorists or suspected terrorists. Israeli forces undertook many of these targeted killings in areas where civilian casualties were likely, killing 47 bystanders in the process, including children. The Israeli Government said that it made every effort to reduce civilian casualties during these operations.

Israeli security units often used excessive force when confronting Palestinian demonstrations, while on patrol, pursuing suspects, and enforcing checkpoints and curfews, which resulted in numerous deaths. In response to Palestinian attacks on Israeli targets, Palestinian civilian areas suffered extensive damage as a result of IDF retaliation, which included shelling, bombing, and raiding.

Israeli soldiers placed Palestinian civilians in danger by ordering them to facilitate military operations, which exposed them to live fire between armed Palestinians and Israeli soldiers. The Government of Israel said that is has reiterated to its forces that this practice is prohibited unless the civilian gives his voluntary consent; however, in practice, most Palestinians who agreed to assist such operations often did so out of fear of the soldiers even if they were not directly coerced. Palestinians who took part in such operations without being harmed still faced the risk of being branded as collaborators and risked being attacked by other Palestinians.

Israeli forces sometimes arbitrarily destroyed, damaged, or looted Palestinian property during these operations. Israeli security forces often impeded the provision of medical assistance to Palestinian civilians by strict enforcement of internal closures that prevented passage of ambulances, asserting in some cases that emergency vehicles have been used to facilitate terrorist transit and operations.

Israeli security forces harassed and abused Palestinian pedestrians and drivers who attempted to pass through the approximately 430 Israeli-controlled checkpoints in the occupied territories. Israel conducted mass, arbitrary arrests in the West Bank during military operations, summoning and detaining males between the ages of 15 and 45. Israel provided poor conditions for Palestinians in its prisons.

Facilities were overcrowded, sanitation was poor, and food and clothing at times were insufficient. Israeli security forces and police officers beat and tortured detainees. Prolonged detention, limits on due process, and infringements on privacy rights remained problems.

Israel carried out policies of demolitions, strict curfews, and closures that directly punished innocent civilians. Israel demolished the homes of families and relatives of suspected terrorists as well as buildings suspected terrorists used as hideouts. Israel's demolitions left hundreds of Palestinians not involved in terror attacks homeless.

Israel often demolished homes after suspects had already been killed or arrested. Israel maintained that such punishment of innocents would *serve as a deterrent* against future terrorist attacks.

The IDF destroyed numerous orchards, olive and date groves, and irrigation systems on Palestinian-controlled agricultural land. Israel constructed parts of a large security barrier on land inside the West Bank isolating residents and limiting access to hospitals, schools, social services, and agricultural property.

. . . .

In several instances, Israel killed, injured, and obstructed human rights monitors and NGO workers through the use of excessive deadly force and the imposition of strict closures.

Israel censored Palestinian publications in East Jerusalem, raided and closed media outlets in the territories, blocked publications and broadcasts, and periodically detained or harassed members of the media and clergy. IDF fire allegedly killed two journalists covering clashes between Palestinians and Israeli security forces, both of whom had clearly identified themselves as noncombatants, and injured at least three others. The Israeli authorities placed strict limits on freedom of assembly and severely restricted freedom of movement for Palestinians. Israeli security forces failed to prevent Israelis from entering Palestinian-controlled areas in the West Bank who injured or killed several Palestinians. In some cases, Israeli soldiers escorted Israeli civilians who beat Palestinians and damaged Palestinian property,

. . . .

Israeli civilians, most often settlers, harassed, attacked, and occasionally killed Palestinians in the occupied territories. During the year, settlers attacked and killed at least one Palestinian. Settlers also caused significant economic damage to Palestinians by attacking and damaging greenhouses and agricultural equipment, uprooting olive trees, and damaging other valuable crops. The settlers did not act under government directive in the attacks, and Israeli soldiers sometimes restrained them, but in several cases Israeli soldiers accompanied them or stood by without acting.

. . .

188

Section 1 Respect for the Integrity of the Person, Including Freedom From:

a. Arbitrary or Unlawful Deprivation of Life

Israeli security forces killed at least 573 Palestinians in the West Bank and Gaza. Israeli civilians, mostly settlers, as well as extremist groups believed to be associated with settlers, killed at least one Palestinian. . . . .

Israeli security forces killed most Palestinians during armed clashes, targeted killings, incursions into Palestinian-controlled areas, at checkpoints, or as a result of sometimes excessive or indiscriminate fire toward Palestinian civilian areas. During these incidents, Palestinian protesters frequently threw stones and Molotov cocktails, and in some cases, also fired weapons at IDF soldiers (see Sections 1.c. and 1.d.). Israeli security forces used a variety of means to disperse protesters, including tear gas, rubber-coated metal bullets, and live ammunition. The IDF did not regularly investigate the actions of security force members who killed and injured Palestinians under suspicious circumstances. Since the start of the Intifada, the IDF has opened only 11 investigations into the improper use of deadly force despite the fact that human rights organizations have raised numerous allegations.

Israeli security forces used excessive force against protesters, in response to threats while on patrols, in pursuing fleeing suspects, and in responding to trespassers in restricted areas, at times resulting in death. Israel also used excessive lethal force against rock-throwers in some instances. For example, on September 15, IDF soldiers shot and killed 10-year-old Ahmad Abu Latifa near the Qalandia checkpoint north of Jerusalem. The boy was among a group of youths who were throwing rocks at Israeli soldiers.

IDF soldiers shot and killed suspects who were avoiding arrest, but in a number of cases who posed no apparent mortal threat to the soldiers at the time of the incidents. For example, on February 10, IDF soldiers in Nablus shot and killed PFLP member Imad Mabrouk when he attempted to escape arrest. On July 3, IDF soldiers in Qalqilya shot and killed al-Aqsa Martyrs Brigades militant Ahmad Shawar when he attempted to run away after being ordered to halt.

IDF soldiers fired without warning on unarmed Palestinian trespassers in or near restricted areas, on several occasions killing Palestinians. For example, on March 5, an IDF soldier shot and killed 75-year-old Abdallah Shehadeh al-Ash'hab as he rode a donkey collecting firewood on his property, which was located near the Netzarim settlement in the Gaza Strip.

On November 29, IDF soldiers in Gaza shot and killed Palestinian police officer Sayed Abu Safra when he attempted to prevent a mentally disabled Palestinian from nearing the perimeter fence surrounding the Israeli settlement of Nissanit. The IDF expressed "sorrow and regret" over the incident.

During the year, the IDF *targeted for killing* at least 44 Palestinians suspected of involvement in terrorism. In the process, IDF forces killed more bystanders than targeted individuals, including children.

IDF forces killed at least 47 bystanders of those targeted and injured a number of others, including bystanders, relatives, or associates.

Israel stated that it only targeted individuals believed to be "ticking bombs" on the verge of carrying out terrorist attacks. In practice, however, the IDF targeted some leaders of terrorist organizations generally considered not to be directly engaged in carrying out attacks.

Israeli security forces put large numbers of Palestinian civilian lives in jeopardy by undertaking targeted killings in crowded areas where civilian casualties were likely. For example, on April 9, Israeli forces fired four missiles at a car in a densely populated area of Gaza city in order to kill two suspected terrorists, Sa'ad ad-Din al-Arabeit, 35, and Ashraf al-Halabi, 25. Israeli forces killed five other Palestinians in the effort, including two children, 13-year-old Ahmad Hamsa al-Ashraf, and 16-year-old Samid Hasan Qasem.

Beginning on June 11, Israeli forces conducted 5 targeted killings in Gaza City within 48 hours, killing 23 Palestinians, including 18 bystanders. Israel conducted the fifth such attack on June 12, firing five rockets at a car traveling in central Gaza City. The rockets killed wanted Hamas terrorist Yasser Muhammad Ali Taha, 31, and six bystanders, including an 18-month-old child and a pregnant woman.

Israeli security personnel used excessive force while operating checkpoints, killing a number of Palestinians (see Section 1.g.). On July 25, an IDF soldier at a checkpoint outside Bartaqa ash-Sharqiya near Jenin fired on a car waiting for permission to pass. The shots killed 3-year-old Palestinian Mahmoud Jawadat Sharif Kabaha, who was sitting in the car.

An investigation into the incident was ongoing at year's end.

Israeli forces put civilian lives in jeopardy by using imprecise, heavy weaponry in operations against terrorist infrastructure conducted in civilian areas. Frequently, and often following Palestinian shooting attacks, IDF retaliation excessively damaged Palestinian towns and cities in the West Bank and Gaza. Israeli forces fired tank shells, heavy machine-gun rounds, and rockets from aircraft at targets in residential and business neighborhoods where Palestinian gunfire was believed by the IDF to have originated.

On April 27, the Israeli Supreme Court of Justice ruled in an October 2002 case brought by the Palestinian Center for Human Rights (PHCR) and Physicians for Human Rights-Israel against the IDF's use of flechette tank shells in Gaza. The imprecise anti-personnel munitions launch thousands of small metal darts over an area of several thousand square feet; use of such munitions in densely populated civilian areas makes the **likelihood of civilian casualties very high. The Gaza Strip has a population density of approximately 3,300 persons per square kilometer and is one of the most densely populated areas in the world.** The High Court of Justice denied the petition and stated that it would not intervene in the IDF's choice of weapons. Unlike in previous years, there were no reports that the IDF used flechette shells during the year.

On September 9, Israeli soldiers targeting gunmen hiding in a building in a residential area of Hebron opened fire on the building with tank shells. The shelling continued for more than 4 hours, and shrapnel killed 11-year-old Palestinian Muhammad Mansour Sayouri, who was hit in the head while standing in the kitchen of another residential building approximately 150 feet south of the structure being targeted.

Israeli security forces killed numerous civilians during military incursions into Palestinian-controlled cities and towns.

Such incursions usually were conducted in response to Palestinian suicide bombings, shooting attacks that had killed Israeli civilians, settlers, or soldiers, or to make arrests. Israeli security forces also conducted military incursions on the basis of intelligence information about possible future attacks. Palestinians often responded with gunfire and by booby-trapping civilian homes and apartment buildings with deadly, indiscriminate devices. As part of such actions, the IDF usually raided and often leveled buildings, including homes.

On May 1, the IDF launched an incursion into Gaza City, home to approximately 365,000 Palestinians. The raid in a densely populated neighborhood led to a shootout with Palestinian militants. During the fighting, the IDF killed five innocent Palestinian bystanders, including a 1-year-old boy, a 13-year-old boy, a 14-year-old boy, a 57-year-old man, and a 38-year-old man who attempted to treat the wounded.

IDF fire killed Amir Ahmad Muhammad 'Ayad, the 1-year-old baby boy who was inside his home during the incursion. The IDF also killed seven Palestinian gunmen during the clash. The IDF demolished two homes before withdrawing from the city.

Israeli forces used excessive force to enforce curfews in reoccupied Palestinian areas, resulting in deaths. For example, on April 17, IDF soldiers enforcing a curfew in Tulkarm opened fire on and killed a Palestinian civilian found out of his home.

Israeli security forces at checkpoints often impeded the provision of medical assistance to sick and injured Palestinians. The Government's implementation of control measures resulted in delayed access to medical treatment for at least one Palestinian who subsequently died (see Section 1.g.).

Israel forces allegedly beat and killed a Palestinian prisoner in December 2002. On December 30, 2002, Israeli Border Police in Hebron arrested 'Imran Abu Hamdiyeh, a 17-year-old Palestinian. Palestinians found Hamdiyeh dead in Hebron's industrial area later that day. An autopsy sponsored by Palestinian and **Israeli human rights groups concluded that Hamdiyeh died due to "blunt force injury."** On April 18, Israel arrested four Israeli Border Police officers on charges that they had beaten Hamdiyeh to death. The trial was ongoing at year's end.

. . . .

Israeli settlers, acting individually, or in small groups, harassed, attacked, and occasionally killed Palestinians in the West Bank and Gaza Strip (see Section 1.c.). During the year, settlers killed at least one Palestinian. On April 30, a settler security guard at the Moshav Petza'el settlement in the Jordan Valley shot and killed Palestinian laborer Ra'ik Mas'id Daraghmeh, 35, who had stopped to relieve himself in a field near the settlement.

On January 25, a settler near the West Bank village of Budrus allegedly shot and killed Palestinian shepherd Ahmad Subuh, 24. A companion of Subuh's claims to have seen a settler drive away from the scene, but no suspect had been arrested by year's end.

. . . .

c. Torture and Other Cruel, Inhuman, or Degrading Treatment or Punishment.

Israel employs physical pressure and degrading treatment as interrogation methods against arrested Palestinians in the occupied territories. The law, based on a 1999 High Court decision, prohibits the use of a variety of abusive practices, including violent shaking, painful shackling in contorted positions, sleep deprivation for extended periods of time, and prolonged exposure to extreme temperatures. However, the High Court decision allowed for the security forces to request "special permission" to use "moderate physical pressure" against detainees considered to possess information about an imminent attack. In 2002, the Israeli GSS acknowledged use of physical pressure against 90 Palestinians who had been defined as "ticking bombs."

Interviews and studies by human rights groups during the year claim that torture is employed. The Public Committee Against Torture in Israel assessed that in the beginning of this year hundreds of Palestinians were subjected to torture or other cruel, inhuman, or degrading treatment by Israel security agencies, an increase from the dozens reported in 2002.

Israeli and Palestinian human rights groups noted that jailers made it difficult to visit prisoners during the interrogation period and that some detainees were reluctant to report abuse out of fear of retribution.

The case of Daoud Dirawi was representative of numerous allegations of physical abuse which human rights groups received. For example, on February 21, Israeli authorities arrested Dirawi, a Palestinian lawyer, for being in Jerusalem without proper identification. Police initially detained Dirawi at the al-Qeshle police station in Jerusalem before transferring him to the Asyun military prison in the Negev. Dirawi told his attorney that soldiers beat him severely en route to the Asyun prison. Dirawi sustained serious bruises and a broken lower jaw. Dirawi states that he was tied up upon arrival with his hands locked above him and that he was kept in this position outdoors in the rain through the night. On March 4, Israel sentenced Dirawi to 6 months of administrative detention without pressing formal charges against him and rejected his appeal. Israel renewed his administrative detention for another 6 months. At year's end, Dirawi remained under administrative detention.

The law prohibits the admission of forced confessions as evidence. However, most convictions in security cases before Israeli courts were based on confessions made well before legal representation was made available to defendants. A detainee may not have contact with a lawyer until after interrogation, a process that may last days or weeks.

The Israeli Government did not allow representatives of the International Committee of the Red Cross (ICRC) access to detainees until the end of their legal period of isolated detention. Detainees sometimes stated in court that their confessions were coerced, but judges rarely excluded such confessions.

The IDF injured approximately 2,992 Palestinians, including innocent bystanders and journalists, during armed clashes, retaliatory strikes, targeted killings, and other military actions. During the year, Israeli gunfire allegedly killed two journalists and injured at least three others during Israeli military actions (see Sections 1.a., 1.g., and 2.a.).

Israeli authorities abused Palestinians at checkpoints, subjecting them to verbal and physical harassment. Each day, tens of thousands of Palestinians traveling between Palestinian towns and villages faced as many as 730 different barriers to movement. At year's end, Israel had established 60 checkpoints, 9 occasionally manned checkpoints, 479 earthen mounds blocking roads, 102 cement roadblocks, 39 road gates, and 41 gates in a separation barrier. As many as several thousand Palestinians encountered some form of abuse from soldiers at checkpoints.

Palestinians were subjected to excessive delays in passing through checkpoints. For example, on May 12, an IDF soldier at the Hawarah checkpoint outside Nablus decided to only let Palestinians pass through who were able to identify the Israeli political figure on the 100 Shekel note. On April 30, an IDF soldier abused Qassem Awisat, 19, a resident of Qalqilya, when he attempted to pass through the Seida checkpoint in the Tulkarm district. **The soldier pulled Awisat aside and etched a Star of David on his arm using shards of broken glass.**

The Israeli human rights organization B'tselem documented Awisat's testimony of the incident and photographed the injury to his arm.

Israeli soldiers forced Palestinian civilians to wait in the rain or inclement weather for excessive periods of time.

The IDF subjected Palestinians in the West Bank and Gaza to beatings, tire slashings, and gunfire directed against them or their vehicles because they were traveling on, or trying to circumvent, roads on which the IDF blocked passage to Palestinians as it attempted to enforce internal closures between Palestinian cities and towns in the West Bank and Gaza (see Section 2.d.).

Israeli security personnel on patrol abused and in some cases tortured Palestinian civilians. For example, Israeli soldiers on patrol in June attacked 20 Palestinian youths who were trying to cross a dirt road near a military checkpoint north of Jerusalem. The soldiers beat the youths with their rifles and threw several of them in a sewage ditch before leaving the scene.

In June, Israeli Border Police in Tulkarm took the identity card of shepherd Nazih Salah 'Awad Damiri, 24, and forced him to mime sexual intercourse with his donkey.

Israeli fire injured seven Palestinian medical personnel. Israeli fire also damaged 12 Palestinian Red Crescent Society (PRCS) ambulances (see Sections 1.a and 1.g.).

. . . .

Some settlers attacked Palestinian homes and damaged crops, olive trees, greenhouses, and agricultural equipment, usually in areas located near settlements, causing extensive economic damage to Palestinian-owned agricultural land and depriving innocent farmers of their livelihood. In October, settlers disrupted the Palestinian olive harvest by firing on Palestinians picking olives, beating harvesters returning home and stealing the harvest, and invading Palestinian property and picking the olives themselves. For example, October 23, settlers from the Yitzhar settlement near Nablus threw stones and fired warning shots at Palestinian farmers harvesting olives in the village of Burin. The harvesters were forced to disperse. On October 22, Yitzhar settlers also stole 6 120-pound bags of olives from a farmer in Burin.

Although human rights monitors reported that the IDF provided greater protection to Palestinian farmers than they did in the past, settlers carried out such actions in areas in which the IDF was responsible for security. **Israel often enforced security by applying curfews and closures only to Palestinians, which on occasion prevented Palestinians from defending themselves and their property from attacks by settlers.** Palestinians also complained that when the IDF provided protection it gave insufficient time for Palestinians to complete the harvest. Burin farmers, for example, complained that they only received 2 days of IDF protection to complete a harvest of some 1,000 olive trees.

The Government of Israel generally did not prosecute settlers for their acts of violence against Palestinians, and settlers rarely served prison sentences if convicted of a crime against a Palestinian. However, in August Israel arrested nine settlers for plotting and carrying out attacks on Palestinian civilians. On August 8, two of those settlers were charged with possessing army explosives and preparing for a terrorist attack on Palestinian civilians. Those two were released after a plea bargain. Three other settlers were convicted during the year. In September, two were sentenced to 15 year terms and one was sentenced to 12 years. The remaining detained settlers were still under trial at year's end.

On January 19, a group of settlers in Hebron stabbed Iyad Salhab, 25, three times in the waist, thigh, and face. IDF soldiers stood by while the stabbing attack took place, but intervened when a larger group of twenty or more settlers ran toward the scene. Salhab was treated with stitches and was briefly hospitalized.

. . . .

.Israel provided poor conditions for Palestinians in Israeli prisons. Facilities were overcrowded, sanitation was poor, and at times food and clothing were insufficient. Israel crowded Palestinian prisoners, exceeding capacity of the facilities. Israel was unprepared to accommodate properly the hundreds of Palestinians that were arrested in sweeps that accompanied Israeli operations during the year. In January, Palestinian prisoners in the Ofer prison camp near Ramallah, which held close to 1,000 Palestinian detainees, conducted a protest against poor treatment.

Israel significantly expanded its use of solitary confinement, holding increasing numbers of prisoners in isolation. At year's end, Israel held 120 Palestinian prisoners in some form of solitary confinement compared to 15 at the end of 2002.

Israel neglected the medical needs of some Palestinian prisoners. The Mandela Institute, a Palestinian prisoners advocacy group, alleged that such neglect contributed to at least one death in custody. Bashir Oweiss, a Palestinian from Nablus, died of a stroke on December 8 after allegedly receiving negligent medical care as his condition deteriorated. Oweiss was arrested on November 1 and sentenced on November 27 to 6-months of administrative detention. Oweiss suffered a stroke on December 4. According to the Mandela Institute, poor treatment at the Megiddo hospital caused Oweiss' condition to deteriorate that night. The hospital then transferred him to Afula hospital where he died 3 days later.

Israel permitted independent monitoring of prison conditions by the ICRC and other groups, although human rights groups reported they sometimes encountered difficulties gaining access to specific detainees.

.... d. Arbitrary Arrest, Detention, or Exile

Israeli security personnel may arrest without warrant or hold for questioning a person suspected of having committed a criminal or security offense. During the year, Israel conducted mass, arbitrary detentions in the West Bank. Most of those detained were released several days or weeks thereafter. Israeli Military Order 1507 permits the Israeli army to detain people for 10 days during which detainees were barred from seeing a lawyer or appearing before court. Israel conducted mass detentions under this order's authority. On May 12 and 13, Israeli forces arrested 83 Palestinians in Hebron.

Israel used administrative detention to hold hundreds of Palestinians without trial or charge. At year's end, Israel held 649 Palestinians in administrative detention.

Individual administrative detention orders could be issued for up to 6-month periods and could be renewed indefinitely. A number of Palestinians under administrative detention during the previous several years have had their detention orders renewed repeatedly.

Israel conducted de facto detentions at checkpoints by confiscating Palestinian identification cards and car keys. Palestinians were unable to leave the scene until IDF soldiers returned the items. For example, on the morning of June 3, IDF soldiers confiscated the car keys and identification cards of three Palestinian residents of East Jerusalem driving to Hebron. The soldiers did not return the keys until the afternoon and never returned the identification cards at all.

On November 23, IDF soldiers at the Hawwara checkpoint outside Nablus demanded that two Palestinians stop and clean the checkpoint. When the men refused, the soldiers handcuffed, blindfolded and detained them for several hours. When B'tselem investigated the incident the soldiers admitted to the action and claimed their superiors had ordered them to do it.

Israeli authorities intermittently issued special summonses for those suspected of involvement in or knowledge of security offenses. Israeli military order 1369 provides for a 7-year prison term for anyone who does not respond to a special summons delivered to a family member or posted in the MATAK office nearest the suspect's home address. Bail rarely was available to those arrested for security offenses.

Israel's age standard in prosecuting youth as adults differs based on national origin. Israeli youth under the age of 18 cannot be tried as adults; however, Palestinian youth who are 16 years of age can be tried as adults.

Israeli authorities must inform detainees of their right to an attorney and whether there are any orders prohibiting such contact. Higher-ranking officials or judges may extend the period during which a detainee is denied access to counsel. For example, access to counsel was denied routinely while a suspect was being interrogated, which may last up to several weeks.

Israel hampered or prevented contacts between Palestinians, their lawyers, families, and human rights organizations in Israeli prisons and detention facilities.

The law provides that in the occupied territories, Israeli authorities must inform the family of a person's arrest and place of detention "without delay." Such notification rarely was given, and Palestinian suspects often were kept incommunicado for much longer than 48 hours. Israeli authorities stated that they attempted to post notification of arrests within 48 hours, but that senior officers may delay notification for up to 12 days. Additionally, a military commander may appeal to a judge to extend this period in security cases for an unlimited period of time. Even if family members or others became aware of a person's arrest, it often was difficult for them to obtain information regarding where a detainee was being held or whether the detainee had access to an attorney. Palestinians often located detained family members through alternative means. Palestinians may check with a local ICRC office or the Israeli human rights organization HaMoked to determine whether it has information regarding the whereabouts of a family member.

The Israeli Government routinely transferred Palestinians arrested in the occupied territories to facilities in Israel, especially the prison in Ashkelon and the military detention centers in Megiddo and the Negev Desert.

Israeli authorities in some instances scheduled appointments between attorneys and their detained clients, but subsequently moved the clients to another prison without notice prior to the meetings. Authorities reportedly used such tactics to delay lawyer-client meetings for as long as 90 days. Palestinian prisoners had difficulty obtaining legal representation because of restrictions in place on Palestinian lawyers. Since the Intifada began, only Israeli citizens or Palestinian lawyers with Jerusalem identification cards were permitted to visit Palestinian prisoners in Israeli prisons as advocates or monitors. This significantly reduced the availability and timeliness of legal aid for such prisoners due to a reduction from 1,300 to approximately 100 lawyers available to handle such cases. Lawyers with Jerusalem identification cards reported frequent, repeated, and lengthy delays in meeting with prisoners.

Human rights groups stated that Palestinian lawyers from the Gaza Strip had a more difficult time obtaining permission to meet their clients than their West Bank counterparts, and that they were denied entry into Israel more frequently than West Bank lawyers.

Male family members between 16 and 40 years of age, and any family members with security records, usually were barred from visiting relatives in Israeli facilities. Relatives of Palestinian prisoners also stated that in some instances they learned that visitation rights were canceled only when they arrived at the prison after having traveled for many hours from the occupied territories. Following the outbreak of violence in 2000, the Israeli Government banned all family visits for Palestinian prisoners in Israeli prisons, although some visitation rights were restored intermittently after ICRC intervention (see Section 1.c.).

Evidence used at hearings for administrative detentions in security cases was secret and unavailable to the detainee or his attorney during the hearings; the detainee and defense lawyer were required to leave the courtroom when secret evidence was presented. Israeli authorities maintained that they were unable to present evidence in open court because doing so would compromise the method of acquiring the evidence. Judges, not military officials, may renew administrative detention orders beyond a 6-month period. Detainees may appeal detention orders, or the renewal of a detention order, before a military judge, but their chances for success were very limited. No information was available regarding whether any detainees were successful in such appeals.

During the year, the total number of Palestinian prisoners and administrative detainees in Israeli prisons rose. According to the IDF, there were 5,944 Palestinian security prisoners held in IDF and Israeli Prisons Service jails, compared to 4,511 at the end of 2002. The IDF also held an unspecified number of Palestinian detainees in waiting facilities in the occupied territories.

Israel forcibly transferred 20 Palestinians suspected of terror activity but not convicted in court from the West Bank to Gaza. Israel forcibly transferred three Palestinians in 2002 and none in 2001.

On May 18, Israel transferred Mahmoud Suleiman Sa'id as-Sa'di as-Saffouri, 31, from his home in Jenin in the West Bank to the Gaza Strip. Israel conducted the transfer on the basis of a military order issued on April 10. Israel first detained as-Saffouri on June 19 and held him without charge in the West Bank before expelling him to Gaza for 2 years.

From November to December, Israel relocated 18 Palestinians from the West Bank to Gaza. Israel in mid-October issued military orders calling for the transfers. All of the appeals to the Israeli High Court by the detainees were struck down.

. . . .

e. Denial of Fair Public Trial

Israeli law provides for an independent judiciary, and the Government generally respected this in practice. **Palestinians accused by Israel of security offenses in the occupied territories usually were tried in Israeli military courts. Security offenses are defined broadly and may include charges as varied as rock throwing or membership in outlawed terrorist organizations, such as HAMAS or the PFLP.** Military prosecutors brought charges. Serious charges were tried before three-judge panels; lesser offenses were tried before one judge. **The Israeli military courts rarely acquitted Palestinians of security offenses**, but sentences in some cases were reduced on appeal.

Israeli military trials followed evidentiary rules that were the same as those in regular criminal cases. Convictions may not be based solely on confessions, although in practice some security prisoners were convicted on the basis of alleged coerced confessions of both themselves and others. The prosecution must justify closing the proceedings to the public in security cases, and the Attorney General determines the venue. Counsel may assist the accused during trial, and a judge may assign counsel to those defendants when it is deemed necessary. Charges are made available to the defendant and the public in Hebrew, and the court may order that the charges be translated into Arabic if necessary. Sentencing in military courts was consistent with that in civilian criminal courts. Defendants in military trials had the right to appeal through the Military High Court. Defendants in military trials also may petition to the civilian High Court of Justice (as a court of first instance) in cases in which they believe there are procedural or evidentiary irregularities. The court may hear secret evidence in security cases that is not available to the defendant or his attorney. While a conviction may not be based solely on such evidence, it reportedly may influence the judge's decision.

Trials sometimes were delayed, sometimes excessively, because witnesses, including Israeli military or police officers, did not appear, the defendant was not brought to court, files were lost, or attorneys failed to appear, sometimes because they were not informed of the trial date or travel restrictions prevented Palestinian lawyers from reaching the court (see Section 2.d.). Palestinian legal advocates argued that these delays were designed to pressure defendants to settle their cases without trial or to pressure some defendants to plead guilty to minor offenses so that an expedited trial could be held.

In expedited trials a charge sheet was drawn up within 48 hours and a court hearing was scheduled within days. There frequently was no testimony provided by Palestinian witnesses either for or against Palestinians on trial. Israeli authorities stated that this was due to the refusal of Palestinians to cooperate with the authorities. Palestinian authorities stated that the absence of Palestinian witnesses was due to strict travel restrictions. Tension resulting from the security situation, and the closures imposed on the West Bank and Gaza, posed additional barriers to cooperation.

Confessions usually were given in Arabic but translated into Hebrew for the record because, authorities maintained, many Israeli court personnel could speak Arabic but few could read it. As a result, many Palestinian prisoners signed confessions written in Hebrew, which many could not read or understand.

Crowded facilities and poor arrangements for attorney-client consultations in prisons hindered legal defense efforts. Appointments to see clients were difficult to arrange, and prison authorities often failed to produce clients for scheduled appointments with their attorneys.

Israeli settlers in the West Bank and Gaza Strip accused of security and ordinary criminal offenses were tried under Israeli law in the nearest Israeli district court. Civilian judges presided, and the standards of due process and admissibility of evidence were governed by the laws of Israel, not military orders. Settlers rarely were prosecuted in Israeli courts of crimes against Palestinians, and, in the rare instances in which they were convicted, regularly received lighter punishment than Palestinians convicted in Israeli courts (see Section 1.a.). The Government of Israel maintains a special department within the police force to investigate violence by settlers; however, the establishment of such a unit has not noticeably diminished settler violence. During the year, 9 settlers were indicted for violence in the occupied territories and three were convicted for related crimes.

The Israeli Government maintained that it held no political prisoners, but Palestinians claimed that many of the 553 Palestinian administrative detainees being held without charge were political prisoners.

The Government of Israel held thousands of persons for security related offenses (see Section 1.d.).

. . . .

f. Arbitrary Interference with Privacy, Family, Home, or Correspondence.

Israeli military authorities on many occasions entered private Palestinian homes and institutions without a warrant, citing security concerns. An officer of the rank of lieutenant colonel or above could authorize such action. In conducting searches, both in areas under Israeli control and during incursions into areas ostensibly under PA control, IDF personnel forcibly entered and in some cases, beat occupants and destroyed property.

Israeli forces arbitrarily destroyed or looted Palestinian property and solicited bribes during military operations. A B'tselem investigation revealed that IDF soldiers stationed at the Qalandiya checkpoint outside Jerusalem in October and November solicited bribes from Palestinian truck drivers to facilitate the passage of their vehicles. Authorities stated that beatings and arbitrary destruction of property during searches were punishable violations of military regulations and that compensation was due to victims in such cases. However, the Israeli Government stated that it did not keep consolidated information regarding the claims against the Ministry of Defense for damages resulting from IDF actions.

Israeli security forces demolished and sealed the homes (owned or rented) of Palestinians suspected of terrorism or the relatives of such suspects, without any judicial review (see Section 1.g.). During the year, according to Israeli human rights organization B'tselem, Israeli forces demolished 219 homes (compared to 250 in 2002) and sealed three others as punishment for terror activity and deterrence against future attacks. Israel also demolished many homes in the Gaza Strip between the Rafah refugee camp and the border with Egypt claiming that the houses concealed tunnels used for weapons and other smuggling from Egypt or provided cover for attacks against Israeli soldiers.

The IDF destroyed numerous citrus orchards, olive and date groves, and irrigation systems on Palestinian-owned agricultural land in both the West Bank and Gaza. The IDF destroyed these groves or orchards for security reasons, stating that Palestinians had been shooting from those areas. **The IDF also cleared and took control of West Bank land, including land held by private Palestinians, in order to facilitate construction of the separation barrier. B'Tselem estimated that at least 10,000 dunams of land has been taken over for construction of the separation barrier.** Israel asserts that it has sought to build the barrier on public lands where possible, and where private land was used, provided opportunities for compensation to the owners.

. . . .

g. Use of Excessive Force and Violations of Humanitarian Law in Internal Conflicts

Israeli security forces often used excessive force against Palestinians and others. The IDF killed or injured Palestinians or others in non life-threatening situations. IDF fire killed or injured innocent bystanders, including journalists and Palestinian civilians, when they fired into crowds at demonstrations (see Sections 1.a. and 2.a.). Palestinian medical groups have estimated that approximately 10 percent of the injuries will result in permanent disabilities, and another 10 percent will require medical rehabilitation (see Section 5).

Israel obstructed the movement of and occasionally fired upon and assaulted medical personnel and ambulances. In the past, Israel alleged that terrorists have used ambulances to transport weapons or to commit terrorist acts. During the year, the PRCS reported that ambulances came under fire 57 times and emergency teams came under fire 79 times. The PRCS also reported that IDF soldiers and Israeli settlers injured 7 PRCS medical staff members and damaged 12 ambulances in these incidents. PRCS reported that its ambulances were delayed or denied access to areas on 584 separate occasions.

On March 11, a PRCS ambulance entered an ongoing firefight in Tel al-Sultan in Gaza to retrieve a Palestinian injured in tank shelling and gunfire. When the crew located an injured Palestinian and moved to take him into the ambulance an IDF tank opened fire in the ambulance's direction. The ambulance driver was hit in the left hand by shrapnel from a tank shell before managing to flee the scene.

On February 2, Israeli soldiers raided the medical center of the Union of Palestinian Medical Relief Committees (UPMRC) in the Old City of Nablus. The soldiers destroyed three hospital beds, furniture, a defibrillator, and various containers of medicine.

On May 20, an IDF soldier at the Surda checkpoint in Ramallah assaulted ambulance driver Talal 'abd al-Malek Muhammad 'Ida, 45. A soldier in a jeep summoned 'Ida as he attempted to coordinate his passage through the checkpoint and punched him in the face. 'Ida was treated with stitches at a Ramallah hospital.

On June 14, the UPMRC reported that IDF soldiers outside the village of Deir Ghassaneh halted an ambulance at gunpoint and then boarded it. The ambulance was driving to the town to pick up injured Palestinians. The soldiers hid in the rear of the ambulance and told the ambulance team to drive to the town with them inside. The soldiers told the UPMRC staff not to reveal the soldiers' presence in the ambulance. The soldiers used the cover of the ambulance to arrest people seized the identification cards of the ambulance crew members when they refused to continue driving and did not return until 3 days later.

During the Intifada, the IDF also used excessive force in responding to a number of incidents at checkpoints (see Section 1.a.).

Israeli soldiers placed Palestinian civilians in danger by ordering them to facilitate military operations, which exposed them to live fire between armed Palestinians and Israeli soldiers. Since the beginning of the Intifada, IDF soldiers have ordered Palestinian civilians to enter buildings to check whether they were booby-trapped; to expel their occupants; to remove suspicious objects from the road; and to walk in front of soldiers to protect them from gunfire. For example, on May 14 Israeli Border Police officers forced a Palestinian driving a car in Jenin to park the vehicle in front of a private home and then proceeded to use the car, which held three passengers, as a shield during a gun battle with armed Palestinians. One Border Police officer forced Muhammad Aradeh, 19, out of the car and made him to kneel while firing over his head. On March 6, IDF soldiers conducting an incursion into Awarta village near Nablus ordered 'Ula 'Awad to lead them through an apartment building and a neighboring house and knock on doors as they conducted searches. The officers threatened to shoot 'Awad as he conducted the search.

In 2002, the Israeli High Court of Justice granted an injunction against the use of Palestinians as "shields" for Israeli forces. Israel admitted the use of such practices, in violation of existing procedures, and reiterated that IDF forces "are absolutely forbidden to use civilians of any kind as a means of 'living shield' against gunfire or attack by the Palestinian side, or as 'hostages.'" However, this ruling did not prevent IDF soldiers from carrying out the same practices under another name. IDF soldiers are openly permitted to employ the "neighbor procedure," which allows them to seek the assistance of Palestinian civilians in operations so long as that assistance is consensual. Human rights groups asserted that Palestinians who agreed to assist such operations often did so out of fear of the soldiers even if they were not directly coerced. Palestinians who took part in

Israel also placed civilians in danger by occupying Palestinian homes, quartering soldiers there, and conducting military operations from them. For example, in December, IDF soldiers conducted raids in the Old City of Nablus and detained residents of buildings in a single apartment while using the upper floors for military activities.

The IDF fired tank rounds, as well as rockets from helicopters and military aircraft, on targets in cities and towns in the West Bank and Gaza during operations undertaken in response to attacks on Israeli soldiers, settlers, and other civilians (see Section 1.a.).

Israeli forces demolished the homes of the families and relatives of those convicted of or suspected of committing terror attacks, effectively punishing innocent Palestinians not implicated in the attacks. Israel's demolitions left hundreds of Palestinians not directly implicated in the attacks homeless. During the year, Israeli forces demolished 219 homes and sealed three others for punitive reasons, compared to 250 in 2002, and 10 in 2001. The numbers of such demolitions increased as Israel re-occupied areas previously under exclusive PA control and gained access to such homes. For example, on March 3, Israeli forces in the Bureij refugee camp in the Gaza Strip carried out the punitive destruction of the home of arrested Hamas leader Muhammad Saleh Hassan Abu Taha. The destruction of the home left seven residents of the building homeless and severely damaged an adjacent home, causing a wall to collapse that killed a 40-year-old pregnant woman next door.

Israel demolished entire apartment buildings that had been used as past shooting points by Palestinian gunmen, effectively punishing innocent civilians unconnected with the attacks. For example, on September 5, Israel demolished a seven-story residential building in Nablus after exchanging fire with and killing Muhammad al-Hanbali, 26, a Hamas militant who was hiding inside the building. IDF soldiers removed Hanbali's body from the building and then planted explosives on the first floor of the building and leveled the structure. The demolition left 15 Palestinian families homeless with all of their belongings destroyed.

Israel's extensive curfews on Palestinian towns punished entire innocent populations. The curfews affected every aspect of life for Palestinians, damaging livelihood and causing food shortages. The Israeli

Government's sustained imposition of internal and external closures and curfews in the West Bank and Gaza during the year severely impacted Palestinian society and economy, contributing to shortages of basic food, water, and the provision of medical care and supplies.

The external and internal closures contributed to increased unemployment and poverty in the occupied territories. Approximately 146,000 West Bank and Gaza workers, representing roughly 25 percent of the Palestinian work force, depended on day jobs in Israel, Israeli settlements, and Jerusalem and were prevented from leaving the occupied territories.

The closures on Palestinian cities and towns also impeded Palestinians from reaching jobs or markets in the occupied territories and disrupted internal and external trade. Closures, and the destruction of large swathes of Palestinian-owned agricultural land and economic infrastructure by the IDF and settlers, contributed to an unemployment rate that was estimated at 30 percent at the end of the year.

Closures particularly isolated and hurt the roughly 200,000 Palestinians who lived in rural villages. Rural villages rarely were self-sustaining communities and did not have the full range of services—such as medical care, education, or municipal provision of water—that larger urban areas had, increasing their isolation when community members were not able to travel outside the area to obtain access to services and provisions. Other rural villages under full Israeli control were further isolated from major Palestinian population centers.

Israeli security forces' implementation of control measures at checkpoints often impeded the provision of medical assistance to sick and injured Palestinians. Since the beginning of Intifada, The Government's implementation of control measures resulted in delayed access to medical treatment for at least 39 Palestinian who subsequently died (see Section 1.g.).

The ICRC stated that the prolonged closure of Palestinian cities significantly obstructed the delivery of medical care. The closures made it extremely difficult for patients living outside large cities who need repeated medical treatment, such as dialysis or physical therapy, to reach medical centers on a regular basis. The PRCS has estimated that more than one-third of Palestinians who have been injured in the Intifada required some type of physical rehabilitation and at least 10 percent have permanent disabilities. Medical professionals reported that many Palestinians delayed all but emergency medical care because of the restrictions and economic conditions. Preventive treatment, such as vaccinations, antenatal and postnatal care, and family planning often was postponed; and the number of births at home, in ambulances, and at checkpoints remained high. Medical observers reported that as the Intifada continued, the impact on public health would be negative.

On June 14, Israeli soldiers detained for 1 hour the ambulance of Muhammad Hassan Abu Qibeta, a 65-year-old diabetic Palestinian from Yattaon his way to a hospital in Hebron. Qibeta had reportedly suffered a heart attack before reaching the checkpoint, and died there after waiting at the checkpoint for an hour.

Closures and curfews also have affected the provision of emergency medical care, including by impeding the ability of medical staff to reach work. Israeli security services stopped and searched all ambulances at each checkpoint, which frequently added life-threatening delays in reaching hospitals, due to the fact that some had to use substandard local roads when denied access through any of the checkpoints. Israeli security forces often impeded the provision of medical assistance to Palestinian civilians by strict enforcement of internal closures. The PCRS reported that its average response time to emergency calls in "outer city" areas was 40 to 50 minutes, compared to a past average of 10-15 minutes.

Israeli soldiers frequently harassed and abused Palestinian emergency services staff at the checkpoints (see Section 1.c.).

. . . .

Section 2 Respect for Civil Liberties, Including:

a. Freedom of Speech and Press

The Israeli Government generally respected freedom of speech in the occupied territories; however, **IDF soldiers routinely harassed and occasionally detained Palestinian and other journalists covering stories in the West Bank and Gaza. Israel frequently denied journalists travel permits and revoked or delayed issuing press credentials, all of which amounted to de facto censorship.** Israel censored and prohibited public expressions of anti-Israeli sentiment and of support for Islamic extremist groups. **The IDF allegedly killed two journalists covering clashes between Palestinians and Israeli security**

forces, both of whom were identified as noncombatants, and injured at least four others. During the year, Israel raided the premises of several television and radio stations.

During the year, the Israeli Government continued to enforce selectively its standing prohibition on the display in East Jerusalem of Palestinian political symbols, such as flags, national colors, and graffiti. Such displays were punishable by fines or imprisonment. Israeli enforcement of existing censorship regulations remained stringent regarding press coverage of the Intifada. Israeli authorities monitored Arabic newspapers based in East Jerusalem for security-related issues, and newspapers sometimes were ordered to halt publication of stories about the security situation until the information first appeared in the Israeli media.

Military censors reviewed Arabic publications for material related to the public order and security of Israel. Reports by foreign journalists were subject to review by Israeli military censors for security issues, and the satellite feed used by many foreign journalists was monitored. In periods of heightened security, the Israeli Government often closed areas to journalists when it imposed a curfew or closure. Israeli authorities denied entry permits to West Bank Palestinian journalists traveling to their place of employment in Jerusalem during closures of the territories, and the journalists had difficulty renewing their Israeli issued press credentials (see Section 2.d.).

The IDF required a permit for Palestinian publications sold in areas of the occupied territories under its control. Publications may be censored or banned for content considered anti-Semitic or anti-Israeli. Possession of banned materials was punishable by a fine and imprisonment.

The Israeli Government prohibited the delivery and distribution of publications, including newspapers, in the Gaza Strip on the Jewish holiday of Yom Kippur (when import of any item is prohibited) and on numerous other occasions when the closure of the Gaza Strip was particularly tight. On several occasions during the year, usually following terrorist incidents, the Israelis banned Palestinian daily newspapers from entering Gaza. However, during such periods, Israeli newspapers were allowed into Gaza. During internal closures, the Israeli Government also occasionally blocked the delivery of Palestinian daily newspapers to Palestinian cities in the West Bank.

Israel also harassed Palestinian media organizations. On January 31, Israeli forces conducted an incursion on the city of Hebron and shut down all local radio and television stations in the course of imposing curfew. During the incursion, IDF soldiers raided the offices of the al-Nawras and al-Majd television stations and the Marah radio station.

During the year, Israeli soldiers killed two journalists. On May 3, the IDF killed James Miller, 34, a cameraman for a British television network. Miller was filming a documentary in the Shaja'iya neighborhood of Gaza City and was wearing a vest marking him as a journalist. IDF sources claimed that they were returning Palestinian fire; however, Palestinians at the scene claimed that there was no such fire. Human rights groups rejected Israel's account of the incident after independent investigations of the circumstances of the shooting.

On April 19, an IDF soldier shot and killed Nazeeh Darwaza, 45, a cameraman for the Associated Press Television Network and Palestinian Television. Dawazah was filming a wounded child during an IDF incursion in Nablus and was wearing a jacket labeling him as press. On July 30, Reporters Sans Frontieres released a statement criticizing Israel for an incomplete and botched investigation into Darwaza's death. The IDF did not charge any soldiers in this case.

On March 6, Israeli tank fire in the Jabalya refugee camp in the Gaza Strip injured two Reuters journalists, Ahmad Jadallah and Shams Odeh. Jadallah suffered severe shrapnel injuries and Odeh suffered a fractured foot. On January 28, Israeli gunfire during an incursion into Jenin injured Reuters reporter Seif ad-Din Ad-Daheleh, 20.

Israeli soldiers confiscated journalists' press cards, detained, and beat them on several occasions. For example, on May 19, IDF soldiers in Beit Sahour detained licensed photographers Sha'aban Qandil and Joseph Hadal and beat them. Qandil and Hadal were driving in a car marked "press" and labeled with "TV" stickers. Both men suffered broken bones from the beating.

. . . .

The Israeli Government required one Palestinian-owned newspaper, Al-Quds, to submit its entire contents, including advertising, to the military censor by 4 p.m. each day. The editor claimed that this process caused his journalists to practice self-censorship.

. . . .

Israeli severely restricted academic freedom by disrupting the operations of West Bank and Gaza schools, colleges, and universities during the year. Israel disrupted Palestinian education through closures, curfews, and military actions that shut universities down entirely. Students and staff at all educational levels had difficulty traveling to and from educational facilities because most areas were under some form of internal closure for the entire year. In addition, Israeli forces imposed curfews on many Palestinian areas, some for 24 hours a day, for extended periods (see Sections 2.d. and 5).

Students from Gaza were unable to reach West Bank universities since early October 2000, when Israel closed the safe passage route between Gaza and the West Bank. Israeli shelling and gunfire during military operations damaged a number of schools in the West Bank and Gaza.

In January, Israel shut down the two principal higher education facilities in Hebron by military order. The military order, which was valid for 6 months and was extended in June, closed down Hebron University and the Hebron Polytechnic School. The closure blocked the education of over 5,000 Palestinian students.

The PA Ministry of Education reported that since 2001 the IDF had confiscated 3 schools in Hebron and subsequently quartered soldiers there after converting them to military barracks. T

Those three schools were the Jawhar Girls Elementary School, the Osama Girls Elementary School, and the Ma'arif Boys Elementary School. The Ministry of Education also reported that IDF forces raided schools 26 times during the year. Since the start of the Intifada, the **IDF reportedly raided or fired on schools 295 times, shut down 9 schools completely, and forced the suspension of classes at 1,125 schools and nearly all higher education institutions.**

. . . .

b. Freedom of Peaceful Assembly and Association

The Israeli Government placed severe limits on freedom of assembly for Palestinians in the occupied territories, largely through the imposition of internal closures and curfews (see Section 2.d.). Israeli military orders banned public gatherings of 10 or more persons without a permit. Extensive curfews during the year made assembly of any kind impossible in most major Palestinian cities. Those Palestinians who chose to take part in even peaceful demonstrations often did so only by breaking curfew restrictions and IDF prohibitions against demonstrations.

Israeli security forces killed many Palestinians and injured several thousand during demonstrations and other often violent clashes (see Sections 1.a. and 1.c.). The Israeli and Palestinian authorities regularly disputed whether Palestinians fired at security forces during such demonstrations. Israeli security forces resorted to live fire, even in instances when Palestinians did not direct gunfire at them at them first. In 2001, the IDF changed its definition of "life-threatening" situations to include rock-throwing in some cases.

. . . .

The Israeli Government continued to place severe restrictions on freedom of association in East Jerusalem. In 2001, Israeli forces **closed Orient House, the preeminent Palestinian political institution in Jerusalem,** and other East Jerusalem institutions located in Orient House, including: The Chamber of Commerce, the Land Research Center, the Higher Council for Tourism, a women's center, a prisoner's rights society, and a historical preservation group. Orient House remained closed at year's end; however, during the year, several institutions opened up alternative offices outside Jerusalem in the neighborhoods of al-Ram and Dahiat al-Barid.

During the year, **Israeli police closed the Arab Graduates Club, a social club frequented by Fatah activists** and run by PA Deputy Waqf Minister and Jerusalem Fatah Secretary General Salah Zuheikeh. In 2002, the **Israeli police closed the Multi-Sectoral Review Project, the Land Research Center, the East Jerusalem offices of the Federation of Palestinian Chambers of Commerce, and the Jerusalem Cultural Association and the Union of Sports Clubs.** At year's end, all of these organizations remained closed.

. . . .

c. Freedom of Religion

Israeli law provides for freedom of worship, and the Government generally respected this right in practice in the occupied territories. Israel did not ban any group on religious grounds, and permitted all faiths to operate schools and institutions.

Israel's imposed internal and external closure of the West Bank and Gaza, significantly impeded freedom of worship for Muslims and Christians. Israeli closure policies prevented tens of thousands of Palestinians from reaching their places of worship in Jerusalem and the West Bank, including during religious holidays such as Ramadan, Christmas, and Easter. On numerous occasions, the Israeli Government prevented worshippers under the age of 45 from attending Friday prayers inside the Haram al-Sharif/ Temple Mount, the third holiest site in Islam and the holiest site in Judaism. The Israeli Government stated that such actions were necessary for security reasons. However, in June, armed Israeli police officers began escorting groups of Christian and Jewish tourists into the Haram al-Sharif/Temple Mount against the wishes of the Waqf authorities. Israeli police spokesmen indicated that the visits were an effort by the Government of Israel to re-assert the right of non-Muslims to visit the shrine.

During the year, the Government of Israel's continued closure policy prevented a number of Palestinian religious leaders (both Muslim and Christian) from reaching their congregations.

. . . .

The Israeli Government severely restricted freedom of movement for Palestinians. During the year, Israel prohibited most Palestinians from the West Bank and Gaza from entering Israel, and the IDF continued to enforce a massive network of checkpoints and roadblocks across the occupied territories, which impeded the movement of people and goods between Palestinian cities, villages, and towns. Numerous cities were placed under strict curfews that ran for weeks and even months. Israel lifted some checkpoints and eased some movement following the release of the roadmap in May, but in most cases the restrictions were later reinstituted. During the year, the restrictions on movement were the most severe that Israel had imposed since it occupied East Jerusalem, the West Bank, and Gaza in 1967.

Israel constructed parts of a large security barrier in the West Bank. The result was division of approximately 5,000 Palestinian residents from the rest of the West Bank and severe disruption of their access to hospitals, schools, social services, and agricultural property. At the end of the year, the total land area secluded by the separation barrier from the remainder of the West Bank was approximately 96,000 dunams.

Since 1993, Israel has required that all West Bank and Gaza residents obtain permits to enter Israel and Jerusalem. However, Israel often denied applicants permits with no explanation and did not allow effective means of appeal. Palestinian officials and members of the clergy with VIP passes, including PA cabinet officials, members of the Palestinian Council were regularly subjected to long delays and searches at Israeli checkpoints in the West Bank, despite the fact that they were traveling on special passes issued by the Israeli Government. These practices continued at an increased level from previous years, severely restricting PA officials from conducting administrative functions and implementing reform.

On October 2, Israel issued military orders that required Palestinians residing between the separation barrier and the Green Line to obtain residency permits in order to remain in these areas. At year's end, the permit requirement applied to approximately 5,000 Palestinians who were located in such areas, dubbed "seam zones."

Even in periods before the Intifada, Palestinians in the West Bank and Gaza Strip found it difficult to obtain permits to work, visit, study, or obtain medical care in Israel. Israeli authorities permitted only a small number of Gazans to bring vehicles into Israel and sometimes did not permit West Bank vehicles to enter Jerusalem or Israel. Except for senior PA officials, Palestinians of all ages crossing between the Gaza Strip and Israel were not permitted to travel by automobile across the main checkpoint. Instead they were forced to travel along a narrow walkway almost a mile long. Israelis moving into and out of the Gaza Strip were permitted to use their automobiles. Israeli regulations prohibited Palestinian residents of Jerusalem from entering the West Bank, although this ban only intermittently was enforced. Israeli authorities also required that these Palestinian residents provide written notice to the Israeli Government if they intended to travel to the Gaza Strip; however, provision of such notice did not ensure that the Government would permit the travel.

Since 1993 Israel applied varying levels of "closure," or enhanced restrictions, on the movement of Palestinians and their goods, often for lengthy periods, in response to Palestinian terrorist attacks and other changing security conditions. The Government of Israel imposed a tightened version of closure, called "comprehensive, external closure" during periods of violent protest in the West Bank or Gaza, or when it believed that there was an increased likelihood of such unrest. Comprehensive closures also were instituted regularly during major Israeli holidays and during some Muslim holidays. During such closures, the Israel Government cancelled travel permits and prevented Palestinians—even those with valid work permits—from leaving the occupied territories. During comprehensive closures, the authorities severely restricted the movement of goods between Israel and the occupied territories and between the West Bank and Gaza. Due to the ongoing unrest, Israel imposed strict and consistent external closure throughout the year for the second straight year, compared with 210 days in 2001 and 88 days in 2000.

During periods of unrest in the West Bank and Gaza, in the aftermath of terrorist attacks, or during military exercises, the Israeli Government prohibited travel between towns and villages within the West Bank. These "internal" closures resulted in the cutoff of goods, including food and fuel, and restricted the movement of persons. During the year, Israel expanded internal closures further, sometimes in response to specific acts of violence and sometimes as a preventive measure imposed on entire cities and towns. The internal closures were even more severe when Palestinians were prohibited from using primary roads and physical barricades close off many secondary roads.

The Israeli Government further constrained the movement of Palestinians and goods in the West Bank and Gaza by imposing total closures on specific areas or villages, sometimes for weeks at a time, and by intermittently closing the Allenby and Rafah crossing points to Jordan and Egypt. Israel also consistently imposed curfews in some areas, often for extended periods. During the curfews, Palestinians generally were confined to their homes for all but a few hours per week during which they were allowed to buy food and other provisions.

The prolonged closures and curfews imposed by the Government of Israel on Palestinian cities and towns during the year had a severely negative impact on every sector of the Palestinian economy. They impeded Palestinians from reaching jobs or markets and disrupted internal and external trade (see Section 1.g.).

The prolonged closure also seriously impacted students' ability to attend school and university (see Sections 2.a. and 5.). The Government of Israel stated that they were necessary security measures (see Section 1.g.).

The Israeli Government required all Palestinian residents to obtain permits for foreign travel and restricted the travel of some political activists. Bridge-crossing permits to Jordan may be obtained at post offices without a screening process.

Israel offered East Jerusalem residents Israeli citizenship following Israel's occupation of Jerusalem in 1967. Most have chosen not to accept Israeli citizenship, choosing instead to seek a residence permit or Jerusalem identification card. which Israel occupied during the 1967 War, Israel applied the 1952 Law of Permanent Residency and its 1974 amendments to Jerusalem identification card holders. The law states that a Jerusalem resident loses the right of residence if he or she leaves Israeli territory for more than 7 years, acquires the nationality of another country, or acquires permanent residence in another country. Such persons are permitted to return only as tourists and sometimes are denied entry. The Government of Israel does not apply these same restrictions to Israeli citizens.

In 2000, the Israeli Ministry of Interior published new instructions regarding residency rights in Jerusalem. According to these instructions, permanent residents whose identity cards had been revoked after 1995 but who returned to live in Jerusalem from 1998 on were entitled to restoration of their identity cards, provided that they could demonstrate that Jerusalem was the "center of their lives." In addition to the provision on restoration of identity cards, the new guidelines allowed for the revocation of residency in cases in which East Jerusalem Palestinians obtained new citizenship or residency rights while living abroad. Human rights groups reported that such revocations have taken place infrequently.
. . . .

[END OF 2003 STATE DEPARTMENT REPORT]

AMNESTY INTERNATIONAL

Israel and the Occupied Territories
Surviving Under Siege:
The impact of movement restrictions on the right to work.

September 2003   Executive Summary
AI Index:

_____

MDE 15/064/2003

The restrictions imposed by Israel on the movements of Palestinians in the Occupied Territories have reached an unprecedented level since the beginning of the intifada (Palestinian uprising) in September 2000.(1) Closures, blockades, checkpoints, roadblocks, curfews and other restrictions have had a disastrous impact on the lives of Palestinians in the West Bank and Gaza Strip, and have crippled the Palestinian economy. Unemployment and poverty have spiralled, malnutrition has emerged, anaemia and other health problems have increased and education has been negatively affected.

In law as well as in practice, the Israeli authorities have breached their obligations under international law to respect and protect the rights of the Palestinians in the West Bank and Gaza Strip. The sweeping and indiscriminate restrictions imposed by Israel on the movement of people and goods in the Occupied Territories not only violate the right to freedom of movement, but also infringe the right to work and other economic and social rights of Palestinians in the Occupied Territories.

Some 60 percent of Palestinians now live below the poverty line of US$2 per day and most are forced to depend on aid. The high levels of unemployment, poverty, malnutrition and other health problems afflicting Palestinians are not just a humanitarian problem they are the direct result of the restrictions imposed by Israel on the Palestinians in the Occupied Territories.

"No one is starving in the Gaza Strip and the West Bank. International organizations including UNWRA and the Red Cross operate extensively in the territories." Colonel Shimshon Arbel, Head of Information and Coordination of Government Activities in the Occupied Territories(2)

Charity and humanitarian assistance do not absolve Israel of its obligation to guarantee the Palestinians' right to work under international law, so that they can feed themselves. Moreover, according to international law, Israel's obligations as the occupying power in the West Bank and Gaza Strip include ensuring the food and medical supplies of the occupied population. However, Israel has long relied on international humanitarian organizations to ensure the survival of a significant percentage of some three and a half million Palestinians in the Occupied Territories, while at the same time frequently hindering the work of aid organizations.

Hopes that in the context of the Roadmap peace plan restrictions on the movement of Palestinians in the Occupied Territories would be lifted have not materialized. Only a handful of more than 300 checkpoints and roadblocks have been lifted. In addition, more and more Palestinians are finding themselves trapped in enclaves and separated from their land as the construction of the barrier/fence/wall continues inside the West Bank. Israeli settlements, established in the Occupied Territories in violation of international law, and roads built for the benefit of Israeli settlers continue to expand, resulting in further restrictions being imposed on Palestinians.

This document summarizes Amnesty International's report, Israel and the Occupied Territories: Surviving under siege: The impact of movement restrictions on the right to work (AI Index: MDE 15/001/2003, September 2003) which analyses the impact of movement restrictions on the right to work of Palestinians in the West Bank and Gaza Strip.(3) The report details the findings of the organization's research, describes representative cases in different areas of the West Bank and Gaza Strip, and contains recommendations to the Israeli authorities, the international community, the Palestinian Authority and Palestinian armed groups.

Restrictions on movement
"The directives of the military command are to freeze all traffic on West Bank roads, including taxis, buses, private vehicles and others according to security needs." Binyamin Ben Eliezer, Defence Minister, explaining the Israeli army's policy in the Knesset on 3 October 2002

In the West Bank Palestinian vehicles are prohibited from using main roads, which are used freely by Israeli settlers. Secondary roads which pass near settlements or intersect with roads used by settlers have likewise been blocked. With the spread of Israeli settlements throughout the West Bank and Gaza Strip, the areas where passage is prohibited to Palestinians have multiplied.

When at all possible, traveling even a short distance between West Bank towns and villages usually entails a lengthy, costly and potentially dangerous journey for Palestinians. Detours to avoid closed checkpoints, blockades or areas which are forbidden to them often take travelers miles out of their way, sometimes on tracks over or round steep hills, changing several vehicles and crossing blockades on foot. In addition this involves the risk of being turned back, harassed or even shot. Such detours are difficult or impossible for the sick, the elderly or those carrying heavy packages or small children.

Palestinians may apply to the Israeli army for permits to travel between West Bank towns but the army's criteria for delivering such permits are unclear and requests are frequently refused without explanation. Permits are normally only issued for a limited period and are only valid for travel on certain days and at certain times. When curfews or full closures are imposed, the permits cannot be used and at other times Israeli soldiers may deny passage to those who have permits. Often permit holders limit their travel because they fear soldiers may shoot at them from a distance, before approaching to check whether they have a valid travel permit.

"Every time I drive on these roads and see a tank in the distance I wonder if I'll make it home to see the children again. I have a permit, for a month, but if the soldiers shoot at me and I am killed the permit won't do any good to me or my family. They can always say I was a terrorist, or that I did something suspicious that made them think I was a danger. And even if they admit making a mistake and apologize what good would that be if I am dead? So I try to avoid traveling as much as possible" Human rights lawyer, November 2002

The Gaza Strip has likewise suffered from closures, with the movement of some 1.3 million Palestinians made subordinate to the movement of some 5,000 Israeli settlers. Since October 2000, sections of the two main north-south roads, which run near Israeli settlements, have been completely or partially closed.

Closed areas: In parts of the Gaza Strip, areas where Palestinians live surrounded by settlements, such as al-Mawasi and al-Sayafa, have been declared closed military zones (see cases studies in the report). These enclaves are accessible only to residents, who are only allowed to enter and leave the areas on foot, and only at specified times. A dusk to dawn curfew is often in force and residents are frequently prevented from leaving or returning to their homes for days or even weeks. With the construction of the barrier/fence/wall similar closed enclaves have been created in the western part of the West Bank (see below).

Transporting goods the back-to-back system: When at all possible, the movement of goods is difficult, time consuming and costly, as Palestinian trucks are usually not allowed to travel between towns in the West Bank and in and out of closed areas. Goods must be transferred from a truck on one side of a checkpoint to a truck on the other side of the checkpoint, a procedure known as the "back-toback" system. The process can take hours and as a result the time and cost of transport have increased dramatically, as several vehicles and drivers have to be used, as well as extra people to unload and reload the merchandise at each checkpoint. The repeated handling of goods and the waiting periods cause many of the goods, especially agricultural produce, to get spoilt or damaged. Palestinians medical services are also often forced to use the back-to-back system and transfer patients between ambulances on each side of checkpoints.

Methods of restricting freedom of movement

Physical barriers: The Israeli army controls movement in and out of the main towns and many villages in the Occupied Territories by setting up checkpoints on primary and secondary roads, by blocking other roads with earth barricades and cement blocks and by digging deep trenches to stop Palestinians from opening closed roads or from passing even on foot. During the winter, rain and mud fill the trenches and make the slopes slippery, and sewage is sometimes diverted by the Israeli army into the trenches to obstruct the passage of even the most agile pedestrians.

Some villages have been completely besieged by earth barriers, cement blocks and trenches, making vehicle access impossible, even for ambulances and water tankers. Passage on foot is also far from easy. Taking long detours and climbing up and down dirt mounds or trenches carrying shopping bags and small children is difficult even for the young and able. For the elderly or disabled, movement in such condition is virtually impossible.

In addition to the permanent or long-term closures of roads by checkpoints, blockades, trenches or other physical obstacles, other roads are frequently blocked temporarily by Israeli tanks or other military vehicles. These are usually referred to as "flying" roadblocks. Israeli military and emergency legislation give military commanders the broadest discretion to declare closed military areas, restrict the use of roads and impose curfews.

On 25 October 2002 Amnesty International's delegates negotiated for the passage of a Palestinian human rights fieldworker at a "flying" roadblock. An armed personnel carrier was blocking the road connecting Nablus to a nearby village, near a road used by settlers. The soldier agreed to let him pass but refused to allow anyone else through. Scores of Palestinians had been waiting in the sun for up to three hours. As an old woman, supported by two people, and two women with babies in their arms took a few steps forward, the soldier engaged his rifle and threatened to shoot them. Yet a few minutes later, without contacting anyone by radio or telephone (indicating that he had not received any instructions), he got back inside the armored personnel carrier and the vehicle drove off, leaving the road free for those waiting to cross.

Curfews: West Bank towns and villages have often been placed under curfew, in many cases for prolonged periods. After the Israeli army retook control of the main West Bank towns in the spring of 2002, 24-hour curfews were imposed for days and in some cases weeks. The army almost completely stopped vital service providers and ambulances from functioning. At times curfews were lifted for a few hours to allow Palestinians to purchase essential supplies. Nablus was under curfew for longer than any other city, and remained under 24-hour curfew for five months after 21 June 2002, apart from one month when it was under a night curfew only. In the H2 area of Hebron some 30,000 Palestinians have been under full or partial curfew most of the time in order to allow some 500 Israeli settlers to move freely.

'Abd al-Rahman Jobe' owns the al-Nada factory in Hebron's industrial area in H-2, producing decorative metal objects, such as banisters. Before the intifada, the factory operated two eight-hour shifts each day and employed up to 25 day labourers. Some 40 to 50 percent of production was destined for the market in Hebron governorate, the rest for other areas of the West Bank and for export to Jordan. Output has declined sharply since October 2000, with profits down to an estimated 10 to 20 percent. By October 2002, the factory was employing only four workers with only one shift a day. When curfews were imposed in H-2, the factory was unable to operate.

The barrier/fence/wall

On 14 June 2002, the Israeli government announced that work would begin immediately to build a barrier/fence/wall along the perimeter of the West Bank, and north and south of Jerusalem. The barrier, some 400km long and up to 100m wide, comprises a complex of obstacles, including deep trenches, electric fences, trace paths and patrol roads for tanks.

The stated aim of the project is to prevent Palestinians crossing clandestinely from the West Bank into Israel. However, most of the separation barrier is being constructed on Palestinian land inside the West Bank in order to encompass a number of Israeli settlements. The barrier/fence cuts off scores of Palestinian villages from the rest of the West Bank or from their farming land. The land in these areas is among the most fertile in the West Bank, with better water resources than elsewhere, and agriculture in the region constitutes the main source of income for the Palestinians.

In Qafin, a village west of Jenin with a population of about 9,500, some 600 dunums of land was to be seized on grounds of military necessity to build the barrier/fence. In September 2002, Israeli land bulldozers began to clear the land, tearing down most olive trees before their owners had been able to harvest the crop. In the Qafin area, the barrier/fence lies some three kilometres inside the West Bank and surrounds the village on three sides. Sixty percent of the village's agricultural land and thousands of olive trees are on the other side of the fence. Most of the active population in Qafin used to work in Israel but is no longer permitted to, and the income from the olives harvest is crucial for many residents.

The barrier has serious economic and social consequences for over 200,000 Palestinians in nearby towns and villages. Beyond land confiscation, the construction of the barrier is resulting in increased restrictions on movement. Palestinians who live in these areas have to cross the barrier at designated checkpoints which are only open at certain times to go to work, to tend to their fields, to sell their agricultural produce, and to access education and health facilities. Non-residents require special permits to enter these areas.

The city of Qalqilya, home to more than 40,000 Palestinians, is completely walled in from all sides with a single checkpoint in and out of the city. This is in order for the barrier to encompass the Israeli settlements to the north-east and south-east of the town. The checkpoint is normally open from morning to evening but times vary. When Amnesty International delegates visited the town the Israeli soldiers said that the checkpoint usually closes at 7 or 7.30 pm but on that day it would close at 5.30 pm. Residents coming back after 5.30, expecting the checkpoint to be open, would have to stay outside until the following morning.

The impact of restrictions on movement

No Palestinian has escaped the impact of the severe restrictions on movement imposed in the Occupied Territories. Although less well documented than other human rights violations, such as killings, torture and detentions, the economic and social consequences of the restrictions are devastating.

In 2001 the UN Committee on Economic, Social and Cultural Rights described Israel as perpetrating "continuing gross violations of economic, social and cultural rights in the occupied territories, especially the severe measures adopted by the State party to restrict the movement of civilians between points within and outside the occupied territories, severing their access to food, water, health care, education and work."(4)

Nabil Hani 'Ashur, a self-employed plumber living in Nablus, has four children and also supports his mother. His monthly salary has fallen by some 90 percent since the start of the intifada. There has been little construction in Nablus because of the depressed economic situation and the shortage of building materials. Some months, he earns nothing at all.

Apart from supporting his family, he had to find money to buy drugs for his wife, Suhad 'Ashur, who was suffering from breast cancer. She was unable to receive any treatment for nearly two months because of curfews and closure and the specialist doctor could not reach the hospital in Nablus from his home in Jenin for weeks. She died on 9 July 2002.

Living standards: Some 60 percent of the Palestinian population is living below the poverty level of US$2.1 per day and unemployment has risen to close to 50 percent.(5) There is no unemployment benefit system in the Occupied Territories. An unemployed person's only means of support are from family or community networks and the limited assistance available from the UN Relief and Works Agency (UNRWA), the Palestinian Authority's Ministry of Social Welfare, and charitable and humanitarian organizations. The dramatic decline in the standard of living among Palestinians in the

Occupied Territories has led to increased malnutrition and other health problems.

As Palestinians have increasingly been forced to rely on charity to meet their basic needs, feelings of hopelessness and alienation have grown, damaging the fabric of society and fuelling resentment. In the predominantly youthful Palestinian community, the lack of prospects for the future has contributed to increased radicalism and violence.

The damage inflicted on the Palestinian society and economy by movement restrictions in the past three years will have grave long-term effects. Even if the restrictions were to be lifted immediately, it would take a long time for the economic situation to improve.

Unemployment: Loss of jobs in Israel, where wages are significantly higher than in the Occupied Territories, has been followed by a reduction in demand for goods and services in the Occupied Territories. Closures and curfews have disrupted the import and transport of raw materials, creating shortages and sharp price rises. Most Palestinian export businesses have lost their export markets as a result of the closures and have extreme difficulties transporting their products between the West Bank and the Gaza Strip, or even moving them short distances to local markets. Perishable foodstuffs spoil when repeatedly handled and delayed at checkpoints or border crossings, making them unmarketable or reducing their price.

In addition to increased unemployment, there has been a huge increase in underemployment and a significant drop in wages. Those who still have jobs have often been unable to reach their workplaces because of curfews and closures. For labourers who are paid on a daily basis, failure to show up for work means loss of a day's wages, as well as an increased risk that their place will be filled by others.

'Omar Ahmad Kababji, aged 56, owns a stone factory in Nablus and supports his wife and seven children. Before the intifada, the factory employed five workers to produce stone building blocks for the market in the West Bank and in Israel. The raw materials come from stone quarries near Nablus. 'Omar Kababji had to close the factory and lay off the workers after the Israeli army blocked off the main roads and back roads into Nablus at the start of the intifada. Transport of the raw materials and finished stone became impossible. All 85 quarries and stone factories in Nablus governorate were forced to close.

Impact on farming: Families in rural areas traditionally turn to farming in times of rising unemployment and declining incomes, but farm incomes have also shrank and some operate at a loss because of restrictions on movement. In many areas, farmers do not have regular access to their land because it is within a closed military area or near an Israeli settlement or settlers' roads. They may be barred from it or fear attack by settlers or the army. Lack of access at key times of the year results in crops being lost or damaged or in severely reduced yields.

Expenditure on agricultural inputs such as fertilizers, pesticides and animal feed has risen sharply, as suppliers have passed on increased transport costs. Some such products are no longer available or farmers cannot afford to buy them. Some villages are not connected to a water network and farmers have to buy water. The price of water has increased on average by 80 percent, because of increased transport costs. Some farmers have sold off productive assets, such as livestock and even land, to cover their basic, immediate needs. This jeopardizes their long-term prospects, even in the event of a future improvement in economic conditions.

Sa'id al-Agha is married with nine children. He owns 50 dunums of land in al-Mawasi, a closed military area in the Gaza Strip. The yield from his land has fallen since the Israeli army stopped fertilizer being brought into al-Mawasi. Before the intifada, he would expect to make a profit of US$15,000. In 2002 he made US$ 1,000.

Guavas, his main crop, used to be exported from Gaza to Israel, the West Bank and Jordan. Now it is almost impossible to send the crop even to the West Bank and often even out of al-Mawasi. The price has collapsed because the market in Gaza is flooded with guavas. When Amnesty International visited Sa'id al-Agha's house, a large pile of rotting dates was piled up in front of it. He had not been able to transport them across the checkpoint out of al-Mawasi.

Excessive use of force to enforce closures and curfews

When a town or a village is under curfew, the Israeli army usually schedules to allow the movement of civilians for a few hours during daylight. However, scheduled breaks in the curfew are often cancelled without notice. Members of the Israeli security forces have frequently resorted to lethal force to enforce closures, killing or injuring scores of unarmed Palestinians as a result. Soldiers have opened fire on Palestinians bypassing checkpoints, crossing trenches, removing barriers and breaking curfews. They have fired at ambulance personnel, municipal employees and journalists who had coordinated their movements in advance with the Israeli army.

Jihad 'Abd al-Rahman al-Qurini, a driver for the Nablus municipality, was shot dead by an Israeli soldier on 20 August 2002 during a curfew. The Nablus municipality had coordinated with the IDF to ensure that his vehicle could move during the curfew to carry out electrical repairs. The truck was marked as a Nablus municipality vehicle and had a distinctive crane and flashing light. In Faisal Street, one of four Israeli soldiers searching a Palestinian ambulance indicated that Jihad al-Qurini should reverse. He backed the vehicle about two metres. The soldier indicated that he should drive forward and fired one shot in the air. Jihad al-Qurini drove the truck slowly forward. The soldier reportedly aimed his weapon at the truck, motioned with his right hand that the vehicle should proceed, then fired twice. One bullet hit Jihad al-Qurini in the head.

The Chief Military Prosecutor concluded that the soldiers "did not deviate from the domain of reasonable conduct expected in actions by military forces in the relevant area and circumstances" and declined to open an investigation into the incident.

Justification on security grounds

The Israeli authorities claim that the restrictions imposed on the movement of Palestinians in the Occupied Territories are justified on security grounds, notably to prevent Palestinian armed groups from carrying out suicide bombings and other attacks in Israeli cities. The Israeli authorities have the right to take necessary, reasonable and proportionate measures to protect Israelis from such attacks. However, the sweeping and stringent restrictions imposed indiscriminately on all Palestinians have not put a stop to the attacks. On the contrary, attacks intensified as restrictions on the movements of Palestinians increased, calling into question the effectiveness of indiscriminate restrictions that treat every Palestinian as a security threat and punish entire communities for the crimes committed by a few people.

Moreover, it cannot be said that preventing Palestinians from travelling between Nablus and Ramallah is necessary to prevent attackers from entering Israel to carry out attacks in Jerusalem or Tel Aviv. Yet closures inside the Occupied Territories are often justified on these grounds and are routinely imposed or tightened following Palestinian attacks inside Israel. Like the Israeli bombardments of PA buildings which have usually followed Palestinian suicide bombings or other attacks, closures and curfews often appear to be intended as punishment or retaliation for attacks by Palestinians, as well as to show the

Israeli public that the army is taking action. This is particularly obvious in the Gaza Strip, which has been surrounded by an electric fence for over a decade. None of the Palestinians who have carried out attacks inside Israel in recent years are known to have come from the Gaza Strip. Yet, in the wake of major Palestinian attacks inside Israel the Israeli army has frequently attacked PA installations in the Gaza Strip, such as the airport, the sea port or police stations.

The main reason for the imposition of restrictions on the movement of Palestinians within the Occupied Territories is to keep them away from Israeli settlements and from the roads used by the settlers.

Israeli settlements and human rights abuses in the Occupied Territories

Israeli settlements in the Occupied Territories(6) violate international law, notably Article 49 of the Fourth Geneva Convention, which prohibits an occupying power from transferring its nationals into occupied territory, and the principle of non-discrimination one of the fundamental principles contained in all the major international human rights treaties ratified by Israel. Settlements have repeatedly been condemned as illegal by the international community, including the UN Security Council and other UN bodies.

Settlements and the network of roads built to connect them to each other and to Israel are spread through the West Bank and Gaza Strip and **surround** all the major Palestinian cities and many villages, making it impossible for Palestinians to travel very far without passing close to an Israeli settlement or a road used by settlers.

For example, the built up area of Nablus, including eight villages and two refugee camps, with a total population of about 184,000 Palestinians, is surrounded by eight settlements inhabited by some 6,000 Israeli settlers. The rapid spread of settlements and settlers' roads in the past decade, notably during the Oslo peace process years (1993-2000), has fragmented the Occupied Territories, disconnecting Palestinian communities from each other.

To ensure the freedom of movement of some 380,000 Israeli settlers, the Israeli army has increasingly confined some three and half million Palestinians to some form of house, village or town arrest.

International law

According to international law, an occupying power is required to administer the territory it controls as far as possible without making far-reaching changes to the existing order, while at the same time ensuring the protection of the fundamental rights of the local population.(7) The core idea of the international rule of belligerent occupation is that occupation is transitional, for a limited period, and one of its key aims is to enable the inhabitants of an occupied territory to live as "normal" a life as possible.

While Israel has a right to take certain security measures, including imposing restrictions on those who constitute a security threat, the sweeping restrictions currently imposed on the movement of Palestinians are disproportionate and discriminatory. They violate fundamental freedoms guaranteed in international humanitarian and human rights law.

Freedom of movement: "Everyone lawfully within the territory of a State shall, within that territory, have the right to liberty of movement and freedom to choose his residence". (Article 12.1, International Covenant on Civil and Political Rights (ICCPR)).

Restrictions imposed by Israel on Palestinians in the Occupied Territories consistently violate their right to freedom of movement protected by the ICCPR, to which Israel is party. Restrictions on this right may only be imposed if they are based on law, pursue a legitimate objective, such as protecting public order, and are strictly necessary.

The sweeping restrictions on the movement of Palestinians are disproportionate and discriminatory they are imposed on all Palestinians because they are Palestinians, and not on Israeli settlers who live illegally in the Occupied Territories. Even though the Israeli authorities claim that such measures are always imposed to protect the security of Israelis, the restrictions imposed do not target particular individuals who are believed to pose a threat. They are broad and indiscriminate in their application and as such are unlawful. They have a severe negative impact on millions of Palestinians who have not committed any offence.

The right to work: According to Article 6(1) of the International Covenant on Economic, Social and Cultural Rights (ICESCR): "The States Parties to the present Covenant recognize the right to work, which includes the right of everyone to the opportunity to gain his living by work which he freely chooses or accepts, and will take the appropriate steps to safeguard this right." Article 6(2) specifically requires Israel to: "take steps to achieve the full realization of [the right to work] and full and productive employment under conditions safeguarding fundamental and economic freedoms to the individual".

Israel's restrictions on the movement of Palestinian in the Occupied Territories have dramatically reduced the employment opportunities which existed and have prevented the creation of new ones. These restrictions contravene Israel's obligation to secure the Palestinians' right to work. Closures and curfews in particular have regularly prevented thousands of people from reaching their places of employment. The quality of employment still available has also been affected and many Palestinians have had no choice but to opt for casual jobs or to work for substantially reduced wages. Freedom from discrimination: According to Article 1 of the ICCPR, Israel is obliged to "ensure to all individuals within its territory and subject to its jurisdiction the rights recognized in the present Covenant, without distinction of any kind, such as race, colour, sex, language, religion, political or other opinion, national or social origins, property, birth or other status."

The restrictions imposed by Israel discriminate against Palestinians and are inconsistent with fundamental human rights principles, notably the principle of equality. Restrictions on movement, such as the prohibition on the use of roads and the imposition of curfews in the Occupied Territories are imposed on Palestinians only, not on Israeli settlers. The measures which the Israeli authorities have taken to protect the security and freedom of movement of some 380,000 Israeli settlers, whose presence in the Occupied Territories violates international law, curtail the freedom of movement of some three and a half million Palestinians.

Freedom from collective punishment: " Collective penalties are prohibited Reprisal against protected persons and their properties are prohibited". (Article 33, Fourth Geneva Convention).

Closures and curfews in the Occupied Territories have been routinely increased after suicide and other attacks by Palestinian armed groups inside Israel or in other areas of the Occupied Territories. Such measures constitute a form of collective punishment and appear to be a retaliation intended to intimidate and punish the whole Palestinian community, as well as to show to the Israeli public that the army is reacting to attacks. Such conduct breaches the prohibition on collective punishment contained in the Fourth Geneva Convention and the Hague Regulations.

The applicability of international law: According to the Israeli government, international human rights law applies only to Israeli settlers in the Occupied Territories whose presence there is illegal under international law but not to the local Palestinian population. Israel's position has not been accepted by any of the UN human rights treaty bodies.

Israel contends that the only applicable legal regime for the Palestinians in the Occupied Territories is humanitarian law (and not human rights law), but at the same time Israel also rejects the applicability of the Fourth Geneva Convention to the West Bank and Gaza Strip. The UN, the International Committee of the Red Cross (ICRC) and the international community at large have consistently maintained that the Fourth Geneva Convention fully applies to the Occupied Territories and that the Palestinians are a protected population under the terms of the Convention.

International monitoring

Amnesty International has repeatedly called for an international human rights monitoring presence in Israel and the Occupied Territories. This call has received substantial support both at the local and international level, but the Israeli authorities have consistently refused to accept human rights monitors. In addition, the Israeli army has increasingly targeted international peace activists, whose activities include monitoring restrictions on movement and assisting Palestinians, including medical personnel, who are affected by the restrictions.

Main recommendations

Amnesty International calls on the Israeli authorities:

- To put an end to the regime of curfews and internal closures as currently imposed in the West Bank and the Gaza Strip; to refrain in all circumstances from imposing closures, curfews and other restrictions on movement which constitute collective   punishment; and to ensure that restrictions on movement are only imposed if they are absolutely necessary, are related to a specific security threat and are non-discriminatory and proportionate in terms of their impact and their duration.

- To refrain from constructing separation barriers/fences or other permanent structures inside the West Bank and Gaza Strip which constitute or result in permanent restrictions on the right to free movement of Palestinians within the Occupied Territory or in the arbitrary destruction or seizure of their property;

- To ensure the right of everyone to gain their living by work which they freely choose or accept;

- To stop immediately the use of lethal force to enforce curfews and other restrictions on movement;

- To initiate a full, thorough, transparent and impartial investigation into all allegations of violations of international human rights and humanitarian law, including those documented in this report, and to make the results public;

- To bring to justice those alleged to have committed violations of international human rights or humanitarian law in proceedings that meet international standards for fair trial, and to ensure prompt and adequate compensation and reparation for victims of international human rights or humanitarian law violations;

- To take effective action to prevent, investigate, prosecute and punish human rights abuses committed by Israeli settlers against Palestinians.

- To put an immediate end to the construction or expansion of Israeli settlements and related infrastructure in the Occupied Territories as this violates international humanitarian law and will only lead to further arbitrary restrictions on Palestinians and further human rights abuses;

- To take measures to evacuate Israeli civilians living in settlements in the Occupied Territories, in such a manner as to ensure the human rights of Palestinians are respected, in particular their rights to free movement and to an adequate standard of living. Such measures should include too respect for the rights of those evacuated, including adequate compensation.

- To accept an international monitoring presence in the Occupied Territories with a strong human rights component, which should provide increased security for Israelis and Palestinians.

Amnesty International calls on the international community:

- To ensure that Israel's obligations under international human rights and humanitarian law, most
specifically its obligations as an occupying power under the Fourth Geneva Convention, are met;
- To ensure that human rights are central to all negotiations, interim accords and any final
agreement;
- To bring to justice anyone suspected of war crimes or crimes against humanity who may be within their jurisdiction;
- To set up an international monitoring presence in the Occupied Territories with a strong human rights component, for the security of Israelis and Palestinians.

Amnesty International once again reiterates its call to Palestinian armed groups:
- To put an immediate end to their policy of killing and targeting Israeli civilians, whether inside Israel or in the Occupied Territories.

Amnesty International calls on the Palestinian Authority:
- To take urgent concrete measures to prevent attacks by Palestinian armed groups on Israeli civilians, inside Israel and in the Occupied Territories;
- . To thoroughly investigate any such attacks and ensure that those responsible are brought to justice in proceedings that meet international standards for fair trial.

Background

The human rights situation in Israel and the Occupied Territories has seriously deteriorated in the past three years and violence has reached unprecedented levels. Since the start of the intifada in September 2000, more than 2,100 Palestinians, including some 380 children have been killed by the Israeli army and more than 750 Israelis, most of them civilians, including more than 90 children have been killed by
Palestinian armed groups. Tens of thousands of Palestinians and thousands of Israeli civilians have been injured, many seriously.

In addition the Israeli army has destroyed more than 3,000 Palestinian homes, as well as hundreds of workshops, factories and public buildings in the West Bank

234

and Gaza Strip; they have bulldozed vast areas of cultivated land, uprooting olive groves and orchards and flattening greenhouses and fields of growing crops. Such massive destruction of land and property has damaged the Palestinian economy, but the stringent restrictions imposed on the movement of Palestinians have been the main cause of the severe economic depression and dramatic increase in unemployment and poverty.

Restrictions on Palestinian movement pre-intifada

The Oslo Agreements created the widespread impression that Palestinians had gained "autonomy" or "self-rule". However, despite the creation of the Palestinian Authority (PA) and the redeployment of the Israeli army from some areas of the Occupied Territories, this was not the case. Palestinians soon found that their newly acquired freedom extended no further than the confines of overcrowded refugee camps and disjointed enclaves.

The 1995 Oslo II Agreement established three zones in the West Bank. The PA was given jurisdiction over the densely populated areas while Israel retained full control of some 60 percent of the West Bank, including all the main roads linking these Palestinian population centres, interspersed with Israeli settlements. In the Gaza Strip, the PA had jurisdiction over some 60 percent of the land. Again, densely populated Palestinian areas were separated from each other by 17 Israeli settlements and their "bypass" roads. An electrified perimeter fence was built along the eastern side of the Gaza Strip adjoining Israel.

Thus, virtually all movement in the West Bank and Gaza Strip remained under Israeli control. Moreover Palestinian land continued to be frequently seized by Israel for settlements and roads built to connect the settlements to each other and to Israel.

Following the establishment of the PA, the Israeli army started to impose so-called "internal closures", stopping all movement of Palestinians between different areas of the West Bank for days, sometimes weeks. The closures demonstrated how Israel, despite its withdrawal from some 40 percent of the West Bank, could easily bring Palestinian life to a halt and the Palestinian economy to its knees.

Amnesty International's research

Amnesty International delegates have frequently visited Israel and the Occupied Territories to carry out field research and discuss the organization's concerns with Israeli and Palestinian authorities. It has published numerous reports on different aspects of the human rights situation and on abuses by the Israeli security forces, by Palestinian armed groups and by the Palestinian Authority.

For this report the organization's delegates have interviewed Palestinians, Israelis and others whose lives have been affected by closures, curfews and other restrictions on their movement or who have been subjected to or witnessed abuses. They include medical professionals, human rights and humanitarian workers, journalists, trade unionists, community leaders, businesspeople, workers and self-employed people in various towns and villages, as well as diplomats, government officials and Israeli soldiers.

Over the years, Amnesty International delegates have frequently witnessed Israeli soldiers harassing, threatening and blocking the passage of Palestinians at checkpoints throughout the West Bank and Gaza Strip. They have themselves experienced similar treatment and lengthy travel delays between towns and villages caused by closures and curfews, on occasion being threatened and fired at by soldiers.

This document summarizes a 79-page report: Israel and the Occupied Territories: Surviving under siege: The impact of movement restrictions on the right to work (AI Index: MDE 15/001/2003) issued by Amnesty International on 8 September 2003. The full report and extensive range of our materials on this and other subjects is available at http://www.amnesty.org. Amnesty International news releases can be received by email: http://web.amnesty.org;ai.nsf/news.

INTERNATIONAL SECRETARIAT, 1 EASTON STREET, LONDON WC IX ODW, UNITED KINGDOM********

(1) Palestinians have had their movement restricted to varying degrees since Israel's occupation of the West Bank and Gaza Strip in 1967. Such restrictions increased in the past decade and reached an unprecedented level in the past three years.

(2) In an interview with Israel Radio on 13 October 2002.

(3) Different legislation and policies apply in East Jerusalem, which is part of the occupied West Bank. For the purposes of this report, references to the West Bank do not include East Jerusalem.

(4) E/C.12/1/Add.69, para. 13.

(5) Two Years of Intifada, Closures and Palestinian Economic Crisis; An Assessment. World Bank, 5 March 2003.

(6) The total number of settlers is about 380,000. Of them, some 5,000-6,000 live in the Gaza Strip, some 198,000 in the West Bank and the rest in East-Jerusalem settlements. There are 123 officially recognized settlements in the West Bank (excluding East Jerusalem) and 17 in the Gaza Strip. In addition there are some 100 small settlements, known as "illegal outposts", which were recently established without the approval of the Israeli government, but which benefit from Israeli army protection and other public services.

(7) The sources for the obligations under international humanitarian law applicable to belligerent occupation are found in: The Hague Convention (IV) respecting the Laws and Customs of War on Land (Hague Convention) and its annexed Regulations respecting the Laws and Customs of War on Land (Hague Regulations) of 18 October 1907; The Fourth Geneva Convention relative to the Protection of Civilian Persons in Time of War (Fourth Geneva Convention) of 12 August 1949; Article 75 of the 1977 Protocol Additional to the Geneva Conventions of 12 August 1949 and relating to the Protection of Victims of International Armed Conflicts (Protocol I); Rules of customary international law.

15/091/2003 13 October 2003
AMNESTY INTERNATIONAL
PRESS RELEASE

AI Index: MDE 15/091/2003 (Public) News Service No: 234 13 October 2003
Israel/Occupied Territories: Wanton destruction constitutes a war crime [Demolitions]

Amnesty International condemns in the strongest terms the large-scale destruction by the Israeli army of Palestinian homes in a refugee camp in the southern Gaza Strip town of Rafah, which made homeless hundreds of people, including many children and elderly people.

"The repeated practice by the Israeli army of deliberate and wanton destruction of homes and civilian property is a grave violation of international human rights and humanitarian law, notably of Articles 33 and 53 of the Fourth Geneva Convention, and constitutes a war crime," said Amnesty International. This last wave of destruction between 10 and 12 October is part of a policy which the Israeli army has been carrying out in the Occupied Territories for decades and increasingly so in recent years. In the past three years the Israeli army has destroyed some 4,000 Palestinian homes in the West Bank and Gaza Strip, as well as vast areas of cultivated land, hundreds of factories and other commercial properties, roads and public buildings.

The Israeli authorities have frequently contended that the destruction of Palestinian homes and other properties was necessary for the success of their military/security operations, and that therefore it was permitted by international humanitarian law. However, investigations by Amnesty International and other organizations, including Israeli NGOs, have shown a recurring pattern of destruction of homes and property as a collective punishment, to punish local residents for attacks by Palestinian armed groups.

On this occasion Israeli officials justified the destruction of more than 100 Palestinian homes as due to the presence in the area of three tunnels reportedly used by Palestinian armed groups to smuggle weapons from Egypt into the Gaza Strip. No weapons were reported to have been found. Israeli officials have not explained why the threat posed by the tunnels could not have been tackled by proportionate means that did not recklessly endanger the lives of civilians and did not render hundreds of Palestinians homeless. The army also claimed that armed Palestinians used the now-destroyed homes to fire on Israeli soldiers. However, they have not claimed that the inhabitants of these homes were themselves involved in any shooting or armed resistance.

The Israeli army says it has uncovered 70 smuggling tunnels in Rafah in the past three years and in the same period it has destroyed more than 1,000 homes in the area.

"In most cases examined by Amnesty International, the extensive destruction of Palestinian homes and properties repeatedly carried out by the Israeli army was not justifiable on grounds of absolute military necessity," said Amnesty International. "Such wanton destruction is unlawful and constitutes a war crime."

Amnesty International calls on the Israeli authorities to put an immediate end to the practice of destroying Palestinian homes and other properties, and of using excessive, disproportionate and reckless force against unarmed Palestinians and in densely populated residential areas, which frequently result in the killing and injuring of unarmed civilians, including children.

The organization has repeatedly condemned the deliberate killings of Israeli civilians by Palestinian armed groups as a crime against humanity and reiterates its calls on these groups to immediately halt such practices.

Background:
Much of the destruction of homes and agricultural land in recent years has been in the Gaza Strip, one of the most densely populated areas in the world, where more than two thirds of the population now live under the poverty line (of US $ 2 per day).

238

According to the United Nations Relief and Works Agency (UNRWA), the body which cares for Palestinian refugees, 76 homes were completely destroyed, 44 were partially destroyed and 117 damaged, and the number of refugees left homeless by this latest wave of home demolitions may be over 1,000.

On this occasion, as in many previous operations by the Israeli army involving the destruction of homes, at least six Palestinians, including two children were killed and scores of others, many of them children, were injured during the period of 10 to 12 October.

Article 33 of the Fourth Geneva Convention on the Protection of Civilian Persons in Time of War clearly states that "collective penalties are prohibited... Reprisal against protected persons and their properties are prohibited." **Article 53 of the same Convention states that "any destruction by the Occupying Power... is prohibited,** except where such destruction is rendered absolutely necessary by military operations." Amnesty International condemns the deliberate killings of Israeli civilians by Palestinian armed groups as a crime against humanity.

Public Document
****

For more information please call Amnesty International's press office in London, UK, on +44 20 7413 5566
Amnesty International, 1 Easton St., London WC1X ODW. web: http://www.amnesty.org

ll INDEX: MDE 15/099/2003 7 November 2003

AMNESTY INTERNATIONAL

PRESS RELEASE

Al Index: MDE 15/099/2003 (Public) News Service No: 254
Embargo Date: 7 November 2003 09:00 GMT
Israel/OT: **Israel must immediately stop the construction of wall**

Published

Amnesty International is adding its voice to worldwide protests against Israel's construction of the fence/wall in the Occupied West Bank. The organization calls on the Israeli authorities to stop the construction of the fence/wall in the West Bank that is affecting the lives of hundreds of thousands of Palestinians.

Israeli, Palestinian and international organisations are participating in or supporting the "Stop the Wall Campaign" that has declared 9 November "the International Day of Action against the Wall". The weeklong protests start on Sunday in many countries, including Argentina, Australia, Bangladesh, Belgium, Brazil, Canada, Chile, France, Germany, Holland, Italy, Jordan, Norway, South Africa, Spain, Sweden, the United Kingdom and the USA.

"This fence/wall is having devastating economic and social consequences on the daily lives of hundreds of thousands of Palestinians, separating families and communities from each other and from their land and water - their most crucial assets," said Amnesty International.

Israel is continuing the construction of the fence/wall, with the second phase running even more deeply than the first phase into the West Bank. This is cutting many more thousands of Palestinians off from their land and essential services in nearby villages and towns and further restricting the movements of all Palestinians in these areas.

The Israeli authorities' claim that the fence/wall is being constructed to prevent potential Palestinian attackers from entering Israel to carry out suicide bombings and other attacks is not borne out by the reality on the ground. The fence/wall is not being constructed on the Green Line separating Israel from the West Bank, but mostly on Palestinian land several kilometers inside the

West Bank, in order to isolate Palestinians away from Israeli settlements illegally built in the Occupied Territories.

"The construction of this fence/wall in its current location must be halted immediately," said Amnesty International. "As the fence/wall continues to snake through Palestinian land, more and more Palestinians find themselves trapped into enclaves and cantons, unable to have any semblance of a normal life."

"Israel has the right to take reasonable, necessary and proportionate measures to protect the security of its citizens and its borders. These include measures to prevent the entry into Israel of Palestinians or others who are reasonably suspected of intending to carry out suicide bombings or other attacks," Amnesty International said.

"However, Israel does not have a right to unlawfully destroy or confiscate Palestinian land and property and hinder the movements of Palestinians inside the Occupied Territories in order to consolidate its control over land which is being used for illegal Israeli settlements."

In order to build the fence/wall, large areas of mostly cultivated Palestinian land have been destroyed. The land on which it is constructed has been seized by the Israeli military authorities for "military needs". Although the seizure orders for the land are generally "temporary", usually until the end of 2005, they can be renewed indefinitely. Over the decades, Palestinian land "temporarily" seized by Israel has been used to build permanent structures, including settlements and roads for settlers, and has never been returned to its owners.

The very expensive and sophisticated structure of the fence/wall indicates that it is likely intended as a permanent structure. Affected Palestinians have to cross the fence/wall at designated checkpoints or gates to reach the rest of the West Bank - to go to work, to tend their fields, to sell their agricultural produce, and to access education and health centres in nearby towns and villages.

The Israeli authorities have consistently refused to provide advance information about the route of the fence/wall and information about the precise routing only become available when preparation work for the fence/wall begins on the ground or when the authorities deliver seizure orders to the local Palestinian communities whose land is going to be seized for the construction of the fence/wall.

For more information, please see:

Israel and the Occupied Territories: Surviving under siege: The impact of movement restrictions on the right to work, September 2003 (Al Index: MDE 15/001/2003)

Israel and the Occupied Territories: Surviving under siege: The impact of movement restrictions on the right to work: Executive Summary, September 2003 (Al Index: MDE 15/064/2003)

Public Document

************************************#**

For more information please call Amnesty International's press office in London, UK, on +44 20 7413 5566
Amnesty International, 1 Easton St., London WC1X ODW.
web: http://www.amnesty.org For latest human rights news
view http://news.amnesty.org ********
Amnesty International - Library - Israel/Occupied Territories: The fence/wall violates inte... Page 1 of 2 AI INDEX: MDE 15/018/2004 19 February 2004
AMNESTY INTERNATIONAL
PRESS RELEASE

Al Index: MDE 15/018/2004 (Public) News Service No: 034 19 February 2004

Israel/Occupied Territories: **The fence/wall violates international law**

On the eve of the International Court of Justice's (ICJ) opening hearing on the construction of the fence/wall by Israel, Amnesty International calls on the Israeli authorities to immediately dismantle the sections already built inside the West Bank and halt the construction of the fence/wall and related infrastructure inside the Occupied Territories.

The Israeli government objects to the ICJ hearing the case, claiming that the issue is "political".

"The construction by Israel of the fence/wall inside the Occupied Territories violates international law and is contributing to grave human rights violations. Therefore, it is appropriate that a court of law examines this matter," said Amnesty International.

On 8 December 2003 the United Nations General Assembly, exercising its power under Article 96 of the Charter of the United Nations (UN), passed a resolution requesting the ICJ to issue an Advisory Opinion on the legal consequences of the construction by Israel of the fence/wall inside the Occupied Territories. The Israeli authorities claim that the fence/wall is "a defensive measure, designed to block the passage of terrorists, weapons and explosives into the State of Israel".

However, most of the fence/wall is not being built on the Green Line between Israel and the West Bank. Close to 90% of it is on Palestinian land inside the West Bank, encircling Palestinian towns and villages and cutting off communities and families from each other. It separates farmers from their land and cuts off Palestinians from their places of work, schools, health care facilities and other essential services.

"Israel's legitimate needs to secure its borders and prevent access to people who may constitute a threat to its security do not justify the building of such a fence/wall inside the Occupied Territories. This could be built on Israeli territory on the Green Line, where mechanisms to control entry of outsiders could also be strengthened if deemed necessary," said Amnesty International.

The building of this fence/wall inside the Occupied Territories has severe negative consequences for hundreds of thousands of Palestinians. It imposes unprecedented disproportionate and discriminatory restrictions on their movements within the Occupied Territories and causes other violations of their fundamental rights, including the right to work, to food, to medical care, to education and to an adequate standard of living.

"Any measure Israel undertakes in the Occupied Territories in the name of security must comply with its obligations under international law," said Amnesty International. The route of the fence/wall has been designed to encompass more than 50 Israeli settlements in the Occupied Territories, in which the majority of Israeli settlers live and which are illegal under international law.

"The security exceptions in international law cannot be invoked to justify measures that benefit unlawful Israeli settlements at the expense of the occupied Palestinian population. The construction of the fence/wall inside the Occupied Territories is such a measure and in its present configuration it violates Israel's obligations under international humanitarian law," said Amnesty International.

International human rights and humanitarian law requires Israel, as the occupying power, to protect and ensure the rights of the Palestinian population in the Occupied Territories.

Amnesty International urges the international community to ensure that Israel fulfils its obligations under international human rights and humanitarian law, including its obligations as an occupying power under the Fourth Geneva Convention.

"Attempts to resolve the conflict between Israel and the Palestinians through political negotiations must address and ensure respect for the fundamental human rights of both populations," said Amnesty International. The organization also reiterates its call on the Palestinian armed groups to put an immediate end to their policy of killing and targeting Israeli civilians, inside Israel and in the Occupied Territories, and on the Palestinian Authority to take urgent concrete measures to prevent attacks by Palestinian armed groups on Israeli civilians.

Further information: "The place of the fence/wall in international law"
      Video: Rabbi Arik Ascherman from the
      organization Rabbis for Human Rights
      (Real Player required)   Public Document

      For more information please call Amnesty International's press office in London, UK, on +44 20 7413 5566
      Amnesty International, 1 Easton St., London WC1X ODW. web: http://www.amnesty.org

      For latest human rights news view http://news.amnesty.org

Amnesty International - Library - Israel/Occupied Territories: Israel must facilitate, not hi... Page 1 of 2 AI INDEX: MDE 15/036/2004 2 April 2004
AMNESTY INTERNATIONAL
PRESS RELEASE

AI Index: MDE 15/036/2004 (Public) News Service No: 77 2 April 2004
Israel/Occupied Territories: Israel must facilitate, not hinder, relief for the occupied population

Amnesty International today expressed deep concern for the health and well-being of some 600,000 refugees in the Gaza Strip, and called on Israel to immediately lift unlawful and disproportionate restrictions on movement which are hampering relief efforts by humanitarian organizations.

Yesterday the United Nations Relief and Works Agency (UNRWA) announced that it had stopped distribution of emergency food aid to the refugees following restrictions introduced by Israeli authorities at the sole commercial crossing through which UNRWA can bring in humanitarian assistance.
"Israel, as the occupying power, must take immediate measures to comply with international law and ensure that the basic needs of the Palestinian population, including access to food, are met," said Amnesty International.
"Israel has consistently failed to meet these obligations for decades, leaving the international community to shoulder the burden of providing food, medical care, education, and shelter for Palestinians living under Israeli occupation in the West Bank and Gaza Strip."
In the past three years, Palestinians' ability to work and earn a living has been dramatically reduced by unprecedented stringent restrictions imposed by Israel on their movements within the Occupied Territories. This has caused a dramatic increase in unemployment and poverty. According to the World Bank and UN agencies, two out of three Gazan households now live below the poverty line. Chronic malnutrition is spreading, especially amongst children.

Although restrictions on movement have most affected Palestinians, international humanitarian and human rights workers have been frequently prevented from carrying out their duties because of restrictions imposed on their movements by the Israeli authorities. Only last week, UN agencies in the Occupied Territories protested the increased restrictions on their movements and activities.

Background
Israel's duties as an Occupying Power in the Gaza Strip and West Bank under international law include ensuring food and medical supplies to the occupied population, ensuring and maintaining medical services, public health and hygiene in the occupied territory, and ensuring that medical personnel can carry out their duties.

Articles 55, 56 and 59 of the Fourth Geneva Convention relative to the Protection of Civilian Persons in Time of War (Fourth Geneva Convention)stipulate that Israel allows and facilitates relief on behalf of the occupied population. Article 60 clarifies that relief provided by others in no way relieves the occupying power of any of its responsibilities under the above-mentioned Articles.

The Israeli army has dramatically restricted the movement of people and goods in and out of the Gaza Strip. Passage is limited to selected personnel of intergovernmental and international humanitarian and human rights organizations. Palestinians from the Gaza Strip are only allowed entry into Israel in exceptional cases, and goods are subjected to strict and lengthy security checks and restrictions.

Restrictions were increased following a Palestinian suicide bomb attack which killed 10 Israeli civilians at the Israeli port of Ashdod on 14 March. This was the first time since the beginning of the intifada in September 2000 that Palestinians from the Gaza Strip carried out an attack inside Israel. The attackers are believed to have reached Israel from the Gaza Strip by hiding in a container.

AMNESTY INTERNATIONAL

Public Statement

Al Index: IOR 41/012/2004 (Public) News Service No: 080 6 April 2004
**UN Commission on Human Rights, 60th Session (15 March - 23
April 2003)**
**Agenda item 8: Question of the violation of human rights in the
occupied Arab territories,**
including Palestine
ORAL STATEMENT BY AMNESTY INTERNATIONAL

Delivered by Peter Splinter.

Mr. Chair:

In the past three and a half years, since the beginning of the ongoing
intifada (uprising) violence and human rights violations have reached a level
unprecedented in the 37 years of Israel's occupation of the West Bank and
Gaza Strip. The Israeli army has killed more than 2,300 Palestinians, most of
them unarmed and including more than 400 children and Palestinian armed
groups have killed some 900 Israelis, most of them civilians and including 100
children.

The Israeli army has also destroyed more than 3,000 Palestinian homes,
and hundreds of workshops, factories and public buildings, as well as large areas
of cultivated land in the Occupied Territories. In the Gaza Strip alone, one of the
most densely populated areas in the world, more than 10 percent of the
agricultural land has been destroyed. In his 2003 annual report UNRWA's
Commissioner-General, commenting on the rhythm of destruction of refugee
homes in the Gaza Strip, noted that UNRWA "was not able to keep up with the
pace of shelter destruction". The extent of the destruction has left tens of
thousands of Palestinians homeless and/or destitute.

Increasingly stringent restrictions imposed by the Israeli army on the
movement of Palestinians within the Occupied Territories have curtailed their
access to work, education and medical care. As a result, poverty and
unemployment have spiraled. Two thirds of Palestinians now live below the
poverty line and malnutrition and other health problems are spreading.
The humanitarian crisis has been exacerbated by the construction of a fence/wall
large parts of which lie within the West Bank, as documented by the

Commission's Special Rapporteur. Israel claims that the fence/wall is intended to prevent entry into Israel to Palestinian suicide bombers and other attackers. However, most of the fence/wall is being constructed inside the West Bank — not on the Green Line between Israel and the West Bank.

Close to 90% of the route of the fence/wall runs through the West Bank, encircling Palestinian towns and villages and cutting off communities and families from each other, separating Palestinians from their land and their places of work, education and health care facilities. The route of this fence/wall has been designed so as to encompass more than 60 Israeli settlements, comprising approximately 80 percent of Israeli settlers in the Occupied Territories. The international community has long recognized the unlawfulness of the Israeli settlements in the Occupied Territories.

In its current location the fence/wall causes extreme hardship to a large number of Palestinians. Sections completed to date have already had very serious consequences for tens of thousands of Palestinians who live in the affected areas, confined to enclaves encircled by the fence/wall and cut off from the rest of the West Bank.

Israel's legitimate need to secure its borders and prevent access to people who may constitute a threat to its security do not justify the building of such a fence/wall inside the Occupied Territories. Security measures which comply with international law, including the building of a fence/wall, could be taken on Israeli territory.

Mr Chair,

In recent years, the Commission has repeatedly expressed its concern about the deterioration of the human rights situation in Israel and the Occupied Territories. Israel, however, has consistently failed to implement the Commission's resolutions and cooperate with its mechanisms. Words of concern and condemnation sound increasingly hollow in the face of the inaction of the international community.

The Commission collectively and member states individually have a responsibility to take measures to ensure that the Israeli and Palestinian sides comply with their obligations to abide by international law and respect fundamental rights. Disregarding or subordinating human rights and respect for international law to political considerations has brought neither peace nor security.

The concerns arising from the current situation in Israel and the Occupied Territories must be addressed within the framework of international law. A crucial factor in the collapse of previous peace initiatives, including the recent 'Roadmap' has been their failure to address key human rights issues. A human rights agenda alone may not be sufficient, but it must be a central part of any solution to the conflict.

The international community must also act to support Israelis and Palestinians who refuse to participate in violations and who are taking courageous steps to promote justice and human rights.

Thank you Mr. Chair.

Amnesty International - Library

- Israel and the Occupied Territories:

AI INDEX: MDE 15/001/2003 8 September 2003

The ceasefire reached in the context of the Roadmap peace initiative has resulted in a marked reduction in violence and killings, and has brought a welcome respite to the Israeli and Palestinian civilian populations. Even though the overwhelming majority of Palestinian detainees remain behind bars in Israeli prisons and military detention centres, the release of some detainees who had been held without charge or trial has raised hopes for further releases.

However, hopes that, as part of the implementation of the Roadmap, Israel would lift the closures and movement restrictions which have paralyzed life and the economy in the Occupied Territories have not materialized. By the beginning of August 2003, the Israeli army had lifted only some four checkpoints, out of a total of more than 300 checkpoints and roadblocks.

Even if all the blockades were lifted immediately and free movement allowed in the Occupied Territories it would take years for the Palestinian population to resume a normal life and to rebuild the economy which has been virtually destroyed by years of siege. Long term investments and efforts will be required to reverse the dramatic increase in poverty and unemployment levels of the last few years. These efforts will only be possible if Israel restores freedom of movement in the Occupied Territories.

Restrictions imposed by Israel on the movement of Palestinians within the Occupied Territories reached an unprecedented level in recent years. The effect has been to deprive Palestinians not only of their freedom of movement but of other basic human rights -in particular, their right to work and to provide a living for themselves and their families.

Palestinians have had their movement restricted to varying degrees of restrictions since Israel's occupation of the West Bank and Gaza Strip in 1967. Such restrictions increased in the past decade and have reached an unprecedented level in the past three years, since the September 2000 renewal of the Palestinian uprising against Israeli occupation, known as the intifada or the al-Aqsa intifada.(2) Since then, increasing restrictions and new measures adopted to tighten and enforce closures (the prohibition of movement within and/or between areas) and curfews have all but destroyed the Palestinian economy.

Freedom of movement for people and goods, at least within borders, is an essential requirement for any functional economy, particularly so for a new economy trying to develop and establish itself against the backdrop of dependency created by 36 years of occupation. Yet some 3.5 million Palestinians who live in the Occupied Territories are often effectively confined to their towns and villages by closures enforced by Israeli military checkpoints and roadblocks.

Some villages have been completely sealed off and urban areas are frequently placed under 24-hour curfew, during which no one is allowed to leave the house, often for prolonged periods. Palestinians have been prohibited from driving on main roads connecting one part of the West Bank to another. Trips of a few kilometres, where they are possible, take hours, following lengthy detours to avoid the areas surrounding Israeli settlements and settlers' roads (known as "bypass roads"), which connect the settlements to each other and to Israel and which are prohibited to Palestinians.

With the spread of settlements and bypass roads throughout the Occupied Territories, the prohibited areas have multiplied. Where the settlements are closest to Palestinian villages, movement in and out of these villages is even more restricted than elsewhere. In parts of the Gaza Strip, areas where Palestinians live surrounded by Israeli settlements have been declared closed military zones. These are only accessible, and only at specific times, to the residents, who are also often stopped from leaving or returning to their homes for days or even weeks.

In addition to the increased time, effort and cost involved, journeys are also not without risk. To enforce closures and curfews, Israeli soldiers routinely fire live ammunition, throw tear gas or sound bombs, beat and detain people, and confiscate vehicles and documents (IDs). Ordinary activities, such as going to work or to school, taking a baby for immunization, attending a funeral or a wedding, expose women and men, young and old, to such risks. Hence, many people limit their activities outside the home to what is absolutely essential.

Closures and curfews have prevented Palestinians from reaching their places of work and from distributing their products to internal and external markets, and have caused shortages. Factories and farms have been driven out of business by the losses incurred, dramatically increased transport costs and loss of export markets. As a result, unemployment has soared to over

50% and more than half of the Palestinian population is now living below the poverty line. With the sharp decline in the standard of living in the Occupied Territories, malnutrition and other illnesses have increased. Closures and curfews have prevented Palestinian children and youths from attending classes for prolonged periods, violating their right to education and undermining their future professional prospects.

Amnesty International has documented in numerous reports the deterioration of the human rights situation and the violence that has reached a level unprecedented in the 36 years of Israel's occupation of the West Bank and Gaza. In the past three years more than 2,100 Palestinians have been killed by the Israeli army in the Occupied Territories, including some 380 children. Palestinian armed groups have killed some 750 Israelis, most of them civilians, and including more than 90 children. Tens of thousands of people have been injured, many maimed for life. The Israeli army has destroyed more than 3,000 Palestinian homes, and hundreds of workshops, factories and public buildings in the West Bank and Gaza. They have bulldozed vast areas of cultivated land, uprooting olive groves and orchards and flattening greenhouses and fields of growing crops.

These abuses, notably the destruction of land and property, have contributed to damaging the economy in the Occupied Territories. However, the stringent restrictions on the movement of Palestinians imposed in the past three years have been the main cause of the severe economic depression and the increase in unemployment.

Israel has a right and a duty to protect people from repeated bombings and other attacks by Palestinian armed groups from the Occupied Territories, including by restricting access to its territory. However, under international human rights and humanitarian law, it is obliged to ensure freedom of movement, an adequate standard of living, and as normal a life as possible to the population in occupied territories. International law also prohibits an occupying power from imposing collective punishment on the occupied population.

This report analyses the impact of movement restrictions on the right to work of Palestinians in the West Bank and the Gaza Strip.(3) It details the findings of Amnesty International's research and describes representative cases in different areas of the West Bank and Gaza. The report contends that the widespread and prolonged closures, curfews and other restrictions on movement currently imposed cannot be justified on security grounds, and discriminate against Palestinians, and are often used as a form of collective punishment in reprisal for attacks committed by Palestinian armed groups.

Among its recommendations, Amnesty International urges the Israeli government to lift the restrictions on movement that constitute collective punishment and to make every effort to enable as normal a life as possible for the inhabitants of the Occupied Territories.

It calls for the evacuation of Israeli settlers from the West Bank and Gaza Strip, on the grounds that their residence in the Occupied Territories violates international law, and that measures purportedly taken to protect the security and freedom of movement of Israeli settlers impose serious human rights abuses against Palestinians.

Restrictions on the movement of Palestinians and goods should be imposed only in relation to a specific security threat and if they are non-discriminatory and proportionate in impact and duration. They should not obstruct the freedom of movement required to maintain an adequate standard of living or have a negative impact on the Palestinians' fundamental rights, including the right to work.

Amnesty International's research

Amnesty International delegates have frequently visited Israel and the Occupied Territories to carry out field research and to discuss the organization's concerns with Israeli and Palestinian authorities. It has published numerous reports and statements on different aspects of the human rights situation and on abuses by the Israeli security forces, by Palestinian armed groups and by the Palestinian Authority (PA). (4).

In October and November 2002, Israeli government officials and representatives of the Israeli Defence Forces (IDF) did not respond to repeated requests by Amnesty International delegates for meetings and information about policies and practices relating to restrictions on movement in the Occupied Territories.

The delegates were able to interview Palestinians, Israelis and others who have lived or worked in the Occupied Territories, and whose lives have been affected by closures, curfews and other restrictions on their movement or who have witnessed or been subjected to abuses. They included medical professionals, human rights and humanitarian workers, journalists, trade unionists, community leaders, businesspeople, workers and self-employed people in various towns and villages, as well as diplomats, government officials and Israeli soldiers. Over the years, Amnesty International delegates have frequently witnessed Israeli soldiers harassing, threatening and blocking the passage of Palestinians at checkpoints in the West Bank and Gaza. They have themselves experienced similar treatment and lengthy travel delays between towns and villages caused by the sudden imposition of closures and curfews, on occasion being threatened and fired at by soldiers.

In compiling this report, Amnesty International has drawn on information from international organizations and agencies, including the United Nations (UN), the International Committee of the Red Cross (ICRC), the World Bank, the International Monetary Fund (IMF), the International Labour Organization (ILO) and the European Union (EU), as well as Israeli and Palestinian governmental and non-governmental organizations and institutions.

[Background: After the 1948 Partition and the creation of the State of Israel . . .]

Protests against partition were followed by war between Arab and Israeli armies. Israel emerged victorious, expanding its de facto frontiers beyond those proposed by the partition plan. Two parts of mandate Palestine remained outside Israel: the Gaza Strip, which came under Egyptian administration, and the eastern part adjacent to the River Jordan. The latter was annexed by Jordan in 1950 and became known as the West Bank.(5)

Hostilities between Israel and Egypt, Syria and Jordan in June 1967 ended in Israel's occupation of the West Bank, East Jerusalem and the Gaza Strip. Israel unilaterally annexed part of the West Bank including the Old City of Jerusalem and incorporated it into the Jerusalem Municipality; this area is known as East Jerusalem. Syria's Golan Heights were annexed by Israel in 1980. The Sinai Peninsula, also annexed, was later returned to Egypt.

Peace talks between Israel and the Palestine Liberation Organization (PLO) began in 1991. A Declaration of Principles signed in 1993 envisaged a five year interim period in which the Israeli military government in the Occupied Territories would transfer some functions to an elected PA in parts of the West Bank and Gaza. Negotiations on a permanent settlement and an end to Israeli military occupation were to be concluded by 1999. Discussion was specifically deferred on Jerusalem, (the Israeli colonies established in the Occupied Territories), borders and refugees (Palestinians forced off their land since 1948) pending negotiations on a permanent settlement.

An Interim Agreement on the West Bank and the Gaza Strip (Oslo II Agreement) in 1995 defined the network of zones in the Occupied Territories over which the PA would have jurisdiction in the interim period and the functions it would take over. Negotiations broke down after the start of the current intifada in September 2000.

East Jerusalem was excluded from the Oslo II Agreement and remains subject to the internal laws of Israel. Its Palestinian population are regarded as "permanent residents" and carry blue Israeli identity cards. Palestinians residing elsewhere in the West Bank and in the Gaza Strip carry green Palestinian identity cards; they are not allowed access to the city without a permit.

Duties of an occupying power

According to international law, an occupying power is required to administer the territory it controls as far as possible without making far-reaching changes to the existing order, while at the same time ensuring the protection of the fundamental rights of the inhabitants of the occupied territory.(6) The core idea of the international rule of belligerent occupation is that occupation is transitional, for a limited period, and one of its key aims is to enable the inhabitants of an occupied territory to live as "normal" a life as possible.

The duties of an occupying power include:

> - treating the occupied population humanely at all times (Article 27, IV Geneva Convention);

> - ensure the food and medical supplies of the occupied population (Article 55, IV Geneva Convention);

> - ensure and maintain the medical services, public health and hygiene in the occupied territory, and ensuring that medical personnel of all categories can carry out their duties (Article 56, IV Geneva Convention);

> - allow and facilitate relief for the occupied population (Article 59, IV Geneva Convention).

Relief provided by others in no way relieves the occupying power of any of its responsibilities under Articles 55, 56 and 59 (Article 61, IV Geneva Convention).

An occupying power may NOT:

- use collective punishment or intimidation against the occupied population (Article 33, IV Geneva Convention);

- forcibly transfer inhabitants of the occupied territory to its territory or elsewhere nor transfer parts of its civilian population into the territory it occupies (Article 49, IV Geneva Convention);

- take measures aiming at creating unemployment or at restricting employment opportunities in the occupied territory, in order to induce the occupied population to work for the occupying power (Article IV Geneva Convention);

- destroy private or public property, except where absolutely necessary for military operations (Article 53, IV Geneva Convention);

- appropriating private or public property or natural resources, for which the occupying power shall be regarded only as administrator (Article 55, Hague Regulations).

Restrictions on movement

For more than three decades, and especially in the past 15 years Israel has imposed varying degrees of restrictions on the movements of Palestinians, and in the past three years it has increased these restrictions to an unprecedented level. Such restrictions, as imposed in recent years, contravene Israel's obligations under international human rights and humanitarian law to protect freedom of movement and not to discriminate against or inflict collective punishment on the population of an occupied territory.

The right to freedom of movement

"Everyone lawfully within the territory of a State shall, within that territory, have the right to liberty of movement and freedom to choose his residence". (Article 12.1, International Covenant on Civil and Political Rights [ICCPR]).

Security measures taken by Israel in the Occupied Territories consistently violate the right to freedom of movement of Palestinians protected by the ICCPR, to which Israel is party.

Already in 1998, prior to the outbreak of the current uprising, the Human Rights Committee, the UN body of experts that monitors states' compliance with the Covenant, expressed concern about the grave consequences of restrictions on movement in the Occupied Territories:

> "While acknowledging the security concerns that have led to restrictions on movement, the Committee notes with regret the continued impediments imposed on movement, which affect mostly Palestinians travelling in and between East Jerusalem, the Gaza Strip and the West Bank and which have grave consequences affecting nearly all areas of Palestinian life. The Committee considers this to raise serious issues under article 12. In regard to persons in these areas, the Committee urges Israel to respect the right to freedom of movement provided for under article 12... " (CCPR/C/79/Add. 93, para 22). [

Restrictions on the right to freedom of movement and the right to work may only be imposed if they are based on law, pursue a legitimate objective, such as protecting public order, and are strictly necessary. Israeli military and emergency legislation give military commanders the broadest discretion to declare closed military areas, restrict the use of roads and impose curfews. According to the UN Human Rights Committee: "The application of the restrictions permissible under article 12, paragraph 3, needs to be consistent with the other rights guaranteed in the Covenant and with the fundamental principles of equality and non-discrimination. Thus, it would be a clear violation of the Covenant if the rights enshrined in article 12, paragraphs 1 and 2, were restricted by making distinctions of any kind, such as on the basis of race, colour, sex, language, religion, political or other opinion, national or social origin, property, birth or other status" . (7)

The sweeping restrictions on the movement of Palestinians are disproportionate and discriminatory –they are imposed on all Palestinians because they are Palestinians, and not on Israeli settlers who live illegally in the Occupied Territories.

Even though the Israeli authorities claim that such measures are always imposed to protect the security of Israelis, the restrictions imposed within the

Occupied Territories do not target particular individuals who are believed to pose a threat. They are broad and indiscriminate in their application and as such are unlawful.

They have a severe negative impact on the lives of millions of Palestinians who have not committed any offence.

Freedom from collective punishment

"....Collective penalties.. ...are prohibited... Reprisal against protected persons and their properties are prohibited" (Article 33, IV Geneva Convention).

Curfews have been routinely imposed and closures tightened in the Occupied Territories, often after suicide bombs and other attacks by Palestinian armed groups inside Israel or in other areas of the Occupied Territories. Such measures constitute a form of collective punishment and appear to be a retaliation designed to intimidate and punish the whole Palestinian community, as well as to show to the Israeli public that the army is reacting to attacks. In June 2003 the UN Relief and Works Agency (UNRWA) described the situation as "approaching three full years of what can only be characterized as collective punishment. "(8)

Such conduct breaches the prohibition on collective punishment contained in the Fourth Geneva Convention and the Hague Regulations. As early as February 2001, the ICRC was expressing concern that closures contravened the Fourth Geneva Convention, including by the imposition of collective punishment and the obstruction of food, healthcare and education. Such restrictions on movement have since been dramatically increased.

"The ICRC views the policy of isolating whole villages for an extended period as contrary to International Humanitarian Law (IHL) particularly with respect to those aspects of IHL which protect civilians in times of occupation. Indeed, stringent closures frequently lead to breaches ofArticle 55 (free passage of medical assistance and foodstuffs), Article 33 (prohibition on collective punishments), Article 50 (children and education), Article 56 (movement of medical transportation and public health facilities) and Article 72 (access to lawyers for persons charged) of the Fourth Geneva Convention. While accepting that the State of Israel has legitimate security concerns, the ICRC stresses that measures taken to address these concerns must be in accordance with International Humanitarian Law. Furthermore, these security measures must allow for a quick return to normal civilian life. This, in essence, is the meaning of the Fourth Geneva Convention, which is applicable to the Occupied Territories. " ICRC, "Israel and Occupied/Autonomous Territories: The ICRC Starts its 'Closure Relief Programme'," 26 February 2001.

Freedom from discrimination

"...all protected persons shall be treated with the same consideration by the Party to the conflict in whose power they are, without any adverse distinction based, in particular, on race, religion, or political opinion". (Article 27, IV Geneva Convention).

The restrictions imposed by Israel discriminate against Palestinians and are inconsistent with fundamental human rights principles, notably the principle of equality. Restrictions on movement, such as the prohibition on the use of roads and the imposition of curfews in the Occupied Territories are imposed on Palestinians only, not on Israeli settlers.

The measures which the Israeli authorities state are taken to protect the security and freedom of movement of some 380,000 Israeli settlers(9), whose presence in the Occupied Territories violates Article 49 of the Fourth Geneva Convention,(10) curtail the freedom of movement of some three and a half million Palestinians. Even in cases where Israeli settlers have attacked Palestinians or their property, it is the Palestinians who have been placed under curfews or denied access to the areas, while no such restrictions have been imposed on the Israeli settlers.

According to international human rights law, it is only acceptable for a state to treat people differently on grounds that are reasonable, objective and fulfil a legitimate purpose, such as protecting public order. The restrictions on the movement of Palestinians imposed in the Occupied Territories are unreasonable, disproportionate and constitute discrimination, prohibited by the International Covenant on Civil and Political Rights, the International Covenant on Economic, Social and Cultural Rights and the International Convention on the Elimination of All Forms of Racial Discrimination.

The International Red Cross

2002 ANNUAL REPORT **OF THE INTERNATIONAL COMMITTEE OF THE RED CROSS ON ISRAEL, THE OCCUPIED TERRITORIES AND THE AUTONOMOUS TERRITORIES.**

CONTEXT

The year under review was one of the most violent and destructive in Israel and the occupied Palestinian territories since Israel occupied the West Bank and Gaza in 1967. By the end of 2002, spiraling hostilities were reported to have claimed the lives of more than 1,700 Palestinians and some 700 Israelis since the current Palestinian insurgency against occupation erupted in September 2000.

In the first half of 2002, an unprecedented wave of indiscriminate and devastating Palestinian suicide attacks caused deep psychological trauma in Israeli society and prompted the most massive action by the Israeli Defense Forces (IDF) in the Palestinian territories in 35 years. By the end of June the IDF had redeployed in seven of the West Bank's eight major cities. It imposed the most stringent security clampdown ever in the troubled territory, plunging Palestinian society into even deeper socio-economic disarray, isolation and dependency.

The almost hermetic blockade was still in force as 2002 ended but this did not put a total stop to attacks by armed Palestinian militants in either the occupied Palestinian territories or in Israel.

IDF troops, backed by tanks, combat helicopters and armoured bulldozers, engaged in heavy fighting in densely populated urban areas in the course of a search-and-destroy mission targeting what they described as an infrastructure of terror responsible for the attacks against Israelis.

 In the process, many civilians were killed and thousands of suspected militants were arrested. Hundreds of houses and other buildings were destroyed, leaving thousands homeless, and extensive damage was inflicted on vital public utilities such as the water supply and electricity system. In the Gaza Strip, IDF airstrikes and incursions by ground forces against militant Palestinian strongholds also continued throughout the year.

These caused considerable incidental damage, including many civilian deaths.

In June, work started on the construction of a security barrier between Israel and the West Bank in response to mounting Israeli public and political pressure to physically separate the country from Palestinian communities in the occupied territory as a means of preventing infiltration by armed Palestinian militants.

The development of infrastructure for Israeli settlements continued with the building of more settler-only bypass roads and enlarged buffer zones around settlements. This resulted in further expropriation of Palestinian land and destruction of Palestinian farmland.

As a result, tensions continued to run high between Palestinian communities and the estimated 400,000 Israelis living in 145 locations in the West Bank and Gaza Strip. Violent incidents between settlers and neighbouring Palestinians were reported almost daily, ranging from simple harassment and stonethrowing to shootings with deaths on both sides.

Rigid curfews, stepped up closures and other severe constraints on the movement of people and goods confined much of the population of two million to their homes for prolonged periods, with no access to basic items such as health care, education and work.

Unemployment and poverty rates soared as traditional coping mecha-nisms eroded further. Meanwhile concern mounted about the nutritional status and health of the population, particularly children, the elderly and the sick.

In March, the **Israeli parliament passed an "unlawful combatants" law** designed to legalize the indefinite detention of any person suspected of engaging in "hostile activity" against Israel, whether direct or indirect.

During a visit to the region in October, the ICRC president noted that the situation in humanitarian terms had grown worse than at any time since the ICRC established a constant presence there in 1967.

While stressing Israel's primary responsibility for the welfare of the civilian population under its occupation, the ICRC was swift to react to the worsening situation by greatly increasing its presence on the ground and vastly expanding aid in an ever more precarious economic security and health environment. Meanwhile, on the Israeli-Lebanese border, the situation remained tense between Hezbollah and the IDF especially in the disputed Shebaa Farms area.

ICRC ACTION

Key points in 2002

- ICRC protection staff were doubled
- ICRC visited more than 13,000 Palestinians detained in 39 Israeli places of detention and hundreds of detainees held by the Palestinian Authority
- both sides were repeatedly urged to respect IHL [International Humanitarian Law]
- ICRC food-relief and hygiene-parcel programmes tripled to cover 30,000 of the most vulnerable families in rural West Bank villages
- an innovative urban voucher scheme was implemented to provide food and meet the other basic household needs of 20,000 particularly vulnerable families in besieged West Bank towns
- food-parcel distribution programme was doubled to cover 2,000 of the most needy families in Hebron's old town
- basic shelter kits were distributed to thousands of Palestinians whose homes were destroyed or expropriated
- ICRC surgeons enhanced the skills of Palestinian war surgeons at peripheral hospitals and clinics in order to reduce the need to transfer patients to referral centres in urban areas
- a new water-distribution programme was started in response to a chronic shortage of drinking water in hundreds of isolated West Bank villages
- support was stepped up to both the PRCS and the MDA

CIVILIANS

Protecting civilians

In 2002, the ICRC documented a significant increase in both the scale and types of IHL violations by the IDF and armed Palestinian militants.

Protecting the civilian population remained central to the work of the ICRC as it operated in an ever more volatile security climate, particularly during "Operation Defensive Shield" in early spring when the organization made repeated appeals to the Israeli authorities, in particular to allow unimpeded medical work and to spare the lives of civilians not taking part in the hostilities.

In response to the upsurge of violence, the ICRC in May decided to expand its field presence and protection work. Its purpose was to put more staff on the ground as a means of better assisting the victims of the violence and enhancing its ability to deal with numerous issues of urgent humanitarian concern, document IHL violations and make timely representations to the Israeli and Palestinian authorities and armed groups. Throughout the violence, ICRC staff remained present in the occupied Palestinian territories, furnishing whatever aid and protection it could within the limits imposed by the security situation.

ICRC dialogue with the Israeli authorities facilitated some Palestinian economic activities. For example, the organization secured relatively safe access by Palestinian farmers to olive groves in order to harvest the fruit for oil production, which has become the main source of income for many Palestinians who have lost their jobs since the second *intifada* started in September 2000.

During a six-day visit to Israel and the occupied and autonomous territories in October, the ICRC president met Israel's president and prime minister as well as the chairman of the Palestinian Authority. The ICRC president also held talks with key military and civilian officials on both sides. In all meetings he conveyed the ICRC's grave concern about the growing crisis which he described as the worst situation from a humanitarian viewpoint since the ICRC had established a presence in the region in 1967.

While acknowledging Israel's security concerns, the ICRC president urged the Israeli authorities to fully implement the provisions of the Fourth Geneva Convention, that is "to take measures that will enable the civilian population living in the occupied territories to resume as normal a life as possible, and to respond to their humanitarian needs". He pointed out the harmful impact of mobility restrictions on civilians.

A key issue raised by the ICRC president in all his talks was the absolute necessity, as laid down by IHL, to draw a clear distinction between combatants and unarmed civilians, and to respect at all times the principle of proportionality in the use of force. He also appealed for the red cross and red crescent emblems to be respected and the need to facilitate the work of the Palestine Red Crescent Society and the Mogen David Adom, stressing that in times of conflict and other violence medical staff must be allowed to carry out their life-saving work unhindered.

ICRC representations to both the Israeli and Palestinian authorities resulted in some improvements, particularly with regard to the ability of emergency medical services to carry out their work. However, as 2002 drew to a close the security climate remained precarious for both Israeli and Palestinian civilians, as well as for humanitarian workers.

Expanding aid
For most of the year hundreds of thousands of West Bank Palestinians were confined to their homes for prolonged periods, leading to the near total socioeconomic collapse of Palestinian society. In response, new and expanded ICRC aid programmes sought to help 50,000 of the most needy families, representing more than 300,000 people or some 15% of the total West Bank population.

The ICRC viewed its relief programmes as extraordinary and temporary measures to meet emergency needs, and not as a substitute for Israel assuming its responsibil-ity, as the occupying power, to ensure the welfare of the Palestinian population. The ICRC stressed that the worsening situation for the inhabitants of the occupied Palestinian territories was largely attributable to Israeli security restrictions imposed there and strongly urged Israel to adjust its security policy in order to minimize its devastating impact on the entire civilian population.

Assisting families in the West Bank
An innovative urban voucher programme, the largest of its kind ever launched by the ICRC, started in July 2002 in the nine largest towns of the West Bank. Its aim was to provide basic food and other relief for 20,000 families, or some 20% of the urban population. Under the scheme, beneficiary families received monthly vouchers worth US$ 90 to purchase basic food and other

essential household items from pre-selected local retailers. Apart from the primary objective of helping destitute families, the project also provided a stimulus to the local economy by ensuring that the product mix available in exchange for ICRC vouchers contained certain items supplied by local producers. By the end of 2002, an average of two distributions had been carried out in each of the nine towns involved. A tightly controlled monitoring system was put in place to oversee the scheme, which was set to run until June 2003.

At the start of 2002, the ICRC launched a large-scale economic-aid programme in the form of monthly relief packages (food and hygiene parcels and sports/school kits) for 10,000 particularly needy families living in isolated West Bank villages. In May 2002, the number of beneficiaries was increased to 30,000 families in some 300 villages and a bulk-food component was added. By 1 December 2002, the first distribution of bulk food (50 kg of wheat flour, 50 kg of sugar and 50 kg of rice per family) had been completed in all rural areas covered by the programme, and a second round was under way (bulk food comprising flour, rice, sugar, oil and lentils) in coordination with the World Food Programme. The programme was set to continue until the end of June 2003.

Both of the above-mentioned programmes were delayed by mobility constraints imposed by closures and curfews.

Extending food aid in Hebron

The living conditions for residents of Hebron's old town continued to deteriorate as a result of almost round-the-clock curfews, frequent violence between Israeli settlers and Palestinian militants, and IDF operations.

In mid-2002, the ICRC doubled the monthly food-parcel programme in Hebron's old town to cover 2,000 families. Eleven distributions were completed in 2002 despite continuous disruptions caused by the unpredictable pattern of the stringent curfew regime and recurrent violent incidents involving Israeli settlers, the IDF and armed Palestinian militants.

Shelter for the homeless

The scale of ICRC shelter aid grew sharply in response to the increased number of Palestinian families rendered homeless by the demolition or expropriation of their dwellings during IDF operations and Israeli settlement expansion, particularly in the Gaza Strip.

More than 2,300 Gaza families received either a full or partial ICRC house destruction relief kit (comprising emergency shelter and basic household items) from July to November 2002. In the West Bank, similar aid was provided to some 400 people over the same period under a programme that will continue in 2003.

Water distribution

Hundreds of isolated rural villages not connected to water supply systems continued to face chronic shortages as the long, dry summer months depleted reserves accumulated in underground cisterns during the rainy winter. The ICRC identified some **270** such villages that in summer were almost totally dependent on increasingly expensive tanker deliveries which most of the population could no longer afford. The problem was further aggravated by the questionable quality of water trucked to villages, which was reflected in an increased incidence of water-borne diseases. To ensure that rural villages had sufficient quantities of clean water during the summer months, the ICRC introduced a new water distribution programme between August and November 2002, targeting 2,500 households in nearly 300 isolated villages.

To supplement its water distribution programme, the ICRC laid the groundwork for enhanced rainwater storage capacity in selected West Bank communities by installing storage cisterns.

At the height of the violence in the second quarter of the year, the ICRC regularly facilitated the safe passage of municipal repair and maintenance staff in West Bank and Gaza Strip towns where water supply facilities had either **been** destroyed or severely damaged during IDF operations. ICRC engineers were also directly involved in emergency repair work..

Restoring family links

More than 2,000 Lebanese nationals who fled southern Lebanon following the Israeli withdrawal in May 2000 remained in Israel in 2002 and required help maintaining contact with their families in Lebanon, with which Israel has no formal ties. Family links were ensured through the Red Cross message (RCM) service.

The RCM service also served to enable Palestinians detained by the Israeli authorities to restore and maintain contact with their families. A total of 5,009 such messages were collected and 3,432 were distributed in 2002.

In addition, the ICRC introduced a system for the issuing of power-of-attorney documents and arranged for their exchange, together with other official documents, between Lebanese families living in Israel and others in Lebanon.

When requested by the families, the ICRC transferred the remains of deceased Lebanese civilians from Israel to Lebanon in order to provide them with a dignified funeral in their country of origin.

ICRC delegates pursued a dialogue with the relevant authorities regarding Lebanese civilians in Israel who expressed the wish to return to their country of origin.

The 16,000 Syrian nationals in the Israelioccupied Golan who had been separated from their families in Syria since 1967 continued to benefit from (CRC efforts to ensure that they were able to travel to Syria for educational or religious purposes, or to get married in the separation zone with persons from Syria.

PEOPLE DEPRIVED OF THEIR FREEDOM

The ICRC considerably enlarged its protection role in response to mass arrests of suspected Palestinian militants by Israeli security forces. Increased (CRC staff levels enabled the organization to regularly visit growing numbers of people held in detention centres in Israel and the occupied Palestinian territories in order to assess their treatment and living conditions and help them maintain contact with their families.

Detainees held by Israel

As 2002 drew to a close, the Palestinian detainee population totalled 5,444, including security and administrative detainees, ordinary detainees and detainees of undetermined status, including foreigners. The ICRC conducted weekly visits to four Israeli interrogation centres and made regular visits to six provisional detention centres, as well as to 19 prisons and some police stations.

Israel reopened the Ofer and Qetziot reserve military detention centres to accommodate the growing number of arrested Palestinians. The (CRC was able to visit both camps shortly after they opened and continued to monitor treatment and conditions there throughout the year.

In all, the ICRC visited 13,118 detainees in 39 Israeli places of detention, focusing primarily on interrogation centres and the Ofer and Qetziot camps. In the latter camp, Israel was holding nearly 900 Palestinian administrative detainees by the end of the year. Visits were also carried out to Israeli prisons, the Meggido military camp, provisional detention centres and some police stations.

Almost 50 foreign detainees whose States had no diplomatic relations with Israel were regularly visited by ICRC delegates to assess their treatment and living conditions and also to determine whether they wished to return home and, if so, to facilitate that process. (Several foreign detainees were repatriated under ICRC auspices.) In other cases it helped arrange resettlement in third countries.

The Central Prison in Jericho was still holding six detainees at the end of the year, transferred from Ramallah on 5 June as part of the resolution of the spring siege of the Palestinian Authority's presidential compound. All six were held by the Authority under the supervision of a joint US and British monitoring team requested by Israel.

ICRC discussions with Israeli authorities to improve the detainee-notification system resulted in some progress. Weekly visits to the four interrogation centres run by the Israeli Security Authority remained a priority.

Following a decision by the Israeli Supreme Court on 23 August 2001 to grant them the right to be visited, the ICRC was finally allowed access to two Lebanese administrative detainees on 23 June 2002, one of whom had never been visited by the ICRC since his arrest in 1994. At present, 17 Lebanese nationals are still being held in Israel after being arrested in southern Lebanon and sentenced by a court in Israel.

Detainees held by the Palestinian Authority

The number of people held by the Palestinian Authority dropped significantly following the large-scale destruction of Palestinian detention facilities, particularly during IDF incursions into the West Bank in early spring. The precarious security situation brought ICRC detainee-welfare work in the West Bank to a near halt following "Operation Determined Path." In the Gaza Strip, the Palestinian Authority's security services managed to maintain a limited detention capacity and regular visits to places of detention continued.

At year's end, the ICRC was assessing the treatment and conditions of 277 persons held by the Palestinian authorities, mostly alleged collaborators with Israel, compared with 799 at the start of the year. With the near-collapse of the central prison system in the West Bank, many detainees were under house arrest or being held in police stations. Some alleged collaborators were the victims of extrajudicial executions, prompting ICRC representations to the Palestinian Authority.

Despite continued representations to the authorities concerned, the ICRC was unable to gain access to places of detention run by the Palestinian Authority's Military Intelligence Services.

Missing Israelis

The ICRC continued its efforts to determine what had happened to nine missing Israeli nationals. Despite repeated ICRC representations to the relevant authorities, no progress was made on this issue in 2002. During his visit to Israel and the occupied Palestinian territories in October, the ICRC president met with the families of the missing Israelis, who were desperate to know what had happened to their loved ones. He reiterated the organization's commitment to resolving this issue and reaffirmed the prisoners' right to family visits. He told the families that "the ICRC

Helping detainees deprived of family visits

Palestinian detainees are entitled to maintain family contacts, in accordance with the relevant provisions of the Geneva Conventions. However, IDF military operations and tight closures continued to severely disrupt the ICRC's family-visit programme for Palestinian detainees. In the West Bank the programme was operational for only about 20 days in 2002. In the Gaza Strip, family visits resumed in August, having been suspended since June, and continued throughout the year despite considerable implementation difficulties and delays.

The lack of family visits in the West Bank also deprived detainees of a source of essential material support. This prompted the ICRC to distribute clothing, medical and recreational items to special hardship cases in various places of detention. The ICRC also provided supplies to canteens and newspaper subscriptions in more than 20 places of detention.

The ICRC continued to urge the Israeli authorities to enable a full resumption of family visits in a manner that ensured the safety and dignity of families involved.

WOUNDED AND SICK
Ensuring access to victims

270

Emergency medical services encountered some of the worst security problems that they had ever faced in the entire history of the Israeli-Palestinian crisis, particularly during "Operation Defensive Shield". As a result, the ICRC had to remind the Israeli authorities of the paramount importance of ensuring those services safe and unhindered access to the victims and to hospitals.

Stringent mobility restrictions imposed by the IDF enabled the Palestinian Red Crescent to respond to only 10% of emergency calls at the height of violence during IDF military incursions into the West Bank in the spring. The ICRC was frequently forced to change the way its emergency services operated owing to the increasingly precarious security environment that resulted in its staff and ICRC ambulances encountering threatening behaviour from IDF troops. Scores of Red Crescent staff were arrested, including the Society's president, and in four separate incidents four emergency medical workers - three of them from the Red Crescent - were killed while carrying out their medical duties.

Despite the serious mobility constraints, the ICRC delivered many truckloads of emergency medical supplies for the Palestinian Ministry of Health and the Red Crescent within the West Bank itself and between the West Bank and Gaza. This was in addition to the many emergency transports of supplies for other humanitarian organizations and for individual patients, carried out particularly during the IDF's five-week incursions into the West Bank, launched on March 29.

Security-clearance delays for ambulances eased somewhat after an enquiry was carried out by Israel into IDF conduct during "Operation Defensive Shield" vis-a-vis humanitarian organizations and their medical services in particular. In the Gaza Strip, however, more constraints were imposed on already hard-pressed medical services by a new military security regulation requiring a minimum of three persons in vehicles seeking to cross checkpoints dividing the Strip.

Reducing dependency on referral hospitals
The ICRC expanded its surgical training and support programme in peripheral hospitals to reduce the need to transfer patients to urban centres. ICRC war surgeons working at hospitals in both the Gaza Strip and the West Bank assisted their Palestinian counterparts by providing expertise in vascular, neurological and reconstructive surgery, as well as intensive and post-operative care.

In cooperation with the Palestinian Ministry of Health, the ICRC held four war-surgery seminars in **October for** some 200 surgeons and other medical staff from hospitals across the Gaza Strip and West Bank. More such seminars are planned for 2003. The hospitals were also provided with surgical instruments and oxygen concentrators.

AUTHORITIES

The ICRC strongly condemned Palestinian attacks on Israeli civilians and stepped up its representations to the Palestinian Authority and militant groups claiming responsibility for many of these attacks.

It also repeatedly urged Israel to ensure that dealing with legitimate security concerns did not prevent it from meeting its overriding responsibility to see to the security and welfare of the civilian population under its occupation, as this was gravely affected by stringent closure and curfew measures that denied people access to the basic necessities of life.

These priority concerns were the subject of wide-ranging discussions held by the ICRC president during his meetings in October with the Israeli and Palestinian authorities. These talks led to improved dialogue with the Israel Civil Administration and, to a lesser extent, the IDF, but by the end of the year had nevertheless failed to bring about any tangible improvement in the occupied Palestinian territories from a humanitarian point of view. Similarly, the ICRC president's appeal to Palestinian militants to cease attacks against Israeli civilians failed to stop that violence.

Israel ratified the Geneva Conventions in 1951 but has not incorporated them into domestic law. Nor has it ratified a number of other humanitarian treaties, including Protocols I and II additional to the Geneva Conventions, the Ottawa Convention and the Rome Statute of the International Criminal Court.

In March, the Israeli parliament passed a "detention of unlawful combatants" law defined as targeting any person having taken part directly or indirectly in "acts of hostility" against Israel, or belonging to a force which carries out such acts against Israel and not fulfilling the conditions needed for prisoner-of-war status. According to this law, the detention of such a person can last as long as his or her release is deemed to endanger Israel's security. The ICRC reminded the Israeli authorities that its application must not deprive persons protected by the Fourth Convention of the rights afforded to them therein.

Finally, nineteen high-ranking Palestinian Authority officials attended a talk on the role of the ICRC in implementing IHL.

ARMED FORCES
AND OTHER BEARERS OF WEAPONS

The year saw continued constructive dialogue with the IDF with a view to improving respect for IHL and increasing knowledge of its provisions among the force's rank and file.

Efforts were stepped up to have IHL incorporated into the IDF's theoretical and practical training. The ICRC for the first time organized a talk for commanders at the IDF junior officers school. A presentation on the ICRC and basic IHL was held for 25 Israeli police officers stationed in the northern sector of the occupied Palestinian territories. Cooperation continued with Israel's military law school on the production of a self-training CD-ROM on IHL.

IHL dissemination courses were also held for over 90 members of four different branches of the Palestinian Authority security services in the Gaza Strip.

CIVIL SOCIETY

The ICRC continued to promote knowledge of the basic principles of IHL among opinion makers, the media and academic circles in both Israel and the occupied Palestinian territories
.

In Israel, delegates gave a briefing on IHL and the ICRC to 19 trainee diplomats at the Israeli Ministry of Foreign Affairs. Frequent exchanges of information took place between the ICRC and legal-affairsoriented NGOs, and the ICRC organized a one-day seminar for representatives of five Israel-based NGOs specializing in human rights law. Legal texts and ICRC lawpromotion kits were regularly distributed to NGOs.

The ICRC also continued discussions with the Israeli Ministry of Education on integrating "Exploring Humanitarian Law" (EHL) into some secondary-school curricula. EHL modules were translated into Hebrew and in conjunction with the ICRC and the Mogen David Adom, the Ministry of Education organized the first in a series of four seminars on EHL for 49 of its national supervisors. In addition, 25 EHL modules in Arabic were supplied to the education authorities for the Arab sector of Israeli society.

EHL modules were presented to the Palestinian authorities, who agreed to work toward EHL's inclusion in the mainstream curricula of secondary education. The process was initially due to start in 2002 but was deferred to the 2003-2004 academic year owing to the disruption of the education system that resulted from the upsurge in violence. In November, four representatives of the Ministry of Education participated in a 10-day training seminar organized in Robot by the Ministry of Education of Morocco and the ICRC, under the auspices of the League of Arab States.

In cooperation with various NGOs focusing on this issue, a presentation on IHL and the ICRC mandate was given to 20 Palestinian lawyers and a study was completed on the involvement of Palestinian children in violence. Several presentations were organized for Palestinian journalists to improve their understanding of the ICRC mandate and activities and increase reporting on the subject.

The impact of the troubles had a devastating impact on Palestinian children, who continued to be exposed to traumatizing acts of violence. While most Palestinian children were victims of the violence, some continued to be involved in acts of violence, either incited by others or acting spontaneously.

In response, the ICRC worked closely with three NGOs to sponsor activities in Palestinian summer camps that heightened awareness of basic human values. Twenty young staff from one NGO attended an ICRC workshop on film-animation techniques and subsequently helped set up four animation workshops in the Gaza Strip during which scores of children produced cartoon films on humanitarian topics of their choice. In the West Bank, the ICRC worked with a local NGO to raise awareness of these same human values

among some 1,000 youths in 20 summer camps, with the help of 20 students trained in IHL by the ICRC.

More than 150 lecturers and students at the Islamic University in Gaza and the Arab-American University in Jenin received basic IHL instruction. Seminars were held for 20 practising Palestinian lawyers, in partnership with the Gaza-based Palestinian Bar Association. Several presentations were also made for Palestinian journalists to improve their understanding of and reporting on the principles of IHL as well as the ICRC's mandate and activities.

One Palestinian and one Israeli university professor were invited to attend the 4th Training Seminar on IHL for University Teachers, organized in September in Geneva by the ICRC and Geneva University.

NATIONAL SOCIETIES
Acting as lead agency in Israel, the occupied and the autonomous territories, the ICRC endeavoured to ensure a coordinated approach among all components of the Movement and their respective activities. Priority was given to the institutional development of the Palestine Red Crescent Society and the Mogen David Adorn in order to enhance their ability to deliver effective emergency humanitarian services.

During his October visit to the region, the ICRC president assured the presidents of the Palestinian and Israeli Societies of the ICRC's commitment to supporting their ambulance services. He also reaffirmed ICRC determination to resolve the emblem issue with a view to integrating the MDA into the International Red Cross and Red Crescent Movement.
In 2002, the ICRC increased its already substantial financial, technical and material support for the Palestine Red Crescent Society (PRCS), in particular the Society's emergency medical services (EMS). The ICRC funded EMS training courses both at technical and management levels and reinforced the EMS structure through the provision of conflict-preparedness and EMS specific equipment (ambulances and pre-hospital medical care equipment, radio communication devices, generators, etc.). Furthermore, the ICRC provided EMS training and teaching material to the PRCS Emergency Medical Technician training centre and supported EMS information and education campaigns aimed at enhancing general public knowledge about the PRCS ambulance services. . . . .

UNITED NATIONS

RESOLUTIONS, REPORTS AND DEBATES

United Nations Security Council Resolution 242

November 22, 1967

The Security Council,
Expressing its continuing concern with the grave situation in the Middle East,

Emphasizing the inadmissibility of the acquisition of territory by war and the need to work for a just and lasting peace in which every State in the area can live in security,

Emphasizing further that all Member States in their acceptance of the Charter of the United Nations have undertaken a commitment to act in accordance with Article 2 of the Charter,

Affirms that the fulfillment of Charter principles requires the establishment of a just and lasting peace in the Middle East which should include the application of both the following principles:

Withdrawal of Israeli armed forces from territories occupied in the recent conflict; Termination of all claims or states of belligerency and respect for and acknowledgement of the sovereignty, territorial integrity and political independence of every State in the area and their right to live in peace within secure and recognized boundaries free from threats or acts of force;

Affirms further the necessity

> For guaranteeing freedom of navigation through
> international waterways in the area;

> For achieving a just settlement of the refugee
> problem;

> For guaranteeing the territorial inviolability and political
> independence of every State in the area, through measures
> including the establishment of demilitarized zones;

> Requests the Secretary General to designate a Special
> Representative to proceed to the Middle East to establish and
> maintain contacts with the States concerned in order to promote
> agreement and assist efforts to achieve a peaceful and accepted
> settlement in accordance with the provisions and principles in
> this resolution; . . . .

United Nations Security Council Resolution 452

JULY 20, 1979

The Security Council,

Taking note of the report and recommendations of the Security Council Commission established under resolution 446 (1979) to examine the situation relating to settlements in the Arab territories occupied since 1967, including Jerusalem, contained in document S/13450,

Strongly deploring the lack of co-operation of Israel with the Commission,

Considering that **the policy of Israel in establishing settlements in the occupied Arab territories has no legal validity and constitutes a violation of the Fourth Geneva Convention** relative to the Protection of Civilian Persons in Time of War of 12 August 1949,

Deeply concerned by the practices of the Israeli authorities in implementing that settlements policy in the occupied Arab territories, including Jerusalem, and its consequences for the local Arab and Palestinian population,

Emphasizing the **need for confronting the issue of the existing settlements and the need to consider measures to safeguard the impartial protection of property seized,**

Bearing in mind the **specific status of Jerusalem**, and reconfirming pertinent Security Council resolutions concerning Jerusalem and in particular the need to protect and preserve the unique spiritual and religious dimension of the Holy Places in that city,

Drawing attention to the **grave consequences which the settlements policy is bound to have** on any attempt to reach a peaceful solution in the Middle East.

1. Commends the work done by the Commission in preparing the report on the establishment of Israeli settlements in the Arab territories occupied since 1967, including Jerusalem;

2. Accepts the recommendations contained in the above mentioned report of the Commission.

3. **Calls upon the Government and people of Israel to cease, on an urgent basis, the establishment, construction and planning of settlements in the Arab territories occupied since 1967, including Jerusalem;**

4. Requests the Commission, in view of the magnitude of the problem of settlements, to keep under close survey the implementation of the present resolution and to report back to the Security Council before 1 November 1979.

United Nations Security Council Resolution 605

DECEMBER 22, 1987

The Security Council,

Having considered the letter dated 11 December 1987 from the Permanent Representative of Democratic Yemen to the United Nations, in his capacity as Chairman of the Arab Group for the month of December,

Bearing in mind the inalienable rights of all peoples recognized by the Charter of the United Nations and proclaimed by the Universal Declaration of Human Rights,

Recalling its relevant resolutions on the situation in the Palestinian and other Arab territories, occupied by Israel since 1967, including Jerusalem, and including its resolutions 446 (1979), 465 (1980), 497 (1981) and 592 (1986),

Recalling also the Geneva Convention relative to the Protection of Civilian Persons in Time of War, of 12 August 1949,

Gravely concerned and alarmed by the deteriorating situation in the Palestinian and other Arab territories occupied by Israel since 1967, including Jerusalem,

Taking into account the need to consider measures for the impartial protection of the Palestinian civilian population under Israeli occupation,

Considering that the current policies and practices of Israel, the occupying Power, in the occupied territories are bound to have grave consequences for the endeavours to achieve comprehensive, just and lasting peace in the Middle East,

1. **Strongly deplores those policies and practices of Israel, the occupying Power, which violate the human rights of the Palestinian people** in the occupied territories, and in particular the opening of fire by the Israeli army, resulting in the killing and wounding of defenceless Palestinian civilians;

2. **Reaffirms that the Geneva Convention relative to the Protection of Civilian Persons in Time of War, of 12 August 1949, is applicable to** the Palestinian and other Arab territories occupied by Israel since 1967, including Jerusalem;

3. **Calls once again upon Israel, the occupying Power, to abide immediately and scrupulously by the Geneva Convention relative to the Protection of Civilian Persons in Time of War,** of 12 August 1949, and to desist forthwith from its policies and practices that are in violation of the provisions of the Convention;

4. Calls furthermore for the exercise of the maximum restraint to contribute towards the establishment of peace;

5. Stresses the urgent need to reach a just, durable and peaceful settlement of the Arab-Israeli conflict;

6. Requests the Secretary-General to examine the present situation in the occupied territories by all means available to him, and to submit a report no later than 20 January 1988 containing his recommendations on ways and means for ensuring the safety and protection of the Palestinian civilians under Israeli occupation;

7. Decides to keep the situation in the Palestinian and other Arab territories occupied by Israeli since 1967, including Jerusalem, under review.

United Nations Security Council Resolution 607

JANUARY 5, 1988

The Security Council,

Recalling its resolution **605** (1987) of 22 December 1987, Expressing grave concern over the situation in the occupied Palestinian territories,

Having been apprised of the decision of Israel, the occupying Power, to "continue the deportation" of Palestinian civilians in the occupied territories,

Recalling the Geneva Convention relative to the protection of civilian persons in time of war, of 12 August 1949, and in particular articles 47 and 49 of same,

1. **Reaffirms once again that the Geneva Convention relative to the protection of civilian persons in time of war, of 12 August 1949, is applicable to Palestinian and other Arab territories, occupied by Israel since 1967, including Jerusalem,**

2. Calls upon Israel to refrain from deporting any Palestinian civilians from the occupied territories;

3. **Strongly requests Israel, the occupying Power, to abide by its obligation arising from the Convention;**

. . . .

United Nations Security Council Resolution 799

December 18, 1992

The Security Council,

Recalling the obligations of Member States under the United Nations Charter,

Reaffirming its resolutions 607 (1988), 608 (1988), 636 (1989), 641 (1989), 681 (1990), 694 (1991) and 726 (1992),

Having learned with deep concern that **Israel, the occupying Power, in contravention of its obligations under the Fourth Geneva Convention of 1949,** deported to Lebanon on 17 December 1992, hundreds of Palestinian civilians from the territories occupied by Israel since 1967, including Jerusalem,

1. Strongly condemns the action taken by Israel, the occupying Power, to deport hundreds of Palestinian civilians, and expresses its firm opposition to any such deportation by Israel;

2. **Reaffirms the applicability of the Fourth Geneva Convention of 12 August 1949 to all the Palestinian territories occupied by Israel since 1967, including Jerusalem**, and affirms that deportation of civilians constitutes a contravention of its obligations under the Convention;

3. Reaffirms also the independence, sovereignty and territorial integrity of Lebanon;

4. Demands that Israel, the occupying Power, ensure the safe and immediate return to the occupied territories of all those deported;

. . . .

Security Council 4945th Meeting (PM)

SECURITY COUNCIL URGED TO CONDEMN EXTRAJUDICIAL EXECUTIONS FOLLOWING

ISRAEL'S ASSASSINATION OF HAMAS LEADER

Keep Focus on Palestinian Terrorism,
Not Acts of Self-Defence, Says Israel's Representative

As the Security Council met this afternoon, less than a month after it failed to condemn the killing of Hamas leader **Sheikh Ahmed Yassin**, it was once again called on to condemn extrajudicial executions by Israel, the most recent of which was Saturday's assassination of Yassin's successor, **Abdel Aziz Al-Rantisi**.

Urging the Council to take "bold and courageous action", the **Observer for Palestine** said that last month's failure of the Council to condemn the extrajudicial execution of Sheikh Yassin, due to the veto by the United States, had further emboldened Israel to continue carrying out such illegal actions with impunity. Without concern for reproach and punishment or for the consequences of its actions, Israel continued to behave as a State that was above the law.

He said that any parallels drawn between Israel's actions against the Palestinians and the war against global terrorism was inappropriate and completely erroneous. Israel's constant attempts to draw such parallels and to exploit the international fight against terrorism must be rejected.

Prime Minister Ariel Sharon's announced unilateral withdrawal from Gaza was an attempt to confer legitimacy on some of Israel's illegal settlements, to negate the rights of Palestine refugees and to dilute international opposition to the catastrophic expansionist separation wall. The proposal fell far short of any real withdrawal, keeping control of international borders, airspace and water in the hands of the occupier and maintaining the so-called "right" to military attacks against Gaza.

Israel's representative said it was regrettable that the Council had been compelled to convene again, not to condemn the murder of innocent civilians by organizations such as Hamas, but to denounce the demise of a key architect of those massacres. Just hours before the targeted counter-terrorist operation against Mr. Rantisi, "a trader in death", the organization which he had headed had claimed responsibility, together with the Al-Aqsa Martyrs Brigade, for yet another suicide attack at the Erez Crossing, killing a guard and injuring others.

Those acts of terror should be the focus of the Council's specific attention, not the acts of self-defence necessary to prevent them, he said. Mr. Rantisi had been a radical terrorist leader who had joyfully and publicly celebrated the murder of innocent men, women and children, called for the destruction of Israel by force of arms, and believed that violence was the "only option". . . .

The majority of the speakers who addressed the meeting, held at the request of the Arab Group and the League of Arab States, strongly condemned the most recent extrajudicial execution, saying that the Council's failure to act last month had sent the wrong message to Israel, which had essentially been given the green light to continue its illegal policies.

It was not too late, said Algeria's representative, for the Council to reassert its authority, to put an end to Israel's policy of escalation, provocation and defiance, and to reaffirm once and for all that a genuine, just and lasting peace could only be achieved through the implementation of the Quartet's Road Map.

Many speakers agreed that, while Israel had the right to defend itself and protect its citizens, it must act in accordance with international law. The fight against terrorism, Spain's representative stressed, must take place in an environment of international legality.

The appeal for vengeance following Mr. Rantisi's killing forecast an increase in violence.

The reactions to Israel's disengagement plan were mixed, with some speakers warning that such unilateral actions might prejudge the final status negotiations, while others felt it would be a significant step forward. Council President Gunter Pleuger (Germany), speaking in his national capacity, welcomed any Israeli withdrawal from settlements as long as it took place in the context of implementation of the Road Map. Only a negotiated settlement on Gaza would receive the necessary international support for the maintenance of security and the rehabilitation and reconstruction.

Calling an Israeli withdrawal from Gaza a rare opportunity for progress, the representative of the United States said it was noteworthy that the initiative was being put forward by Prime Minister Sharon, a principal architect of the Israeli settlement policy.

Israel's planned disengagement from Gaza, the representative of the United Kingdom added, gave the international community an opportunity to help the Palestinian Authority with the measures it needed to get to the point where the concept of a viable Palestinian State became a real possibility. It was not prejudging the final status negotiations or pushing the Road Map to the side. Instead, it was a way back to the Road Map, which remained the correct route to a just and lasting solution.

Also making statements today were the representatives of Benin, Angola, Brazil, Russian Federation, Pakistan, Philippines, China, Chile, Romania, France, Egypt, Syria, Ireland (on behalf of the European Union and associated States), Yemen, Morocco, United Arab Emirates, India, Malaysia, Libya, Sudan, Bahrain, Kuwait, Saudi Arabia, South Africa, Lebanon, Tunisia, Jordan, Japan, Cuba, Indonesia, Iran, Mauritania and Norway.

In addition, the Observer for the League of Arab States and the Chairman of the Committee on the Exercise of the Inalienable Rights of the Palestinian People also addressed the Council.

The meeting, which began at 3:15 p.m., adjourned at 6:35 p.m.

Background

The Security Council met this afternoon to consider the situation in the Middle East, including the Palestinian question.

Before the Council was a letter dated 19 April from the Permanent Representative of Egypt to the United Nations addressed to the President of the Security_ Council (document S/2004/303), in which he requests, in his capacity as Chairman of the Arab Group for the month of April, and on behalf of the States members of the League of Arab States, the holding of an immediate meeting of the Council to consider Israel's grave violations of international humanitarian law, the most recent of which is the extrajudicial execution of

Abdel Aziz al-Rantisi in Gaza, and the escalation of its military attacks against the Palestinian people and their leadership, and to take the necessary measures in that regard.

STATEMENTS:

NASSER AL-KIDWA, Observer for Palestine, said the Council was meeting again after less than one month, because Israel continued its reign of terror against Palestinian people. Israel had not ceased its campaign of death and destruction in the occupied Palestinian territory. It continued to carry out the extrajudicial executions of Palestinian leaders and to kill, wound and maim defenceless Palestinian civilians, including women and children, in grave breach of international law, including international humanitarian law and human rights law.

Two days ago on 17 April, he said, less than four weeks after the extrajudicial execution of Sheikh Ahmed Yassin in Gaza, the Israeli occupying forces had committed yet another extrajudicial execution by killing Abdel Aziz al-Rantisi, a political leader of Hamas. The occupying forces had fired missiles at the vehicle in which he was riding, killing Dr. Rantisi, as well as two other Palestinian men who had been with him. That was the second time that the occupying forces had targeted Dr. Rantisi for assassination, the first being in June 2003.

He said that latest in a long series of war crimes committed by the occupying Power had been carried out in fulfillment of the repeated threats of Israeli Prime Minister Sharon and other Israeli Government and military officials to continue targeting Palestinian leaders for assassination in flagrant violation of international law and in complete and total disregard for the condemnation, pleas and demands by the international community for the cessation of such an illegal and barbaric policy. Indeed, following the attack on Saturday, Mr. Sharon and other high-ranking Israeli officials had publicly boasted and congratulated themselves on the success of the operation and proceeded to declare more threats against Palestinian leaders.

Without a doubt, he said, the recent failure of the Council to condemn the extrajudicial execution of Sheikh Yassin and to take urgent measures to address the deterioration of the situation, due to the veto of one of the Council's permanent members, had further emboldened the Israeli Government to continue carrying out such illegal actions with impunity. Without concern for reproach and punishment or for the consequences of its actions, Israel continued to behave as a State that was above the law. Unable to uphold its duties for the maintenance of international peace and security, the Council had allowed Israel to continue acting beyond the parameters of international law, permitting it to use the most oppressive measures and practices to impose more death and destruction and loss on the Palestinian people under its occupation.

Parallel to, and in conjunction with, its illegal actions against the Palestinian people, he said, the Israeli Government had intensified its attempts to carry through unilateral actions intended to further entrench the illegitimate measures already taken by Israel on the ground in the occupied Palestinian territories. The meeting last week of Prime Minister Sharon and President Bush and their exchange of letters and assurances had taken those attempts to impose a unilateral "disengagement" one step further. The content of those letters violated relevant provisions on international law and violated the rights of the Palestinian people.

He said it was an attempt to confer legitimacy on some of Israel's illegal settlements, to negate the rights of the Palestine refugees and to dilute international opposition to the catastrophic expansionist Wall. The content was also in complete departure from the Road Map, and as such made the work of the Quartet extremely difficult, if not impossible, to carry out. Even with regard to Gaza, the proposal fell far short of any real withdrawal, keeping control of international borders, airspace and water in the hands of the occupier and maintaining the so-called "right" to military attacks against Gaza.

Any parallels drawn between Israel's actions against the Palestinians and the war being waged against global terrorism was inappropriate and completely erroneous, he said. Israel's constant attempts to draw such parallels and to exploit the international fight against terrorism must be rejected.

The time was long overdue for the international community to take urgent measures to address the ongoing tragedy. The Council must take the lead in that regard. The Council must take bold and courageous actions to ensure compliance with its resolutions, adherence to international law, and to bring an end to the cycle of violence and bloodshed that had prevented the two peoples and the entire region from realizing genuine peace, freedom and security for so many decades.

DAN GILLERMAN (Israel) noted that the people of Israel commemorated Holocaust Remembrance Day today. It was with regret that the Council had been compelled to convene again on the Day, not to condemn the murder of innocent civilians by organizations such as Hamas, but to denounce the demise of a key architect of those massacres. Just hours before the targeted counter-terrorist operation against Mr. Rantisi, the organization which he had headed had claimed responsibility, together with the Al-Aqsa Martyrs Brigade, for yet another suicide attack at the Erez Crossing. The attack had killed a guard at the crossing and injured others. In recent days, there had also been repeated Qassam rocket fire at civilian communities in Israel. Those acts of terror should be the focus of the Council's specific attention, not the acts of self-defence necessary to prevent them.

Were the current Palestinian leadership a genuine partner in peace, defensive actions would not have been necessary, he said. The Palestinian obligation to dismantle the terrorist infrastructure, arrest terrorists, confiscate illegal weapons and stop incitement was as obvious and fundamental a legal imperative as it was a moral one. Under the Road Map, Council resolutions, signed agreements and international law, the Palestinian Authority was required to arrest murderers like Mr. Rantisi, not give them protection and safe haven. It there was something "extrajudicial", it was the total refusal of the Palestinian leadership for years to act against terrorism.

He said Mr. Rantisi had been a radical terrorist leader who had joyfully and publicly celebrated the murder of innocent men, women and children and called for the destruction of Israel by force of arms. He had believed that violence was the "only option". He had developed alliances with terrorist groups around the world, supported by regimes in Syria and Iran, and had been committed to fostering terrorism in Iraq and throughout the Western world. Mr. Rantisi had been a trader in death, a doctor of death, and no one should be surprised that he had paid the price. In the absence of any cooperation from the Palestinian Authority, and any viable means of arrest, Israel was sometimes left with no choice but to target those who planned and executed the murder of innocent civilians.

Israel was engaged in armed conflict against terrorism on an unparalleled scale, he said. It was not good enough to affirm in theory Israel's right to defend itself in the conflict, but then in practice seek to deny it the right to specifically target those illegal combatants directly responsible. Israel did so in a manner that was both necessary and proportionate, and when there was no other realistic option of detention or prevention. In those circumstances, such actions were wholly consistent with international law.

The targeting of Mr. Rantisi had not merely been a necessary defensive act to prevent ongoing and planned attacks against civilians, but a part of the global struggle against terrorism, he said. In line with Council resolutions 1368, 1373, 1377 and others, that action made clear that those who harboured terrorists must be held accountable. The Palestinian leadership could not brazenly violate international law by supporting terrorists and then seek to deny Israel the right to protect itself against them, guaranteed under that same law.

The entire world knew that Hamas was a terrorist organization committed to the destruction of Israel and of the hopes of peace by the deliberate massacre of innocent civilians, he said. The entire world, including the Arab world, knew that Hamas was the enemy of peace and stability in the region. The death of Mr. Rantisi was no doubt a relief for many innocent Palestinians whose lives he had endangered by the strategy of terrorism and the rejection of peace he had championed. The text presented to the Council was yet another example of misrepresentation and double standards, focusing yet again on the response to terrorism rather than the terrorism itself. It grossly distorted reality and sought to bully the Council to score political points.

As the struggle against terrorism continued, he said, Prime Minister Sharon had launched a bold and unprecedented initiative to bring new hope and opportunity to the peace process. The disengagement plan, when approved, would lead to the evacuation of settlements and military installations in the Gaza Strip and parts of the West Bank. The move was not required by the Road Map, but was an opportunity to restart the Road Map process to which Israel remained committed. Prime Minister Sharon's bold initiative deserved the international community's support and that of the Council. While in the absence of a peace partner Israel had been compelled to propose the unprecedented initiative itself, it hoped to implement it in a coordinated fashion that would ensure stability and security for both Israelis and Palestinians, provide a sound humanitarian infrastructure and rekindle the peace process.

The initiative was wholly consistent with Council resolutions 242 (1967) and 338 (1973), could facilitate the two-State solution in the context of the Road Map and was consistent with previous peace proposals, he said. Israel remained committed to a negotiated solution to permanent status issues that would guarantee peace, security and stability for both peoples, as well as secure borders. No permanent peace agreement could be imposed; it must be negotiated between the parties.

He said the initiative was a moment of opportunity, a chance for the Palestinian side to prove finally that it was capable of a new and responsible leadership that fought terrorism and preferred the welfare of its people. The initiative was the evacuation of settlements, something the Palestinian side had long called for. The Palestinian leadership must make a choice and the international community should encourage it to make the right one. Israel was ready to be a partner for peace with such a leadership.

ABDALLAH BAALI (Algeria) said that three weeks ago he had warned the Council that its failure to act would send the wrong message to Israel, which would abusively take it as a licence to kill. In fact, immediately after the vetoing of the draft resolution that would have condemned the assassination of Sheikh Ahmed Yassin and called for the cessation of all acts of violence, including acts of terrorism, the representative of Israel, in addition to insulting the Council, had made it clear that his country would continue to "take out the Palestinian leaders".

Again, Israel had struck and killed, remaining defiant in spite of almost unanimous condemnation, he continued. Its Prime Minister, after praising the army for Abdel Aziz al-Rantisi's assassination, had vowed yesterday to "hit the terror organizations and their leaders". And again, the Council found itself confronted with yet another Israeli provocation and challenge to its authority and credibility. Was it going, this time, to assume its responsibilities and condemn the killing in a clear and unequivocal fashion, calling for respect for international law? Was it going to come, at last, to the conclusion that civilian population in the Palestinian territory was in great danger and needed to be protected by an international force, to be urgently dispatched?

He said that, this time, the Council had to make the right decision and call upon Israel to cease its policy of targeted assassinations and abide by international law. If no action was taken and Israel got away with its horrendous crimes again, the situation in the Palestinian territory might deteriorate very rapidly and go out of control. Israel could not keep violating international law with total impunity and must be stopped before the peace process was put to death. It was not too late for the Council to reassert its authority, to put an end to Israel's policy of escalation, provocation and defiance, and to reaffirm once and for all that a genuine, just and lasting peace could only be achieved through the implementation of the Road Map. He hoped this time the Council would live up to its responsibilities and to the expectations of those who had kept faith in it.

Jean-Francis REGIS ZINSOU (Benin) said the critical situation in the Middle East, in particular on the Palestinian front, had continued to deteriorate in the past few months. His delegation had exhorted all parties to show restraint and commitment to the Road Map. **The execution of Mr. Rantisi had taken place less than a month after the killing of Sheikh Yassin. Those executions were a new challenge to international legality.** The continuation of such killings, targeting Palestinian leaders, did serious damage to the efforts of the international community to restore peace.

Renewing his urgent appeal to all parties to return to the path of dialogue to implement the shared vision of two States living side by side in peace, he also urgently demanded that the Quartet make use of its influence with the parties to end the cycle of violence in the Middle East. The partial disengagement would not be a positive step in the right direction.

JULIO HELDER DE MOURA LUCAS (Angola), expressing regret at the prevailing situation, said any signal of hope was immediately destroyed by terror, by policies of collective punishment and by revenge. Angola wished to see both sides enjoying peace and conviviality. Unfortunately, all efforts remained engulfed in deadlock, causing despair and frustration for the entire international community.

The Angolan delegation was totally opposed to extrajudicial killings, and had expressed regret at recent events in Gaza City, he said. It was necessary to break the cycle of violence. An investment in peace would be more rewarding than the actions the world had witnessed. Terrorism and occupation fed conflict and closed windows of opportunity for peace. Angola called on both sides to end terror and occupation, and to avoid steps that could escalate violence. For its part, the international community must persevere in efforts to bring the parties to the negotiating table. Both sides must take risks for peace, not unilateral action.

RONALDO MOTA SARDENBERG (Brazil) said the extrajudicial killing of Mr. Rantisi and other Palestinians last Saturday should be condemned by the Council as it ran counter to international law. It damaged the prospects for peace in the Middle East and undermined international efforts, including those of the Council, to bring the parties to the negotiating table. He called on all sides to use restraint at such a critical stage

ANA MARIA MENENDEZ (Spain) expressed concern about the recent extrajudicial killing, following the killing of Sheikh Yassin, which was part of an attempt in recent months to do away with the Palestinian leaders. Such killings did not contribute to creating a climate of peace and obstructed the implementation of the Road Map. Indiscriminate violence could not promote coexistence. The fight against terrorism must take place in an environment of international legality. The appeal for vengeance following Mr. Rantisi's killing forecast an increase in violence.

She condemned all terrorist actions that took innocent lives, made the peace process difficult and damaged the Palestinian cause. The present circumstances must be brought to an end. Appealing to both sides for restraint, she said the only solution was the coexistence of two States in the framework of global peace, as set forth in the Road Map and supported by the Council in resolution 1515 (2003). The Road Map set the priorities for both parties.

Regarding the announced unilateral withdrawal, she said it must have the support of the international community for a peaceful and orderly transition.

GENNADY GATILOV (Russian Federation) said serious concern was being expressed in Moscow about the possible consequences of the recent event in Gaza. Russia had repeatedly declared its rejection of targeted eliminations. While not casting doubt on Israel's right to self defence, that right **must be implemented within the framework of international law.** During the course of upcoming contacts with parties to the Quartet, there would be discussions of specific modalities for linking the Israeli plan with the Road Map.

He stressed that the modalities for a solution to such sensitive issues, including the fate of refugees and East Jerusalem, must be determined through agreement between the two sides. The legal basis for a settlement had been defined in Council **resolutions 242, 338, 1398 and 1515, which demanded compliance with the principle of the inadmissibility of acquiring territory by force.** The world organization had a responsibility for the implementation of the Road Map. The key to success was in joint actions. The Russian Federation favoured a speedy meeting of the Quartet, at which time it would be possible to discuss issues related to the Israeli proposal and the Road Map.

MUNIR AKRAM (Pakistan) condemned Israel's most recent extrajudicial execution, saying that despite international condemnation of a similar killing of Sheikh Yassin a few weeks ago, Israel had refused to heed the wishes of the international community that it stop acting in defiance of international law. The extrajudicial killings were clear violations of international law, especially the Fourth Geneva Convention. No interpretation of the principle of self-defence could justify such extrajudicial killing. Peace and the rule of law could not be established by those acting outside the law. Israel's actions had greatly damaged international endeavours to break the cycle of violence and put the peace process back on track.

The international community supported a two-State solution and that vision could only be achieved through the implementation of Council resolutions and the Quartet's Road Map. It must not be forgotten that the root cause of all the violence in Palestine was foreign occupation by Israel. If an initiative for greater stability in the region was to be taken, it must address that cause and end the occupation.

JAMES B. CUNNINGHAM (United States) noted that on Saturday the terrorist organization Hamas had claimed responsibility for a suicide attack at the Erez Crossing. A second bombing attack had been foiled. Both had been designed to perpetuate conflict and prevent progress towards the steps outlined in the Road Map. The attacks had occurred before the leader of Hamas had been killed. The United States had urged Israel to consider the consequences of its actions and had stressed the need to exercise restraint.

An Israeli withdrawal from Gaza would be a significant step forward, presenting a rare opportunity for progress, he said. It was noteworthy that the initiative was being put forward by Prime Minister Sharon, a principal architect of the Israeli settlement policy. That was an important development that should be commended. Israelis and Palestinians had important obligations under the Road Map, including Israel's commitment to take actions in the West Bank and to improve the humanitarian situation by easing restrictions on Palestinians not engaged in terrorist activities. Palestinians must stop acts of violence and incitement against Israel, and their leadership must take institutional reform. The United States had no intention of prejudicing the outcome of permanent status negotiations.

ADAM THOMSON (United Kingdom) **condemned the targeted killings as unlawful** and counterproductive. While **Israel** had the right to defend itself and protect its citizens, it **must act in accordance with international law**. The United Kingdom had repeatedly condemned terrorist acts against Israeli citizens and condemned the attack on Saturday. Terrorism inflicted huge suffering and loss and tried to undermine the true Palestinian cause. The Palestinians must take immediate and effective action to stop terrorist acts emanating from the Palestinian territories, and both parties must exercise restraint and stop escalating violence.

Israel's planned disengagement from Gaza and parts of the West Bank gave the international community an opportunity to help the Palestinian Authority with the measures it needed to get to the point where the concept of a viable Palestinian State became a real possibility, he said. It was not prejudging the final status negotiations or pushing the Road Map to the side. Instead, it was a way back to the Road Map, which remained the correct route to a just and lasting solution. The focus should be on getting the Road Map back on track. A comprehensive settlement was the only way either side would find peace and security.

LAURO L. BAJA, JR. (Philippines) called on all sides to exercise restraint and to refrain from events that would cause an escalation of violence. The new equation for peace in the Middle East, notwithstanding its noble intentions, was not a product of negotiation by the parties on the ground. He urged the restart of the Middle East process as set out under the Road Map and endorsed by Council resolution 1515 (2003).

ZHANG YISHAN (China) said his delegation expressed deep shock over the assassination, saying he was gravely worried about the prospects of tension between Israel and Palestine. **Israel must stop such assassination operations immediately.**

Noting that the question of the Middle East was complicated, he said the only way to peace lay in a comprehensive settlement under Council resolutions. Tit-for-tat violence would not contribute to a solution of the issue, but lead only to more violence and conflict. The international community must take practical measures to bring Israelis and Palestinians back to peace talks at an early date.

CHRISTIAN MAQUIEIRA (Chile) condemned the killing, saying that extrajudicial executions were reprehensible, a violation of international law and an obstruction to the peace process, which was based on the Road Map. That applied to all acts of violence and terrorism. The central question today involved the announcement of the Israeli Prime Minister's plan to proceed with withdrawal from Gaza and possibly some parts of the West Bank. The sense of that proposal was not clear enough. The last monthly report of the Secretary-General on the situation in the Middle East stated that for a successful withdraw of Israel, the following aspects must be included: compliance with the Road Map, cooperation with the Palestinians; withdrawal must be total and complete; and it must be a first step to end the occupation in accordance with Council resolutions.

The withdrawal, he continued, must be consistent with those parameters. Chile's position was based on strict compliance with the norms of international law and implementation of Council resolutions, particularly 242, 338, 1397 and 1515. Chile viewed the immediate future with skepticism. Regarding extrajudicial executions, who would decide where the limits would be? How long would that practice be resorted to? The Quartet must renew its efforts to keep the Road Map alive and to ensure that the announced withdrawal would be within that framework.

MIHNEA MOTOC (Romania), aligning himself with the European Union, expressed concern over the deterioration of the situation in the Middle East following the targeted killing of Abdel Aziz al-Rantisi. The Government of Israel had to examine very carefully the consequences of that act, because such operations did not provide more security. Rather, they fuelled tension and hatred that in turn generated even more violence. **Romania recognized the right of**

Israel to self-defence, but extrajudicial killings were contrary to international law and totally unacceptable.

In the present complicated and volatile situation, both parties must do their utmost to refrain from acts that could escalate violence and compromise any chance to revive the prospects for peace, he said. Fighting terrorism effectively, dismantling its infrastructure, and ending incitement to violence remained top priorities.

Expressing concern over the gravity of the humanitarian situation in the Palestinian territories, he said that due to the confrontations and security restrictions, Israel must refrain from actions that embittered the daily life of the inhabitants there, increased their economic hardship or induced a sense of humiliation or despair. A just, comprehensive and lasting peace could be achieved only through negotiations, as envisaged in the Road Map and in accordance with relevant Council resolution.

JEAN-MARC DE LA SABLIERE (France) condemned the 17 April attack, saying that the practice of extrajudicial killings violated fundamental principles of the rule of law. The disproportionate use of force in populated areas endangered efforts to obtain a ceasefire of Palestinian movements, and could only lead to the radicalization of the Palestinian people and undermine the prospects for a resumption of dialogue.

France recognized Israel's right to self-defence and had condemned attacks against Israeli civilians, he said. However, the fight against terrorism must be conducted with strict respect for the rule of law. Violence was not a solution. Only a negotiated agreement based on the principles of international law could allow the Israeli and Palestinian people to live side by side. Nothing lasting would be done without negotiation between the parties. Only a just and negotiated solution based on Council resolutions would provide the security to which all Israelis had a right. Peace must involve all the parties to the conflict, including Syria and Lebanon..

He noted that the withdrawal from Gaza could be positive, as the withdrawal fromPalestinian territories had been repeatedly urged. Hopefully, such a withdrawal would form a stage of the implementation of the Road Map, which was part of the context for the creation of a Palestinian State. The Road Map had been achieved as a result of international consensus, and France was ready to contribute to making the withdrawal a success. The Security Council also had particular responsibility and could not remain silent. France hailed the efforts of Egypt and Jordan and counted on the next Arab Summit to make a substantive effort to launch the peace process.

Speaking in his national capacity, **Council President GUNTER PLEUGER (Germany)** associated himself with the European Union saying he was concerned about the possibility of a further new spiral of violence and urged both sides to break the cycle of terror and violence. Calling on both sides to resume negotiation, he said that **his country, recognizing Israel's legitimate right to self-defence, had never accepted extrajudicial killings, which were contrary to international law.** The continuation of the practice endangered the successful implementation of any disengagement plan in Gaza or elsewhere.

Urging the Palestinians to resume talks on a ceasefire embracing all parties and group, he said he expected the Palestinian Authority to demonstrate its determination in the fight against extremist violence and to confront individuals and groups conducting and planning terrorist attacks. He welcomed any Israeli withdrawal from settlements as long as it took place in the context of implementation of the Road Map. Only a negotiated settlement on Gaza would receive the necessary international support for the maintenance of security and the rehabilitation and reconstruction. It was worth noting, in addition, that final status issues in general were a matter for negotiation and agreement between the parties themselves. They must not be prejudged.

AHMED ABOUL GHEIT (Egypt) condemned and deplored the extrajudicial killings of Palestinians by the Israeli army, which contravened all humanitarian considerations and norms of international law. The Israeli Government had not helped or contributed to the settlement of the Palestinian dispute. With its irresponsible acts, it had deepened the lack of trust in its policies and prompted more violence. The international community had worked to reach an agreed basis for the settlement of the Israeli-Palestinian question, but every time the potential for a breakthrough was on the horizon, Israel took measures to abort the general situation and any possibility for movement.

The demand for a full withdrawal to the pre-1967 borders was the main requirement of that settlement, he continued. Achieving a just settlement for Palestinian refugees was another important question that must be tackled in negotiations between the two parties. The Road Map was the internationally agreed machinery to achieve a settlement without selectivity or deviation and without undermining its principles. Any Israeli withdrawal from Palestinian territories must be coordinated with the Palestinians.

A viable Palestinian State must be established on the land occupied before 1967 and based on resolutions 242, 338 and other United Nations resolutions, the principle of land for peace and other agreements. The implementation of the Road Map required the rejection of violence, the lifting of the blockade and ending the suffering of the Palestinian people, as well as the dismantling of barriers. Egypt called on the Council to reject and condemn all extrajudicial killings and once again declare the terms of reference agreed upon to secure the right to live in peace for the people of Israel and Palestine.

YAHYA MAHMASSANI, Observer for the League of Arab States, said Israel was continuing its policy of killing Palestinians with impunity, the most recent such act being the execution of Mr. Rantisi, another act of State terrorism by Israel. Condemning that heinous crime, he said, Israel's actions, including the building of a separation wall, threatened peace and security and were undermining the peace process.

The crux of the conflict was the occupation of Arab and Palestinian territories, he said. The occupation was at the heart of the Arab-Israeli problem. The use of force was only worsening the situation in the region. The Council must force Israel to cease its policy of extrajudicial killings. Israel must return to the negotiating table.

PAUL BADJI, Chair of the Committee on the Exercise of the Inalienable Rights of the Palestinian People, said the targeted assassinations of Palestinians, be they leaders or members of Palestinian organizations, had been condemned on many occasions by the international community. The Committee had firmly condemned all extrajudicial executions, and it was with that same energy that it condemned the most recent execution. The Israeli Government, in disregard of international opinion, was continuing its vicious policy. Like all acts of that type, such executions were a clear violation of international law and did not respond to the aspirations of Palestinians or Israelis.

Israel had once again poisoned an already volatile situation by assassinating the leader of Hamas, he said. The Committee once again demanded that Israel end the untold suffering of the Palestinian people and called for the dismantling of the wall of separation, as well as an immediate end to the siege on the Palestinian Authority and its President. The Committee urged both parties to refrain from any action that might aggravate the situation and invited the Quartet to apply all its influence on the parties to implement the Road Map, the only viable option to ensure the security of both parties.

FAYSSAL MEKDAD (Syria) condemned the assassination, saying that when the Council met a month ago, all speakers, including some of Israel's friends, had also condemned the extrajudicial killing of Sheikh Yassin. Some had believed that the Israeli Government would hesitate before committing another such crime. The assassination just perpetrated showed that the Israeli leaders did not heed international humanitarian law, nor respect the international community's will. Israel did not hesitate to use its senseless terrorist force for the realization of its purposes.

He said Israel was the party that had brought terror to the region and that pursued terror with the sole purpose of distracting attention from its actions, including the building of settlements and the racist separation wall. Israel's promotion of its actions as the right to self-defence was nothing more than a promotion of its policy of killing and annexation. Israel's new attempts regarding the right of return represented a grave violation of Council resolutions on the Arab-Israeli conflict and the Palestinian question.

The time had come for the Council to adopt decisive resolutions that would end Israeli war crimes, including it's defiance of international humanitarian law, he said. Was not the Council duty bound to enforce its resolutions? Israel — indebted to the United Nations for its creation — did not respect the United Nations or its resolutions. Comprehensive and just peace could not be settled without the right of return.

RICHARD RYAN (Ireland), speaking on behalf of the European Union and associated States, **condemned both the assassination and the suicide bombing at the Eretz crossing.** The European Union reaffirmed that the Road Map represented the only route to a two-State solution agreed between the parties and resulting in a viable, contiguous, sovereign and independent Palestinian State existing side by side and in peace with an Israel living within recognized and secure borders.

He said the Union would not recognize any change to the pre-1967 borders other than those arrived at by agreement between the parties. The refugee question and the manner in which the right of return might be realized was also a final status issue, as set out in the Road Map. In that context, final status issues were a matter for negotiation and agreement between the parties and must not be prejudged.

The European Union welcomed the prospect of Israel's withdrawal from the Gaza Strip, but such withdrawal should be properly orchestrated with the international community in order to ensure an orderly situation in Gaza, he said. The Union was ready to support the Palestinian Authority in taking responsibility for law and order. The Union urged an end to violence and terrorism, as well as the resumption of a ceasefire embracing all parties and groups. A just, lasting and comprehensive peace must meet the legitimate aspirations of both the Israeli and Palestinian peoples and must include Lebanon and Syria. He called on all States in the region to exert every effort to promote peace and to combat terrorism.

ABDULLAH ALSAIDI (Yemen) said that the heads of Likud were heavily involved in undermining the prospects for peace at a time when the world's gaze was fixed on Iraq. The assassination of al-Rantisi was part of a framework of extrajudicial executions carried out by Israel, taking place at a time when calls were made to Palestinian factions to exercise restraint. Israeli practices in the Palestinian territories were illegal, including those perpetrated in East Jerusalem. Those acts had been condemned by many in the international community, including the Secretary-General. The policy of assassinations by Israel in a frenzied manner dovetailed with its organized campaign to withdraw from Gaza. Israel must be made to respect and implement its duty, in accordance with the Fourth Geneva Convention.

He also emphasized the importance of commitment by all the parties to comply with the Road Map without resorting to unilateral actions, which might endanger the peace process and lead to further instability in the region. In order to put an end to extrajudicial killings, it was clear that the Council must consider seriously the possibility of allowing the International Criminal Court to play a role in the current situation. Therefore, the Council must adopt a firm stand and should have done so on the killing of Sheikh Yassin. The heads of Likud were flouting the will of the international community. He hoped the Council, this time, would adopt a resolution on the situation.

MOHAMED BENNOUNA (Morocco) said the Council was meeting once again to debate the grave situation in the occupied Palestinian territory. The Israeli forces had perpetrated a cowardly act of aggression, which Morocco formally condemned. The international community could not fail to condemn the most recent violation, which could jeopardize the prospects for a negotiated peace. The policy could further aggravate the situation and cause a new cycle of violence.

He urged the international community to shoulder its responsibilities and make every effort to stem the worsening of the situation. It was up to the Council to take a clear stand by condemning the Israeli policy of occupying territories and suppressing those who spoke up against such actions. The strengthening of peace remained the only way of achieving a just and comprehensive settlement in the Middle East, on the basis of relevant council resolutions. Morocco was committed to the Arab peace initiative, which made the principle of land for peace the one and only foundation for a normalization of the situation.

ABOULAZIZ NASSER R. AL-SHAMSI (United Arab Emirates) said that, for the second time in less than a month, the Council was meeting to discuss the latest episode in a series of illegal practices by Israel. The assassination by Israel of the leader of Hamas 26 days after the assassination of the spiritual leader of Hamas not only reflected the Israeli policy of State terror, but also reflected the irresponsible and dangerous approach by Israel aimed at obstructing prospects for peace.

He condemned the assassination and threats to further assassinate Palestinians, which constituted not only a violation of international law, but a war crime that could have been averted had the Council undertaken its responsibility a month ago. The failure of the Council to adopt a decisive position sent the wrong message to the Sharon Government. Once again, he appealed to the international community, especially the Council, to interfere urgently and adopt binding measures to protect the Palestinian people and its leadership and bring Israel into compliance with Council resolutions. He also called on the Council not to be duped by distortions by Israel to justify its actions under the cover of self-defence.

V.K. NAMBIAR (India) said that the targeted killing of Mr. Rantisi was unjustified and unacceptable, and could not be condoned under any circumstances. Such action, following closely after the killing of Sheikh Ahmed Yassin, could only lead to a further deterioration of the situation in the region and escalation of the cycle of violence and counter-violence. India was consistently opposed to all acts of terrorism, including cross-border terrorism. There could be no justification for terrorism in any form and from any source.

"The need of the hour" in West Asia was moderation and restraint, he continued, so as to enable peace negotiations to restart at the earliest. The violence must be halted, and both Israelis and Palestinians should work towards a viable negotiating process aimed at a just, lasting and . . . . by side within secure and recognized boundaries, based on Security Council resolutions 242 (1967), 338 (1973), 1397 (2002)and 1515 (2003).

RASTAM MOHD ISA (Malaysia) said the latest Israeli action, the brutal murder of Mr. Rantisi, would only serve to inflame emotions on the ground. As expected, Palestinians were vowing to take revenge. His country unequivocally condemned extrajudicial executions and reiterated its grave concern over the current developments and continuing deteriorating situation in the occupied Palestinian territory. His Government reaffirmed its support for the efforts of the Quartet and firmly believed that confidence-building played a crucial part in the implementation of the Road Map. He urged the leaders, as well as the Secretary-General, to ensure that Israel abided by the Middle East peace plan.

His country believed that Israel's continued resort to acts of State terrorism was a clear violation of international law, he said. Israel must be held responsible and accountable for the cycle of violence. The international community must not allow Israel to repeatedly act with impunity, in complete disregard of international law and public opinion. He called on the Council to reiterate its demand for the complete cessation of all acts of violence, including all acts of terrorism, military attack, provocation, incitement and destruction. The Council should also reiterate its full endorsement of the Road Map.

AHMED A. OWN (Libya) said the Zionists had committed another crime since the murder of Sheik Yassin. In killing Mr. Rantisi and a number of his associates, they committed an extrajudicial killing when the later were only defending their legitimate right to protect their land and holy places. Supported by the United States administration, the Zionists were conducting State terrorism. He called on the international community to condemn the barbaric, inhuman, criminal act and urged the Council to provide the necessary protection to the children of the defenceless Palestinian people, a people targeted by modern aircraft equipped with the most sophisticated United States technology.

The international community had remained silent for more than five decades, he said. If it continued to flout the legitimate right of the Palestinian people, the Road Map that called for Israel's withdrawal from the occupied Palestinian territories and the creation of a Palestinian State would be a source of frustration for Palestinians and would only fuel violence in the entire region. Support for unilateral measures aimed at retaining the Israeli settlements in the West Bank, preventing the right of return, and the building of a separation wall would prepare the way for further acts of violence.

If Israel was honest in its desire for peace, it must withdraw from the occupied Palestinian territories and restore the legitimate rights of the Palestinian people, he said. The continuation of a unilateral peace would not lead to peace, but to violence and instability. The international community, in general, and the Council, in particular, must exert pressure on Israel to cease its practices and withdraw from the occupied Palestinian territories.

OMER BASHIR MOHAMED MANIS (Sudan) said that in the wake of every heinous crime, the Council was unable to take a decision on the side of what was right, whether it was the separation fence, the exiling of the Palestinian President or State terrorism on the part of Israel. The Sudan condemned the unprecedented organized State terrorism used by Israel.

Now before the Council was a colonizing State that violated all norms of international law and crossed all the lines, he said. The Council could put an end to the episodes of State terror or give Israel another green light to commit further heinous crimes. The world's people were looking to the Council, which only talked of the Road Map and the Quartet and other political machinery. It was necessary to address the killing machinery first.

TAWFEEQ AHMED ALMANSOOR (Bahrain) said the convening of today's meeting had come as a response by the Arab Group to the assassination of the leader of the resistance, Dr. Rantisi. Bahrain condemned extrajudicial killings, which confirmed Israel's failure to respect resolutions of international legitimacy and represented State terror. Assassinations were aimed at killing any effort to revive the Middle East peace process.

He appealed to the international community and the Quartet to put an end to the crimes perpetrated by Israel. Bahrain stood by the Palestinian people in their struggle for the recognition of their inalienable rights. The fact that Israel continued to commit such crimes would lead to further instability, as well as the death of any hope for the realization of peace and security.

Ms. AL-MULLA (Kuwait) said Israel's policy had prompted her to wonder about the results of the international community's efforts to fight global terrorism, in light of the State terrorism practised by Israel. The Council was meeting today to discuss one more extrajudicial execution. Kuwait condemned that assassination, which was an act of terrorism committed by Israel, as well as terrorism in all its forms and manifestations. Israel's crime was part of its illegal practices, which were contrary to international law and attempted to torpedo all efforts to achieve a lasting peace in the region.

She called on the Council to act soundly to put an end to Israel's arrogance and its policy of disregarding international agreements, as well as to protect the Palestinian people. That the Council had been unable to adopt a position after the assassination of Sheikh Yassin had only encouraged Israel to continue its illegal practices, thwarting efforts for peace and fuelling the cycle of violence. The Council must encourage all parties to comply with Council resolutions, the Road Map and the principle of land for peace. That was the only way to build peace.

FAWZI BIN ABDUL MAJEED SHOBOKSHI (Saudi Arabia) said that, because the Council had not condemned the killing last month of Sheik Yassin, Israel had assassinated Dr. Rantisi. The Council had been unable to condemn Israeli terrorism and to adopt a position that reflected the interest of peoples. Where was justice in looking at assassination as the law of the jungle? he asked. How could one explain the passivity of the Council before Israel's arrogance? How long would Israel remain above the law?

Saudi Arabia condemned the policy of assassinations, which would only lead to more violence, with disastrous consequences. He called on the international community to provide protection for the Palestinians. The Council must move immediately to stop Israel, make it implement international law and resume negotiations in accordance with the Road Map.

BONGIWE QWABE (South Africa) expressing outrage and condemnation of the assassination of Mr. Rantisi, said that extrajudicial assassination stood in direct contravention of international law and relevant United Nations conventions and served to further fuel the cycle of violence and counter-violence in the Middle East. He called once again on the Council to intervene in the Middle East. Otherwise, the Council might be seen to be sending a disturbing message — a toleration of extrajudicial killings and other violent actions.

He said Prime Minister Sharon's recently announced unilateral disengagement plan would also weaken any possibility of a negotiated settlement of the conflict, because it would fundamentally compromise the inherent rights of the Palestinian people. The withdrawal from Gaza, welcome as it might be, could not be linked to issues such as the right of return and the status of settlements in the West Bank. His Government condemned suicide bombings, extrajudicial executions, collective punishment and all other forms of violence in the Middle East.

SAMI KRONFOL (Lebanon) said that the extrajudicial assassination by Israel two days ago of the freedom fighter Mr. Rantisi in Gaza was another episode in a series of assassinations perpetrated by Israel against Palestinian leaders. Those assassinations, in addition to other Israeli practices, such as collective punishment and the demolition of homes, were a series of war crimes by the Israeli Government carried out so that it could continue to subjugate a whole people. That flood of crimes was terrorism perpetrated by the Israeli military machine. As for the resistance of the Palestinians to that terrorism, it was legitimate and one of the rights of a long-enslaved people. The fact that some Israeli leaders spoke of the continued pursuit of such crimes made the Council duty bound to act. . . . . any chances for peace. What was strange was that some, who were entrusted with peace in the Middle East, would accept such a trick by Israel. The withdrawal would take hostage the work of the Quartet, kill other peace efforts and prevent the return to the negotiating table. The world was watching to see if the Council would act in the face of Israel's actions.

ALI HACHANI (Tunisia) said the Council was holding its meeting in light of the dangerous circumstances in the occupied Palestinian territories. The international community had condemned the assassination of Sheik Yassin a few weeks ago. Tunisia had condemned the assassination of Mr. Rantisi, as targeting Palestinian leaders would only lead to the escalation of the cycle of violence.

Tunisia followed with great concern the serious developments in the occupied Palestinian territories, due to the continuation of the occupying Power's policy of extrajudicial killings. He called on the international community to provide protection for the Palestinian people and underscored his full conviction that resuming peace negotiations was the only way to bring about a permanent peace in the Middle East.

BISHER AL-KWASAWNEH (Jordan) expressed his Government's strongest condemnation of the assassination of Mr. Rantisi, which had taken place under the direct supervision of the highest authority in the Israeli Government. That crime reminded all of the brutal nature of Israel's policy of extrajudicial executions and would only bring about an escalation of violence. It posed, furthermore, a direct threat to the security and stability of the entire Middle East region.

He called upon Israel to fully desist from inflammatory policies and actions and to work with good faith towards restoring calm and stability in the occupied Palestinian territories. He called on the Council to provide adequate protection to the Palestinian population under occupation in accordance with the Fourth Geneva Convention. He called on all parties and on the United Nations through its different organs to work towards reviving the Middle East peace process on the basis of Council resolutions 242 (1967), 338 (1973), 425 (1978), 1397 (2002), 1435 (2002) and 1515 (2003), the Arab peace initiative and the Road Map.

KOICHI HARAGUCHI (Japan) said the killing of Mr. Rantisi was a thoughtless and unjustifiable act, which gravely impaired the realization of peace. Japan condemned the assassination and urged the Israeli Government to exercise maximum self-restraint in order to prevent further deterioration of the situation. The efforts for peace by both the Israeli and Palestinian sides based on the Road Map were virtually suspended.

He said it was important that the Palestinian side make the maximum efforts in the crackdown of the extremists and produce a tangible result. It was also important that the Israeli withdrawal of settlements in the Gaza Strip be implemented in line with the Road Map. Japan strongly hoped that the Government of Israel and the Palestinian Authority would immediately take initiatives to resume dialogue.

ORLANDO REQUEIJO GUAL (Cuba), condemning the most recent selective assassination by Israel in which Mr. Rantisi and others lost their lives, said Israel's State terrorism remained unchecked. It was only part of Israel's other illegal activities, including the demolition of homes and collective punishment. President Arafat still remained confined and was likely to be one of the possible victims of future extrajudicial executions. The crisis in the Palestinian territories had worsened as the figure of deaths and injured grew, the vast majority of them civilians. Israel must respect international humanitarian law.

Reaffirming his full support for the cause of the Palestinian people and his solidarity with their resistance, he condemned suicide bombings against innocent civilians. Violence and the use of force could not resolve the conflict, which could have been resolved long ago if the Council had acted as it should. Half the times the United States had exercised its veto had been in connection with the Middle East. Of those times, 28 were related to Palestine. To make progress, the United States should suspend financial support and military supplies to Israel, which were used to attack civilians. The extrajudicial executions destroyed any hope for achieving peace, which could not be achieved without an end to the occupation or until the Palestinians exercised their right to self-determination and until all Arab land was returned to pre-1967 borders.

REZLAN ISHAR JENIE (Indonesia) expressed shock at the assassination, which had come less than a month after Israel's murder of Sheikh Yassin, his predecessor. Indonesia unreservedly condemned Israel's reckless disregard for human life, and for the views and sensitivities of the international community. The assassination confirmed Israel's loss of interest in and commitment to the peace process, and it was difficult to see how the killing would enhance Israel's security or promote peace.

Calling on Israel to return to negotiations with the Palestinians and not to put its faith in guns or artificial walls of separation and security, he called on the international community to put the necessary pressure on Israel to return to the negotiating table, and to prevent the country from repeating the pattern of extrajudicial executions. It was only in the faithful implementation of the Road Map that a just and comprehensive settlement of the crisis could be realized.

M. DANESH-YAZDI (Iran) said that, once more, another atrocious crime by the Israeli regime had prompted the Council to hold another emergency public meeting. By committing the latest assassination, Israel had registered on its record yet another serious violation of the Fourth Geneva Convention, which amounted to another war crime. The continued criminal acts, coupled with the recent announcement plans to annex part of the occupied territory — which was akin to "killing" the Road Map - indicated that the Israeli regime had always sought to preclude any just and viable peace in the region, thereby restoring the basic rights of the Palestinians.

He said the Israelis were fully aware that each crime they committed would mark the onset of a new cycle of violence. At a time when the international community needed to pull together to effectively combat global terrorism, the Israeli occupation and the criminal acts to sustain it, including extrajudicial killings, undermined the rule of law and cooperation among nations, which were sine qua none in fighting terrorism. There was no doubt that what Israel had done was a "bonanza for the terrorists", unfortunately enabling global terrorism to grow further. Israeli acts were rendering the situation in the region even more tense and explosive.

The assassinations of Sheikh Yassin and Mr. Rantisi could plunge the region into another round of violence, he said. Those deliberate acts were aimed at defeating any attempt to bring peace to the region. It was very sad that the Council had yet to reach an agreement on the way to prevent Israel from committing its numerous crimes. It was even more unfortunate that a single delegation had continued to prevent that body from pronouncing itself on such an important issue relating to international peace and security in one of the most important and sensitive regions. Council members should recognize the need for decisive action in the face of the new tension in the region and avoid the further paralysis and erosion of its authority.

MAHFOUDH OULD DEDDACH (Mauritania) stressed the inalienable rights of the Palestinian people, including their right to establish an independent State. Any agreement must be based on negotiations with the elected leadership of the Palestinian people. Mauritania demanded an end to the occupation and the unconditional and immediate withdrawal of the Israeli Defence Forces from all the occupied Palestinian territories, as well as a just settlement for Palestinian refugees. The Council must take all necessary action so as not to destroy the principle of land for peace.

Calling on the Council and the Quartet to preserve the inalienable rights of the Palestinian people, he strongly condemned extrajudicial assassinations against the Palestinian leadership, as well as any attempt to make the settlements legitimate and reject the right of return. The Council must take up its responsibilities in accordance with the United Nations Charter.

JOHAN LOVALD (Norway) said that Israel's right to defend itself against terror did not justify the action carried out in Gaza last Saturday. The use of extrajudicial killings was not only contrary to international law, but also counter-productive. The vicious cycle of violence and counter-violence must be broken. All parties must refrain from further acts of aggression.

Norway would welcome a withdrawal of all settlers and the Israeli Defence Force from the Gaza Strip, he said. If implemented in an appropriate manner and consistent with the Road Map, the withdrawal plan announced by Prime Minister Sharon could be an important step forward. Final status issues could only be resolved through negotiations between the parties concerned. Unilateral steps could in no manner prejudge their outcome, nor did unilateral measures modify Israel's responsibilities under Council resolutions, including resolutions 242 (1967) and 338 (1973).

Provided certain conditions were met, the international community would support a withdrawal from Gaza and other occupied territories, he said. It would be vital to ensure that the Palestinian Authority was fully capable of taking on the responsibility of governing the territories from which Israel withdrew. The international community must do its share to ensure that the necessary capabilities were created. However, Israel must also contribute to ensuring a smooth transition, including through the necessary coordination with the Palestinian Authority. Only a negotiated twoState solution based on relevant Council resolutions would ensure lasting peace and stability in the Middle East.

HIGH COMMISSIONER FOR HUMAN RIGHTS URGES COMMISSION TO URGENTLY SEND A MISSION TO THE OCCUPIED PALESTINIAN TERRITORIES

Commission on Human Rights
58th session
2 April 2002
Afternoon

Continues Debate on the Situation in
the Occupied Arab Territories

United Nations High Commissioner for Human Rights Mary Robinson this afternoon called on the Commission on Human Rights to dispatch immediately a visiting mission that would travel to the occupied Palestinian territories and return expeditiously to the Commission with its findings and recommendations.

Mrs. Robinson said that efforts of the international community had not brought an end to the hostilities and Palestinians continued to be subjected to a wide range of human rights violations related to the ongoing occupation. Israel also continued to suffer from the deliberate and planned killings of civilians. The last days had brought a frightening increase in the loss of life.

The High Commissioner also repeated that international observers on the ground could be a deterrent to the violations of human rights in the occupied Palestinian territories and could also promote human security against suicide and other attacks on Israeli civilians.

Following Mrs. Robinson's address, a proposal was made by the Malaysian delegation to hold a special meeting devoted to the present situation of the occupied Arab territories, including Palestine. The Chairman of the Commission, Ambassador Krzysztof Jakubowski of Poland, said that the Bureau of the Commission would meet tomorrow morning at 8 p.m. to discuss the High Commissioner's suggestions and this proposal.

Delegations from Malaysia, Algeria, Pakistan, the United States, Cuba, Canada, China, Sudan, Spain (on behalf of the European Union), Egypt (on behalf of the League of Arab States), Iraq and Australia took the floor to comment on the report of the High Commissioner for Human Rights.

Also this afternoon, as it continued with its debate on the question of the violation of human rights in the occupied Arab territories, including Palestine, the Commission heard statements by numerous non-governmental organizations that expressed concerns over the situation in the area. Many said that Israeli forces in the occupied territories had been violating the Fourth Geneva Convention by attacking civilians. Other speakers condemned the Palestinian suicide bombings that had killed many Israelis.

The following non-governmental organizations delivered statements: the American Association of Jurists; the Arab Lawyers Union; the International Fellowship of Reconciliation; the World Jewish Congress; the American Jewish Committee; Defence of Children International; Nord-Sud XXI; Federacion de Asociaciones de Defensa y Promocion de los Derechos Humanos; the World Muslim Congress; the Palestinian Centre for Human Rights; the International Federation of Human Rights Leagues; the International Commission of Jurists; the International League for the Rights and Liberation of Peoples; the World Federation of Democratic Youth; the International Save the Children Alliance; Caritas Internationalis-International Confederation of Catholic Charities; the Commission of the Churches on International Affairs of the World Council of Churches; the Habitat International Coalition; and Medecins du Monde (International).

Israel, Syria and Palestine exercised their right to reply.

The Commission will reconvene at 10 a.m. on Tuesday, 3 April, to hear statements from visiting dignitaries before holding a closed meeting to deal with communications concerning alleged violations of human rights, under its item 9 (b): procedure established in accordance with Economic, and Social Council resolutions 1503 (XLVII) and 2000/3.

Statements

JAIRO SANCHEZ, of the American Association of Jurists, said the Government of Israel was waging a massive, bloody assault against Palestinians on the pretext of eliminating terrorist enclaves; the situation was complicated by a continuing wave of terrorist assaults. Still, Israeli soldiers were carrying out attacks against civilians using tanks and helicopters; Palestinians ordered to leave their homes often refused, and in that case were fired upon. Houses were destroyed; areas were closed down; the Palestinian leadership was blockaded; missiles had been used against the offices of Yasser Arafat, which had been destroyed. It was clear that as long as it had the support of the United States, Israel would continue to avoid negotiations and to wage war against the Palestinians.

It was sad that Israelis, many of them victims of the Holocaust, would use such repression and violence against other people. The Palestinians had an inalienable right to independence; their intifada was justified under the circumstances. Israel should withdraw its military forces from all territories occupied since 1967.

FAROUK ABU EISSA, of the United Nations High Commissioner for Human Rights, said that the Israeli occupying forces had demonstrated total disregard for the plight and rights of the Palestinian people through air, sea and land bombardment of the civilian population, political arbitrary arrests and raids on refugee camps and installations resulting in the death and injury of thousands of innocent civilians. The Palestinian people were a people under foreign occupation fighting a legitimate struggle for their self-determination. The Arab Lawyers Union also stood fast against any proposed United States military strike against the Iraqi people as such a unilateral strike had no moral or international legal basis to justify it.

JONATHAN SISSON, of International Fellowship of Reconciliation, drew attention to the policy of house demolitions and population expulsion that was being carried out by the Israeli Government against the Palestinian community in clear violation of the Fourth Geneva Convention. The house demolitions in the Rafah refugee camp in Gaza and the expulsion of the Palestinian residents of South Hebron were specific examples of that policy. On 10 January 2002, the Israeli defence forces had carried out a massive demolition operation in the Rafah refugee camps in Gaza. Overnight, at least 58 homes were demolished, as a result of which some 520 people, of whom 300 were children, were made homeless in the dead of winter. On numerous occasions, the Israeli policy of housing demolition had been coupled with the expulsion of the local Palestinian population as was the case in South Hebron. House demolitions and population expulsions were instruments of repression in Israel's long-term policy of occupation, which had assumed the dimension of low-intensity warfare.

MASSIMO PIERI, of the World Jewish Congress, said there was no item on the agenda regarding the violations or gross violations of humanitarian law committed with the complicity of the Palestinian Authority by repeated terrorist actions deliberately directed against Israeli civilians. The term "occupied territories" was a misnomer, as Israel had taken them under control following the 1967 conflict in selfdefence, as defined by article 51 of the UN Charter, following violation of the armistice lines of 1941. East Jerusalem could not be included under the category of "occupied Palestinian territories" for several reasons, including lack of any treaty or instrument of international law that supported the contention that East Jerusalem was Palestinian territory. Withdrawal from territories under Israeli control would take place when the two principles established by Security Council resolution 242 were observed.

The right to self-determination did not include the right to destroy the rights of others. The atrocities committed by Palestinian terrorists during the Easter recess should open the eyes of the Commission, which should condemn such conduct. The Commission furthermore should maintain an impartial, fair position with regard to the Middle East. The World Jewish Congress supported the project entitled "Diversity and Peace" in relation to the Middle East conflict.

ANDREW M. SRULEVITCH, of the American Jewish Committee, said that it was concerned about the abuse of the Commission for political attacks against the State of Israel. Israel should be scrutinized as actions of any government were scrutinized. But Israel should be examined under agenda item 9, like every other State. As serious as the situation was in the Middle East, no justification existed for the current discriminatory treatment. The West Bank and the Gaza were not the only territories which were disputed and the subject of accusations of occupation. Tibet, the Western Sahara and Nagorno-Karabakh were just a few examples of current territorial disputes in which one side had been accused of occupation. In these conflicts and others, there had been civilian victims on both sides and allegations of human rights violations. However, none of the parties of these conflicts had a separate agenda item at the Commission. The Commission paid 30 times more attention to the Arab-Israeli conflict than to other conflicts in the world, to the detriment of other pressing situations. If the Commission was concerned about the most sacred of human rights - the right to life - then item 8 might instead be devoted to the pandemic of AIDS in sub-Saharan Africa.

HANAN ELMASU, of the Defence for Children International, said that the Israeli occupation was an all-encompassing system that consistently, repeatedly and intentionally deprived Palestinian children of their rights. The range of those violations was vast and their occurrence well documented. Since September 2000, over 230 children had been killed, 7,000 wounded, 700 arrested and tens of thousands of others traumatized by the ongoing military attacks against their homes and communities. At least 17 children had been killed as a result of Israel's policy of extrajudicial killing of Palestinian activists. Many of those violations constituted war crimes as they were grave breaches of the Fourth Geneva Convention. It was impossible to say that children were not being targeted when the Israel army was repeatedly attacking civilian areas, particularly when children constituted 53 per cent of the population. Israeli authorities had acknowledged that children as young as 13 years old had been detained. Was the State of Israel's security threatened by a sixth grader? For what purposes were those children blindfolded, handcuffed, detained, and, in many instances, tortured?

MANUELA CLAVIJO, of North-South XXI, also speaking on behalf of the InterAfrican Union on Human Rights, said Israel had been an occupying power right from the beginning and had been using military means to prevent the Palestinian people from achieving their objective of self-determination. Offenses had reached the point of bombing towns with helicopters and firing missiles at civilians. These were war crimes; Israel had signed the relevant international convention as a requirement for admission to the United Nations, but it ignored the significance of its own signature. The Palestinian intifada was legitimate as a measure of self-defence. Kamikaze operations, the weapons of the poor, were the cries of a desperate population. Israel, with support from the West, continued to establish illegal settlements, to repress the Palestinians, to destroy schools, and to commit other human rights violations.

The Commission must call for the establishment of a Palestinian State with Jerusalem as its capital, for the dismantling of the settlements, for compensation to be paid by Israel for offenses committed, and for the trial of Ariel Sharon for war crimes against humanity, among other things.

MIGUEL ANGEL SANCHEZ, of the Federation de Asociaciones de Defensa y Promocion de los Derechos Humanos, said that 53 years had elapsed since Israel was created. Half a century on, Israel was violating UN resolutions and jeopardizing peace and stability in the entire Middle East region. During the past 17 months, Israel had stepped up its repression of the Palestinian people, destroying Palestinian infrastructure and confining the Palestinian people to concentration camps. The international community had demonstrated the lack of effectiveness in seeking a viable solution to the Middle East conflict. It was incomprehensible that the international community was so benevolent to Israel. The time had come for the international community to assume its responsibility and help the Palestinians achieve their freedom and independence. The international community should take strong measures against Israel and force it to implement UN resolutions, in particular Security Council resolutions 242 and 338.

M. AHMAD, of the World Muslim Congress, said that it was difficult, if not impossible, to describe the depth of the tragedy of the suffering of Palestinians. The violations of Palestinian human rights in the occupied territories and their consequent effect on the economic and psychological health of the Palestinian nation were too well known to need recounting. Since the 1967 war, when it seized Palestinian and Arab territories, Israel had been following a deliberate policy of deprivation and dehumanisation towards Palestinians. Israeli settlements on occupied Palestinian land were illegal and in flagrant violation of the Fourth Geneva Convention. Each Israeli settlement on Palestinian land deprived the native Arabs of their water and other resources, which were diverted for the use of the settlers. A recent survey by an NGO called Peace Now had revealed that 34 new Israeli settlements had been built in the West Bank under Ariel Sharon; and 7,000 Israeli settlers controlled 20 per cent of Gaza and 42 per cent of its coast line.

JABR WISHAH, of the Palestinian Centre for Human Rights, speaking on behalf of LAW and the Palestinian Society for Protection of Human Rights and the Environment, said they welcomed the Secretary-General's statement on the illegality of Israel's 35-year colonial military occupation and the Special Rapporteur's conclusion that the occupation was responsible for most of the violations of humanitarian law and human rights in the occupied Palestinian territories. The methods now being used were disproportionate and indiscriminate, and effectively and systematically punished the Palestinian civilian population. This intensification was marked by an increasing perpetration of war crimes. There was an urgent need for international intervention; it was the only way to reduce violence and advance hope for peace.

The Commission must reaffirm the illegality of the occupation; provide immediate independent international protection for Palestinian civilians; facilitate a follow-up mission by the human rights inquiry commission; ensure that all peace negotiations were based on human rights and humanitarian law; call upon the High Contracting Parties to the Fourth Geneva Convention to ensure Israel's respect for the Convention; and call on States to donate to international agencies providing humanitarian aid to Palestinian civilians.

ANTOINE MADELIN, of the International Federation of Human Rights Leagues, said that to date, the Israeli military had demolished at least 520 Palestinian homes in the Gaza Strip and 116 in the West Bank, including East Jerusalem. Since 28 September 2000, 802 Palestinians were reported to have been executed. Medical and humanitarian aid agencies were being prevented from delivering medical care and humanitarian assistance. The closure policy imposed by the Israeli occupation forces had left the Palestinian economy largely bankrupt. Palestinians had been denied or delayed access to work, schools, universities, families and friends, and to clinics and hospitals, even in emergency cases. Approximately 3,000 Palestinians from the territories were currently being detained in jails inside Israel, in breach of the Fourth Geneva Convention. The escalation in grave breaches and other violations of the. . . .

IAN SEIDERMAN, of the International Commission of Jurists, said that the horrific developments in Israel and the occupied Palestinian territories were the direct result of impunity for blatant violations of human rights and international humanitarian law. Attacks directed at Israeli civilians by Palestinian armed groups were clearly war crimes under customary international law, whatever the circumstances. Israel had the right to protect itself from such attacks but any security measures should be consistent with Israel's legal obligations under international human rights and humanitarian law. War crimes could not be halted through the perpetration of other war crimes. **The deliberate use of collective punishment by Israel violated article 33 of the Fourth Geneva Convention and a fundamental principle of the rule of law. Statements by Prime Minister Sharon to "hit" Palestinians until it was "very painful" and "to cause them heavy casualties" had found concrete expression in bombing raids against densely populated civilian areas in the West Bank and Gaza, resulting in significant and heavy loss of innocent life.**

JEAN-PIERRE LAGNAUX, of the International League for the Rights and Liberation of Peoples, said civilian missions made it possible to monitor the situation of the Palestinian people despite Israeli restrictions on journalists. Settlements continued to be established; they were created quickly; bulldozers arrived on short notice, settlers arrived and lived briefly in mobile homes, and the perimeter was protected by soldiers. The settlements were tied together by good roads, while Palestinian settlements were increasingly isolated, causing serious problems for health, education, and commerce. The implantation and extension of settlements was based on the routing of peasants and the destruction of their crops. The original Israel had been established by massacres that had caused Palestinians to flee; now settlements were built by the persecution of helpless people by a powerful army.

To ensure the triumph of law and human rights, the truth of facts had to be respected. The Commission must adopt a resolution prohibiting further recruitment of settlers; supporting establishment of a fully independent Palestinian State, including East Jerusalem; demanding that the United States end its massive support, including military aid, to Israel; and demanding a vast financial reconstruction programme for Palestine, with emphasis on education and sanitation.

JAVIER LABRADA ROSABAL, of the World Federation of Democratic Youth, said that the international community had witnessed a massacre of the Palestinian people by Israel over the past 17 months. To date, more than 1,100 Palestinians had been assassinated, 290 of whom were children, and thousands had been wounded. Many buildings of the Palestinian Authority had been destroyed including schools, hospitals and houses. It was ironic and hypocritical that at a time when a war against terrorism had been declared, nothing or very little was being done against the Israeli Government, which was conducting state terrorism against a people fighting for their right to self-determination. It was inconceivable that Israel was receiving millions of dollars from the United States in economic and financial aid which was being used to commit a genocide of the Palestinian people. Israel was called upon, inter alia, to withdraw from the occupied territories, recognize the right of return of all refugees, implement UN resolutions 242, 338 and 194, and free all Palestinians detained in prisons in Israel. The United Nations was also called upon to send an international protection force to protect the Palestinians from aggressions by the Israeli army.

AHMED MOTALA, of the International Save the Children Alliance, said that his organization was extremely concerned about the impact on children, both Palestinian and Israeli, of the increased violence and conflict in the occupied Palestinian territories and Israel. The Alliance condemned violence that targeted children, whether by suicide bombers or by members of the Israeli security forces. The killing and maiming of children could not be justified. The recent increase in the violence in the occupied Palestinian territories and Israel had had a dramatic and negative impact on the lives of children. It had restricted the movement of Palestinian children; increased their pessimism about their ability to shape their own future; affected their ability to obtain education that was relevant and of reasonable quality; and undermined their development. It was the worsening of the human rights situation of children in Palestine that the Alliance brought to the urgent attention of the Commission. The Alliance urged the Commission, among other things, to request its Special Rapporteur on education to visit the Palestinian territories to investigate the impact of the violence and closures on the right to education on Palestinian children.

ALFONS NOLL, of Caritas Internationalis-International Confederation of Catholic Charities, said a velvet genocide was underway; Palestinians had seen the horrific effects of the work of suicide bombers and other militants on the people and cities of Israel, and some had narrowly escaped injury from such bombings; meanwhile Israeli authorities carried out a wide range of violations of Palestinians' basic human rights, including the demolition of houses, the uprooting of trees, attacks with missiles, helicopters, bombers and tanks, indiscriminate shootings at checkpoints, and harassment and obstruction of ambulances. The international community perhaps was seeing with one eye — half the story, half the picture. There were resolutions but no implementation.

There should be international observers dispatched to Palestine; there should be a freeze on settlements on confiscated Palestinian land; there should be an agreement on Jerusalem negotiated between Palestine and Israel in accordance with UN resolutions; there should be a just solution to the refugee problem; and there should be greater involvement by the international community — since it had played a role in creating this problem, it should shoulder responsibility for resolving the decades-old crisis.

AEXANDROS KARIDES, of the World-Council-of-Churches, said that it was with deep concern that the **Council noted the unprecedented escalation of violence and continued grave breaches of the Geneva Convention by Israel, in the form of willful killing and causing of great suffering and serious injury, torture and inhuman punishments, including the bombing and shelling of civilian neighbourhoods, the extensive destruction of agricultural land and homes and the appropriation of property. Moreover, the severe restrictions on the freedom of movement had had a devastating socio-economic effect on the Palestinian population. Even more distressing was the emergence of new patterns of abuses such as the Israeli military reoccupation of Palestinian cities, incursions into refugee camps, mass arbitrary detentions of civilians under degrading circumstances and the deadly attacks on medical and rescue staff.** The attacks on Israeli unarmed civilians were deplorable. The victims of violence on both sides were paying a high price for the policy of occupation and dispossession. The occupation and the impunity enjoyed by Israel . . . .

JOSEPH SCHECHLA, of the Habitat International Coalition, recalled that on 5 March 2002 and before the Israeli Parliament, the Prime Minister had explained his strategy in the occupied Palestinian territories, saying that the aim was to increase the losses on the other side; and that only after they had been battered would Israel be able to conduct talks. That statement had come to characterize the general policy of the Israeli occupation forces as was especially evident at the beginning of March when occupied Palestine had experienced a dramatic upsurge of destruction, bloodshed and trauma. Repeated sieges and closure of villages, towns, and cities constituted a form of collective punishment and a violation of international law. The loss of income to the territories since September 2000 had been estimated at between 2.5 and 3.2 billion dollars. Those closures and undisciplined military action by Israel had impaired economic life and freedom of movement, preventing basic foodstuffs, medicines and even ambulances from moving in and out of municipalities. Dozens of sick or injured Palestinians, as well as pregnant mothers and their newborns, had died in ambulances held up at various checkpoints.

GRACIELA ROBERT, of Medecins du Monde, said the organization had had to partially evacuate its teams from Gaza last week because of renewed violence; they had resumed work this week. Medecins du Monde teams saw first hand the effects of the violence on children. One child had awakened from a failed operation to remove a shell from her skull; a tank had stopped outside her school and started shooting as children were going into class; a 12-year-old girl next to this one had died. The psychological trauma suffered by surviving children was intense. Another child had been seriously burned by a mine on his hands, arms, back and face; he now lived in constant fear and constantly relived his injury; it took his parents hours on foot to reach the hospital to visit him because of Israeli land closures.

Doctors found these things unbearable. The unacceptable injustice of this conflict ould not continue. Medical personnel had been targeted by the Israeli army. And Israeli civilians also were suffering. Civilians on both sides must be protected; the parties to the conflict must not forget this.

MARY ROBINSON, the United Nations High Commissioner for Human Rights, that two weeks ago, she had regretted that efforts of the international community had not brought an end to the hostilities and that **Palestinians continued to be subjected to a wide range of human rights violations related to the ongoing occupation. Israel had also continued to suffer from the deliberate and planned killings of civilians. Early on 29 March, the Israeli Defence Forces (IDF) had occupied Ramallah. On 1 April, the IDF took control of Beit Jala, Qalqilya and Tulkarem. On 2 April the IDF invaded Bethlehem. Movement in all these areas was extremely dangerous due to the operation of IDF tanks and snipers. The last days had brought a frightening increase in the loss of life**. Israeli authorities reported that in the midst of the Passover holiday, 22 people were killed and 140 injured in a suicide bombing in the coastal city of Netanya. Again on 31 March, 14 people were killed and over 40 injured in a bombing in Haifa. As of 5 p.m. on 1 April, 38 Palestinians had been killed and at least 60 persons had been injured. These were tragic examples of a spiral of violence and arbitrary deprivation of life that must be ended.

The High Commissioner said that movement in all the areas of military operations was extremely dangerous. Residents were unable to move about in the streets. The ICRC, the Palestinian Red Crescent Society and other medical personnel, human rights defenders and journalists had all been restricted from carrying out their duties. Some of these personnel had been fired upon and others had been arrested. UNRWA was facing extreme difficulties in operating in the occupied Palestinian territories and responding to the current crisis. On the ground the IDF had often been refusing access to UNRWA staff. Ambulances had been reportedly stopped and prevented from providing assistance.

Mrs. Robinson said that water and electricity systems had been seriously damaged in Ramallah as a result of the recent military operations. Yasser Arafat's headquarters in Ramallah had also had their water and electricity cut after tank movements ruptured lines. According to the Foreign Press Association, since 30 March the IDF had been preventing journalists from entering Ramallah. On 29 March, the IDF took over a building used by Palestinian and foreign media in the city, forcing organizations to abandon the building. Several journalists were reported wounded. Offices of nongovernmental organizations (NGOs), including human rights NGOs, had also reportedly been raided.

Mrs. Robinson said that in her report to the Commission on her visit to the region in 2000, she had asked that the feasibility of establishing an international monitoring presence be explored. That proposal should now be implemented. International observers on the ground could be a deterrent to the violations of human rights in the occupied Palestinian territories and could also promote human security against suicide and other attacks on Israeli civilians.

The High Commissioner said that these events were taking place at the very time when the Commission was in session. That must surely place an urgent duty on the Commission. In the past, she had had the occasion to call for international observers to be stationed in the occupied territories. The Commission should consider dispatching immediately a visiting mission that would travel to the area and return expeditiously to the Commission with its findings and recommendations. Surely the protection of human rights required such a step as a very minimum. She called the Commission to conscience and invited it to let conscience move in this situation taking place before their eyes.

NABIL RAMLAWI (Palestine) said Palestine was grateful for the statement by the High Commissioner; she had gotten rid of any ambiguity that might have been in the minds of people at the Commission. It was clear that grave, serious violations were going on in the occupied Palestinian territories. In view of the proposals made by the High Commissioner, he proposed that tomorrow a special meeting be held to discuss the current situation in the occupied territories and the grave violations of human rights occurring there.

YAAKOV LEVY.(Israel) said that the High Commissioner should have also listened to the views of the other side. She should have spoken not only to her compatriots but also to Israelis. The suicide bombing attacks on restaurants and other terrorist attacks had been incited by the Palestinian Authority led by Yasser Arafat and his supporters. The compilation of the report should have included the Israeli side, particularly those who were not able to go out of their houses due to the terrorist acts of the Palestinians.

COMMISSION ON HUMAN RIGHTS ADOPTS RESOLUTIONS ON SITUATION IN OCCUPIED ARAB TERRITORIES

Commission on Human Rights
59th session
15 April 2003
Morning

The Commission on Human Rights adopted resolutions this morning calling **for Israel to cease repressive measures in the occupied Syrian Golan; end human rights abuses and withdraw from Palestinian territories occupied since 1967; and halt the construction of settlements in the occupied Arab territories**. The three measures, adopted by roll-call votes, were tabled under the Commission's agenda item on the "question of the violation of human rights in the occupied Arab territories, including Palestine".

In a resolution on human rights in the occupied Syrian Golan, adopted by a roll-call vote of 31 in favour and 1 against, with 21 abstentions, the **Commission called upon Israel to desist from changing the physical character, demographic composition, institutional structure and legal status of the occupied Syrian Golan**, and emphasized that the displaced persons of the population must be allowed to return to their homes and to recover their properties; and determined that all legislative and administrative measures and actions taken or to be taken by Israel that purported to alter the character and legal status of the occupied Syrian Golan were null and void.

The lone vote against the resolution was cast by the United States.

A Representative of Israel said Israel had come into possession of the Golan Heights in self-defense against a war initiated by neighbouring Arab countries, that Israel had been negotiating with Syria to reach a peaceful solution to outstanding problems, including the issue of the Golan Heights, and that the resolution was one-sided.

A Representative of the Syrian Arab Republic said Syria wanted to negotiate with Israel, but Israel wanted both peace and the land it had occupied, and should instead manifest its real need for peace.

In a resolution on the question of the violation of human rights in the occupied Arab territories, including Palestine, adopted by a roll-call vote of 33 in favour and 5 against, with 15 abstentions, the Commission among other things reaffirmed the legitimate right of the Palestinian people to resist the

Israeli occupation in order to free their land and be able to exercise their right to self-determination; strongly condemned the violations by the Israeli occupation authorities of human rights in the territory, including East Jerusalem; the Israeli occupation of the Palestinian territory; the war launched by the Israeli army against Palestinian towns and camps which had so far resulted in the deaths of hundreds of Palestinians, including women and children; and the practice of "liquidation" or "extrajudicial executions" carried out by the Israeli army against Palestinians.

A Representative of Israel said that if the resolution really aimed to end violence, it would have included a clear and unequivocal demand for the Palestinian leadership to cease and desist from all acts of violence and would have called upon their followers, including their paramilitary militia groups and security forces, to end the violent armed attacks and suicide terrorist bombings against Israelis that they had initiated in September 2000.

A Representative of Palestine said the situation in the occupied territories had deteriorated under increased military action by Israel and that Israel, through its actions, was practicing what amounted to State terrorism.

In a resolution on Israeli settlements in the occupied Arab territories, adopted by a roll-call vote of 50 in favour and 1 against, with 2 abstentions, the Commission expressed grave concern at continuing Israeli settlement activities, including the illegal installation of settlers in the occupied territories and related activities, such as the expansion of settlements, the expulsion of Palestinians and the construction of bypass roads, which changed the physical character and demographic composition of the occupied territories, including East Jerusalem. The resolution said settlements were a major obstacle to peace and to the creation of an independent, viable, sovereign and democratic Palestinian State.

The United States cast the dissenting vote.

The Representative of Israel said the issue of settlements was one of those difficult issues left to be negotiated with all outstanding issues during permanent status negotiations between Israelis and Palestinians, and the resolution was not about settlements at all, but rather dealt with political and non-human-rights matters under the guise of a discussion of settlements.

The Representative of Palestine said settlements were yet another phase of the Israeli occupation and could not be negotiated as they constituted a war crime and must be dismantled for the sake of a permanent peace.

The Commission also continued general debate this morning on its remaining agenda items. These cover the topics of specific groups and individuals; the report of the Sub-Commission on the Promotion and Protection of Human Rights; the promotion and protection of human rights; advisory services and technical cooperation in the field of human rights; and rationalization of the work of the Commission.

Providing statements were Representatives of Algeria, Pakistan, Syrian Arab Republic, Sri Lanka, Finland, Paraguay (on behalf of the MERCOSUR countries),

Paraguay (national statement), Uruguay, New Zealand, Cameroon, Thailand, Armenia, and Libyan Arab Jamahiriya.

The Commission will reconvene at 3 p.m. to continue its open debate on remaining agenda items.

Action on Resolutions on Question of the Violation of Human Rights in the Occupied Arab Territories, including Palestine

In a resolution (E/CN.4/2003/L.3) on human rights in the occupied Syrian Golan, adopted by a roll-call vote of **31 in favour and I against**, with 21 abstentions, the Commission called upon Israel, the occupying power, to comply with the relevant resolutions of the General Assembly and Security Council, particularly resolution 497 (1981) in which the Council decided that the Israeli decision to impose its laws, jurisdiction and administration on the occupied Syrian Golan was null and void and without international legal effect; called upon Israel to desist from changing the physical character, demographic composition, institutional structure and legal status of the occupied Syrian Golan, and emphasized that the displaced persons of the population must be allowed to return to their homes and to recover their properties; called upon Israel to desist from imposing Israeli citizenship and Israeli identity cards on the Syrian citizens in the occupied Golan and to desist from its repressive measures against them; determined that all legislative and administrative measures and actions taken or to be taken by Israel that purported to alter the character and legal status of the occupied Syrian Golan were null and void, constituted a flagrant violation of international law and of the Geneva Conventions, and had no legal effect; called upon member States not to recognize any of the legislative or administrative measures referred to above; and requested the Secretary-General to bring the present resolution to the attention to all Governments and other relevant organizations.

The results were as follows:

In favour (31): Algeria, Argentina, Armenia, Bahrain, Brazil, Chile, China, Cuba, Democratic Republic of the Congo, Gabon, India, Kenya, Libyan Arab Jamahiriya, Malaysia, Mexico, Pakistan, Paraguay, Russian Federation, Saudi Arabia, Senegal, Sierra Leone, South Africa, Sri Lanka, Sudan, Swaziland, Syrian Arab Republic, Togo, Uganda, Venezuela, Viet Nam, and Zimbabwe.

Against (1): United States.

Abstentions (21): Australia, Austria, Belgium, Burkina Faso, Cameroon, Canada, Costa Rica, Croatia, France, Germany, Guatemala, Ireland, Japan, Peru, Poland, Republic of Korea, Sweden, Thailand, Ukraine, United Kingdom, and Uruguay.

A Representative of Israel, speaking before the vote, said the Commission must remember how Israel came into possession of the Golan Heights. It was in selfdefense against a war initiated by neighbouring Arab countries. Syria lost the war, which she started in 1967, and lost that territory. In recent years, Israel had been negotiating with Syria, attempting to reach a peaceful solution to outstandingproblems including the issue of the Golan Heights. An agreement was almost reached several years ago in a famous meeting between the late President Assad and US President Bill Clinton. This unique opportunity was lost because of Mr. Assad's negative reply to the Israeli proposal. Israel was still committed to negotiating a peace settlement with Syria.

Passing one-sided resolutions that determined the future of one of the outstanding issues, i.e. the Golan Heights, prejudged the outcome of these negotiations and created a disincentive for the Syrians to return to the negotiating table. Israel also called on Syria to close the offices of ten major terrorist organizations in Damascus and to arrest the leaders of these organizations. Syria should also provide information on the whereabouts of three Israeli soldiers who had been missing for 21 years. Israel called on members of the Commission to vote against draft resolution L.3.

A Representative of the Syrian Arab Republic said things seemed to be going upsidedown with Israel accusing its victims of not wanting peace. It would take courage to say that Israel was the aggressor and wished to come to the negotiating table. On the basis of United Nations resolutions, Syria wanted to negotiate with Israel. But Israel wanted both peace and the land it had occupied. It took courage not to expel people in the Golan from their land; it took courage not to kill Palestinians in the occupied territories; and it should be courageous to accept the Arab peace proposal, which aimed at settling the situation in peaceful manner. Israel should manifest its real need for peace. It had killed Egyptian prisoners of war; it had shot down civilian planes; and it continued to kill people in the region. Syria called on Commission members to vote for the resolution.

A Representative of the United States, explaining the country's vote before the vote, said the resolution on the Syrian Golan was another completely one-sided text containing biased and unwarranted criticism aimed at Israel. Its adoption would in no way move the Commission any closer to resolving the status of the Syrian Golan or improving the lives of those individuals resident there. The goal of the United States was a comprehensive peace with security for all States of the region. The United States had not forgotten that Israel still faced hostility from two of its neighbors, Syria and Lebanon. Direct negotiations between the parties were the only viable way to reach a lasting solution to the Arab-Israeli conflict. This resolution on the Syrian Golan again reflected the overriding bias within the Commission on the question of Israel.

One could not but notice that the Arab-Israeli situation was the only regional problem to be the sole subject of an entire item on the Commission's agenda, when it should really fall under item 9. Only a grave distortion of judgment about the relative gravity of human rights abuses worldwide would account for such disproportionate attention by the Commission. The Commission's approach to this matter detracted from its essential role of addressing serious human rights abuses wherever they might occur. The United States urged others to join in rejecting the Commission's biased approach by voting against this resolution.

A Representative of Canada said that while Canada agreed with some elements contained in the resolution, there were others which it could not support. Canada

Israeli control over the territories occupied in 1967. Canada also supported the concept that the peace process must be based on Security Council resolutions 242 and 338. However, the resolution provided neither the full context nor a balanced assessment of the situation of the region. For this reason, Canada would abstain.

A Representative of Guatemala said the delegation was concerned by the wording of some of the paragraphs in the draft resolution. It was of the view that the problem of occupation should be dealt with by the Security Council and not by the Commission. The human rights violations of occupied people were a subject to be dealt with by the Security Council or other United Nations bodies. The Commission should devote its attention to human rights violations in other States. The Guatemalan delegation would abstain in the vote on draft resolution L.3.

In a resolution (E/CN.4/2003/L.12) on the question of the violation of human rights in the occupied Arab territories, including Palestine, adopted by a roll-call vote of 33 in favour and 5 against, with 15 abstentions,

the Commission **reaffirmed the legitimate right of the Palestinian people to resist the Israeli occupation in order to free their land** and be able to exercise their right to self-determination; strongly condemned once more the violations by the Israeli occupation authorities of human rights in the territory, including East Jerusalem;

the Israeli occupation of the Palestinian territory; the war launched by the Israeli army against Palestinian towns and camps which had so far resulted in the deaths of hundreds of Palestinians, including women and children; the practice of "liquidation" or "extrajudicial executions" carried out by the Israeli army against Palestinians;

the establishment of Israeli settlements and other related activities in the occupied Palestinian territory; the expropriation of Palestinian homes in Jerusalem and Hebron, the revocation of identity cards of the citizens of East Jerusalem, and the imposition of fabricated and exorbitant taxes with the aim of driving Palestinian citizens of Jerusalem out of their homes, and called upon the Government of Israel to put an end immediately to these practices;

condemned the use of torture against Palestinians during interrogation; the offensives of the Israeli army of occupation on ambulances and paramedical personnel and the practice of preventing ambulances and vehicles of the International Committee of the Red Cross from reaching the wounded in order to transport them to hospital;

expressed grave concern at the deterioration of the human rights and humanitarian situation in the occupied Palestinian territory, and particularly at the acts of mass killing perpetrated by the Israeli occupying authorities against the Palestinian people; at the military siege imposed on the Palestinian territory and the isolation of Palestinian towns and villages; at the restriction of movement imposed on Chairman Yasser Arafat by the Israeli occupation authorities; at the massive arrests conducted by the Israeli occupying authorities against about 15,000 Palestinians, without trail and without any criminal charges having been brought against them; affirmed anew that the demolition by the Israeli occupying forces of at least 30,000 Palestinian houses was a grave violation of articles 33 and 53 of the Fourth Geneva Convention;

that the Fourth Geneva Convention was applicable to the Palestinian territory occupied by Israel since 1967, and any change in the geographical, demographic and institutional status of the city of East Jerusalem from its status prior to the June 1967 war to be illegal and void; called once again upon Israel to desist from all forms of violation of human rights in the occupied Palestinian territory and to withdraw from the territory occupied since 1967; and called upon the relevant United Nations organs urgently to consider the best ways to . . . .

The results were as follows:

In favour (33): Algeria, Argentina, Armenia, Bahrain, Brazil, Burkina Faso, Chile, China, Cuba, Democratic Republic of the Congo, Gabon, India, Kenya, Libyan Arab Jamahiriya, Malaysia, Pakistan, Republic of Korea, Russian Federation, Saudi Arabia, Senegal, Sierra Leone, South Africa, Sri Lanka, Sudan, Swaziland, Syrian Arab Republic, Thailand, Togo, Uganda, Ukraine, Venezuela, Viet Nam, and Zimbabwe.

Against (5): Australia, Canada, Germany, Peru, and United States.

Abstentions (15): Austria, Belgium, Cameroon, Costa Rica, Croatia, France, Guatemala, Ireland, Japan, Mexico, Paraguay, Poland, Sweden, United Kingdom, and Uruguay.

A Representative of Israel said the wording and implications of the text of L. 12 contributed neither to the advancement of human rights nor to the cessation of violence in the area; nor would L.12 contribute to peace and security through a return to the negotiating table. Were this draft text prepared with the aim of ending violence, it would have included a clear and unequivocal demand for the Palestinian leadership to cease and desist from all acts of violence and would have called upon their followers, including their paramilitary militia groups and security forces, to end the violent armed attacks and suicide terrorist bombings against Israelis that they had initiated in September 2000. Were the authors of this draft resolution committed to ending incitement, hatred and violence, they would call upon the Palestinian leadership, media, the preachers in the mosques, in Gaza and the West Bank, to end their anti-Israeli and anti-Jewish campaign and their rhetoric of hatred. The text before the Commission was completely one-sided and politicized. It was replete with unsubstantiated accusations against Israel, and Israel alone, thus rendering the resolution meaningless.. . .

Whatever the item on the agenda, item 8, item 9, development, housing, whether it related to the Palestinian-Israeli conflict or not, Israel was singled out for different treatment and blamed for all the failures of the Palestinians. Israel suggested to some of the speakers who chose Israel as a scapegoat for the failures of the Palestinian Authority to protect human rights and to deliver humanitarian assistance and social services to their people to pause for a moment of introspection. Funds allocated to the Palestinian Authority were misappropriated. A conscious decision of certain Arab States and of the Palestinian leadership was to perpetuate the plight of those Palestinians who had become refugees in 1948 and their descendent by keeping them in refugee camps as political pawns and agents of incitement to be used against Israel in public, such as in the Commission. If the countries represented in the Commission by such eloquent speakers were really concerned with the plight of these refugees, would they have kept them and their descendents in camps for 55 years?

A Representative of Palestine said the Commission was debating the deterioration of the situation in Palestine while the Israeli delegation was talking the opposite. The army redeployed in 1995. During the Gulf War, 24 hour curfews were imposed for lengthy periods. The IDF also often imposed curfews when carrying out searches and arrests.

1993 - 2000: The peace process years

In 1994 the Israeli military government started to transfer various civil functions to the newly created PA. The 1995 Oslo II Agreement identified the PA's functions and defined the intricate "zoning" of the West Bank and the Gaza Strip that established its interim jurisdiction. However, Israel retained ultimate and effective control of all aspects of Palestinians' movement, both internally and across international . . . .

The situation in the occupied territory had deteriorated with the increased military action by Israel; and the number of martyrs had been increased with many Palestinians being killed. Many villages had been isolated by Israel measures of blockade. Israel, through its actions, had practiced what amounted to State terrorism. The actions taken by Israel had been in violation of all relevant international norms. The occupation itself, let alone the human rights violations of the occupied people, was a violation of international law. The Israel authorities were retreating more and more from peace negotiations.

Palestine once again called on the Commission to adopt draft resolution L.12.

A Representative of the United States said the United States was deeply concerned about violence and terrorist activities in Israel, the West Bank and Gaza and about the human rights violations that had accompanied that violence. However, it was clear that Israel was not responsible for all the ills plaguing the people in the region. Unfortunately, resolution L. 12 failed to recognize that simple fact. This resolution simply ignored the fact that Israeli actions took place in the context of Palestinian terrorist attacks against Israeli civilians. Among the most egregious provisions in all the resolutions considered under this agenda item was the language on right to resistance, which attempted to justify the use of terrorism by Palestinians against Israelis.

The United States found any act of terrorism morally unjustifiable. Palestinian suicide bombers murdered innocent Israeli men, women and children, and these actions must be condemned in the strongest terms. Adoption of such a resolution would be contrary to the very concept of human rights. The actions of this Commission appeared divorced from reality and furthered reduced the credibility of the Commission and increased the mistrust and fear that fueled the region's hatred. The United States would call for a vote and would oppose this resolution.

A Representative of Canada said Canada was deeply concerned about human rights in the Palestinian territories and had consistently called on Israel to comply with its obligations under international law. However, this resolution contributed neither to an improvement of the situation on the ground not towards a solution of the conflict. It contained unacceptable and often inflammatory language directed exclusively at one party to the conflict. The failure of the resolution to condemn all acts of violence, particularly in the context of suicide bombings targeting Israeli civilians, was a serious oversight which rendered the resolution fundamentally unacceptable. Suicide bombings, rocket attacks and other actions intended to harm civilians and sow fear among the civilian population were human rights violations deeply repugnant to the Commission's core values. No claim could ever justify these crimes. For these reasons, Canada would vote against resolution L.12.

A Representative of Guatemala said the delegation was concerned by the pertinence of a resolution that would address the protection of the human rights of the people affected by Israeli occupation of Arab territories. The political character of the occupation should be addressed by other United Nations bodies rather than by the Commission. The resolution also should take into consideration the suffering of both peoples affected by the conflict. Guatemala would abstain from the vote on draft resolution . . . .

In a resolution (E/CN.4/2003/L. 18) on **Israeli settlements in the occupied Arab territories, adopted by a roll-call vote of 50 in favour and 1 against**, with 2 abstentions,

the **Commission called upon the Israeli Government to cooperate with the Special Rapporteur on the situation of human rights in the Palestinian territories occupied since 1967;**

expressed grave concern at the continuation, at an escalated level, of the Israeli-Palestinian conflict; at the continuing Israeli settlement activities, including the illegal installation of settlers in the occupied territories and related activities, such as the expansion of settlements, the expulsion of Palestinians and the construction of bypass roads, which changed the physical character and demographic composition of the occupied territories, including East Jerusalem, as settlements were a major obstacle to peace and to the creation of an independent, viable, sovereign and democratic Palestinian State;

strongly condemned all acts of violence, including indiscriminate terrorist attacks killing and injuring civilians, provocation, incitement and destruction;

expressed concern at the closures of and within the Palestinian territories and the restriction of the freedom of movement of Palestinians;

urged the Government of Israel to comply fully with previous Commission resolutions on the subject of the settlements; to reverse its settlement policy; to prevent any new installation of settlers; to stop the construction of the so-called security fence in the Palestinian territories; to implement the recommendations regarding the settlements made by the High Commissioner for Human Rights; to take and implement serious measures with the aim of preventing illegal acts of violence by Israeli settlers, and other measures to guarantee the safety and protection of Palestinian civilians in the occupied territories;

and urged the parties to cooperate in the early and unconditional implementation, without modifications, of the road map endorsed by the Quartet with the aim of resuming negotiations on a political settlement.

The results were as follows:

In favour (50): Algeria, **Argentina**, Armenia, Austria, Bahrain, **Belgium, Brazil**, Burkina Faso, Cameroon, **Canada, Chile, China**, Croatia, Cuba, Democratic Republic of the Congo, **France**, Gabon, **Germany, Guatemala, India, Ireland, Japan**, Kenya, Libyan Arab Jamahiriya, Malaysia, **Mexico**, Pakistan, Paraguay, Peru, Poland, **Republic of Korea, Russian Federation**, Saudi Arabia, Senegal, Sierra Leone, South Africa, Sri Lanka, Sudan, Swaziland, **Sweden**, Syrian Arab Republic, Thailand, Togo, Uganda, Ukraine, **United Kingdom, Uruguay**, Venezuela, Viet Nam, and Zimbabwe.

Against (1): United States.

Abstentions (2): Australia, and Costa Rica.

A Representative of Israel said the issue of settlements was one of those difficult issues left to be negotiated with all outstanding issues during permanent status negotiations between Israelis and Palestinians. This year, the resolution L. 18 on settlements was not about settlements at all. Rather, it dealt with political and nonhuman-rights matters under the guise of a discussion of settlements.

This resolution criticized the security fence, a defensive measure which Israel had felt bound to introduce because of the continuous wave of violence, the infiltration of terrorists into Israel across the pre-1967 borders, in order to place bombs and dynamite charges. In the absence of any significant counteraction by the Palestinian Authority, Israel had no choice but to establish a defensive mechanism in the form of a security fence. Prior to the current wave of violence, there was no need for restrictions on freedom of movement. What necessitated these defensive measures to protect the right to life of Israeli civilians was the violence imposed upon Israel by a conscious decision of the Palestinian Authority.

A Representative of Palestine said settlements were yet another phase of occupation. It was a military phase since all Israeli settlers in areas implanted in Palestinian territories were military and armed. Settlements had been referred to in international law as a crime of war. The first protocol to the Geneva Conventions reiterated this fact in its article 85. Israel wanted this issue to be discussed and negotiated. Settlements could not be negotiated, they constituted a war crime and must be dismantled for the sake of a permanent peace.

The draft resolution before the Commission included something new compared to previous sessions. In operative paragraph 3 b, it referred to the dismantlement of settlements in order to achieve peace. It was a very important element and a key issue for a long-lasting peace. Operative paragraph 4 stressed the need to adhere to the road map for peace. The Commission was suggesting the acceptance of the road map without amendments, as opposed to the 19 amendments previously suggested by Israel. Palestine stood behind this draft resolution and wished to be a co-sponsor.

A Representative of the United States said resolution L. 18 was inconsistent with the joint statement of the Quartet and the Road Map. It failed to recognize that all sides had responsibilities if the peace process was to move forward. It never once cited the obligations and responsibilities of the Palestinians themselves or criticized those who harboured Palestinian terrorist groups and offered support for their activities. Reducing terrorism and enhancing the security of all parties was something both parties must do.

A Representative of Canada said Israeli settlement activities undermined the hopes of Palestinians and prejudiced the prospects for a fair-minded peace. Canada considered those activities to be contrary to international law and an obstacle to the establishment of a viable Palestinian State. Israel should freeze all settlement activities. Canada would vote in favour of draft resolution L.18.

A Representative of Australia said Australia regarded Israeli settlements as an obstacle to long-standing peace. However, Australia would abstain in the vote on draft resolution L. 18 since the draft resolution did not condemn in equal terms all acts of violence.

A Representative of Algeria said Algeria would vote in favour of draft resolution L. 18. It welcomed it as being one of the most positive texts on the situation in the Middle East. It was clearly stated that the two international Covenants were being violated by the establishment of settlements in the occupied territories. Every day members of the Israeli Government called for the deportation of the Palestinian people and this was also referred to in the text of the European Union. Algeria noted that unfortunately it could not cosponsor the resolution since Paragraph 4 mentioned the Road Map initiative, which Algeria was not familiarized with since it had not read the text of that initiative.

A Representative of Argentina said Argentina would vote in favour of draft resolution L. 18 because of the country's concern about the deteriorating situation in the region. The fact that Argentina supported the resolution should not be interpreted as not condemning all terrorist activities. Argentina supported the proposition that Palestinians and Israelis live in peace within determined territories as two States.

A Representative of Ireland, speaking on behalf of the European Union, explained that the EU had not been able to support resolution on L.3 on the Syrian Golan since a stronger focus was needed on the human rights issue. Concerning resolution L. 12, the European Union was highly disturbed by the on-going cycle of violence, settlements and collective punishments in the occupied Palestinian territories. Israel bore the full responsibility for sanctioning such human rights violations.

At the same time, the Palestinian suicide bombings continued. These acts must be unequivocally condemned and the Palestinian Authority bore the responsibility for preventing such violations of human rights. Whilst the resolution condemned terrorism indirectly, the language of the text was not strong enough. In addition, parts of the language were not appropriate for the Commission.

A Representative of the Syrian Arab Republic said Syria had voted in favour of resolution L. 18 because the text emphasized the illegitimate character of the Israeli occupation of all Arab territories. Syria noted that operative paragraph 4 made reference to the Road Map. Syria did not know what the content of the Road Map was and did not know whether the Road Map was consistent with the relevant Security Council Resolutions and the Madrid Conference for peace in the Middle East based on the principle of land for peace.

A Representative of Brazil said Brazil had supported the resolution on the Syrian Golan to express Brazil's support for the thrust of the draft, in particular for the need to resume peace talks for the establishment of a just and comprehensive peace in the region. However, Brazil wished to stress the position of the Brazilian Government that the frontiers between Israel and Syria were a matter of negotiation between both parties, on the basis of the parameters established by Security Council resolution 242.

Press Release

Fifty-fifth General Assembly
Plenary
78th Meeting (AM)
1 December 2000

The General Assembly this morning adopted six resolutions by recorded vote: - two on the situation in the Middle East and - four on the question of Palestine as it concluded its consideration of those items.

By the terms of a resolution on Jerusalem, adopted with 145 Member States voting in favour, 1 against (Israel) and 5 abstentions (Angola, Federated States of Micronesia, Marshall Islands, Nauru, United States), **the Assembly determined that the decision of Israel to impose its laws, jurisdiction and administration on the Holy City of Jerusalem was illegal** and, therefore, null and void. The Assembly also deplored the transfer by some States of their diplomatic missions to Jerusalem in violation of Security Council resolution 478 (1980). (See Annex I.)

With 96 voting in favour, 2 against (Israel, United States), and 55 abstaining (see Annex II), the Assembly adopted a resolution on the Syrian Golan, by the terms of which it declared that Israel had failed so far to comply with Security Council resolution 497 (1981) and that the Israeli decision of 14 December 1981 to impose its laws, jurisdiction and administration on the occupied Syrian Golan was null and void, and had no validity whatsoever. The Assembly called upon Israel to resume the talks on the Syrian and Lebanese tracks and to respect the commitments and undertakings reached during previous talks. It also demanded that Israel withdraw from all the occupied Syrian Golan to the line of 4 June 1967.

In action on the question of Palestine, the Assembly adopted a resolution on the Committee on the Exercise of the Inalienable Rights of the Palestinian People, in a recorded vote of 106 in favour, 2 against (Israel, United States), and 48 abstentions (see Annex III). By that resolution, the Assembly authorized the Committee to continue to exert all efforts to promote the exercise of the inali-pt}able rights of the Palestinian people, to make such adjustments in its approved programme of work as it may consider appropriate and necessary in the light of developments, and to give special emphasis to the need to mobilize support and assistance for the Palestinian people.

The recorded vote on the Division for Palestinian Rights of the Secretariat was 107 in favour, 2 against (Israel, United States), and 48 abstentions (see Annex IV). By that resolution, the Assembly requested the Secretary-General to continue to provide the Division with the necessary resources and to ensure that it continued to carry out its programme of work.

The resolution on the Special Information Programme on Palestine of the Department of Public Information of the Secretariat was adopted in a recorded vote of 151 in favour, 2 against (Israel, United States) and 2 abstentions (Federated States of Micronesia, Marshall Islands). (See Annex V.) By the terms of the resolution, the Assembly requested the Department to continue, with the necessary flexibility as may be required by developments affecting the question of Palestine, its special information programme for the biennium 2000-2001, and, in particular, to disseminate information on all the activities of the United Nations system relating to the question of Palestine. The Assembly also requested the Department of Public Information to promote the Bethlehem 2000 Project.

A draft text on the peaceful settlement of the question of Palestine (document A/55/L.48) was adopted by a recorded vote of 149 in favour, 2 against (Israel, United States), and 3 abstentions (Federated States of Micronesia, Marshall Islands, Nauru). By the resolution, the Assembly expressed its full support for the ongoing peace process, which began in Madrid and for the Declaration of Principles on Interim Self-Government Arrangements of 1993, as well as the subsequent implementation agreements, including the Israeli-Palestinian Interim Agreement on the West Bank and the Gaza Strip of 1995 and the Sharm el-Sheikh Memorandum of 1999. It expressed the hope that the process would lead to the establishment of a comprehensive, just and lasting peace in the Middle East. It stressed the need for commitment to the principle of land for peace and the implementation of Security Council resolutions 242 (1967) and 338 (1973), and the need for the immediate and scrupulous implementation of the agreements reached between the parties, including the redeployment of Israeli forces from the West Bank.

Responding to statements made during yesterday afternoon's and this morning's debate, the representative of Israel said that, despite recent setbacks, tremendous progress had been made in turning enemies into partners for peace. In May this year, Israel had unilaterally withdrawn its forces from southern Lebanon. In confirming Israel's compliance with Security Council resolution 425, the Secretary-General had specifically determined that the area known as

"Shabaa" was not Lebanese territory. Consequently, subsequent Lebanese claims against Israel regarding that area, justifying aggressive activity by terrorists emanating from Lebanese territory, were in direct contravention of the Secretary-General's findings.

He said any discussion of the situation in the Middle East must not only consider Israel's immediate neighbours, but also address the threats to peace progress this year. He was satisfied with the implementation of Security Council resolution 425, which led to the deployment of United Nations Interim Force in Lebanon (UNIFIL) and established the blue line along the border between Israel and Lebanon, this restoring Lebanese Government control over its territory. He regretted that the Israeli-Syrian track had been stalled for a long time. It was in the interest of all peoples in the region to have the IsraeliSyrian talks on the occupied Syrian Golan resumed without further delay and without preconditions. He called on the Governments of Syria and Israel to further explore the direct talks that followed the Washington summit meeting in December 1999.

MAKARIM WIBISONO (Indonesia) said his country could not but express its dismay at the current state of affairs, where military aggression had been substituted for peace negotiations. Israel must be called upon to cease its aggression without preconditions, as failure to prevent further escalation on the ground would ignite the whole region and result in incalculable consequences, not only for the Middle East but for the world at large. The stakes involved in bringing peace to the Palestinians and to the people of the region were high, for it involved not only the question of peace, territory and settlement, but also the future of an entire people and its never-ending struggle for freedom and independence.

Peace was, however, illusory if it meant unimplemented agreements, broken deadlines and unmet commitments. Neither could peace flourish and grow when accords were reached but untenable policies continued unabated. Those had included the expansion of settlements, confiscation of Arab lands, demolition of houses and property and the economic strangulation of the Palestinian territories. The interests of peace could never be served if its sole purpose was to legitimize occupation and dispossession. A just and lasting settlement in the Middle East, with the question of Palestine at its core, could only be attained by fully taking into account the inalienable rights of the Palestinian people, including the right to their homeland and due recognition of the rights of all States in the region to live within internationally recognized borders.

OLE PETER KOLBY (Norway) appealed to both sides not to respond to provocations. The parties must implement the Sharm el-Sheikh understandings and do their utmost to cease all actions that could escalate the conflict. He said the peace process contained both political and economic elements. Continued economic development in the Palestinian territories was critical to a lasting peace and would also benefit Israel. The violence of the last two months was threatening positive development. If security measures continued to impede the normal functioning of the economy, it might also undermine support for the political process. He, therefore, urged Israel to lift the closure of the West Bank and the Gaza Strip, and, instead, to encourage the development of the Palestinian economy.

His country had always understood and supported Israel's quest for security and had condemned terrorist attacks from any quarters. But lasting security could not be sustained at the expense of others. Israel must respect the safety and security of the Palestinians. Excessive and disproportionate use of forceagainst the Palestinians had exacerbated the tensions and fuelled further violence.

The only long-term solution to the ongoing conflict was a final peace agreement. Such an agreement must be just and fair. Great efforts and sacrifices would have to be made on both sides in order to reach such an agreement, possibly to be preceded by a new interim agreement. Significant progress had been made at Camp David. He urged the Israeli and Palestinian leaders to use that window of opportunity and to take brave steps to ensure peace and stability for all.

. . . .

. . . .

UNITED NATIONS

HIGH COMMISSIONER FOR HUMAN RIGHTS

Israeli settlements in the occupied Arab territories

Commission on Human Rights resolution 2000/8

The Commission on Human Rights,

Reaffirming that all Member States have an obligation to promote and protect human rights and fundamental freedoms as stated in the Charter of the United Nations and as elaborated in the Universal Declaration of Human Rights, the International Covenants on Human Rights and other applicable instruments,

Mindful that Israel is a party to the Geneva Convention relative to the Protection of Civilian Persons in Time of War, of 12 August 1949, which is applicable to Palestinian and all Arab by Israel since 1967, including East Jerusalem,

Recalling its previous resolutions, most recently resolution 1999/7 of 23 April 1999, in which, *inter alia,*

it reaffirmed the illegality of the Israeli settlements in the occupied territories,

1. Welcomes:

(a) The Sharm el Sheikh memorandum of 4 September A , , while noting with concern the delays in its implementation, and calls for the full implementation of the memorandum, as well as of the IsraeliPalestinian Interim Agreement on the West Bank and the Gaza Strip of 28 September 1995 and other related agreements;

(b) The report of the Special Rapporteur on the situation of human rights in the Palestinian territories occupied by Israel since 1967 (E/CN.4/2000/25) and hopes that the Government of Israel will cooperate with the Special Rapporteur to allow him fully to discharge his mandate;

2. Expresses its grave concern:
(a) At the continuing Israeli settlement activities, in spite of the Government's moratorium on new construction permits, including the expansion of the settlements, the installation of settlers in the occupied territories, the expropriation of land, the demolition of houses, the confiscation of property, the

expulsion of local residents and the construction of bypass roads, which change the physical character and demographic composition of the   occupied territories, including East Jerusalem, since all these actions are illegal, constitute a violation of the Geneva Convention relative to the Protection of Civilian Persons in Time of War and are a major obstacle to peace;

(b) At and strongly condemns all acts of terrorism, whilst calling upon all parties not to allow any acts of terrorism to affect the ongoing peace process negatively;

3. *Urges* the Government of Israel:

> (a) To comply fully with the previous Commission resolutions on the subject, most recently resolution 1999/7 of 23 April 1999;

> (b) To match its stated commitment to the peace process with concrete actions to fulfill its obligations and cease completely its policy of expanding the settlements and related activities in the including East Jerusalem;

> (c) To forgo and prevent any new installation of settlers in the occupied territories.

4. *Decides* to continue its consideration of this question at its fifty-seventh session.

52nd meeting
17 April 2000

[Adopted by a roll-call vote of 50 votes to 1, with 1 abstention.

HIGH COMMISSIONER FOR HUMAN RIGHTS

CALLS FOR

SETTING UP INTERNATIONAL MONITORING PRESENCE IN OCCUPIED TERRITORIES

5 December 2001

Following is the statement which the United Nations High Commissioner for Human Rights, Mary Robinson, delivered to the Conference of High Contracting Parties of the Fourth Geneva Convention on 5 December 2001 in Geneva:

"I wish to express my gratitude to the Government of Switzerland for inviting my Office to participate in this important meeting. I commend the Government of Switzerland as the depositary of the Convention, for its efforts to achieve the widest possible consensus.

This Conference of High Contracting Parties, called for by United Nations General Assembly resolution ES-10/6, represents an important opportunity to advance the application of international humanitarian law. Apart from the General Assembly, the fifth Special Session of the Commission on Human Rights, and several mechanisms established by the Commission on Human Rights, including the Special Rapporteur on the situation of human rights in the Palestinian territories occupied since 1967 and the International Commission of Inquiry had also called for the convening of such a Conference. Each of us knows that it is a difficult time, and that words matter and will be noted.

The Security Council, the General Assembly and the Commission on Human Rights have also repeatedly reaffirmed the *de jute* applicability to the occupied Palestinian territories of the 1949 Fourth Geneva Convention relative to the Protection of Civilians in Time of War.

Amongst the mandated responsibilities of the Office of the High Commissioner are: support for the UN human rights system, including the treaty monitoring bodies; the monitoring of human rights violations; and providing technical cooperation to assist governments to implement human rights. OHCHR discharges these aspects of its mandate in disputed and occupied territories, as well as in integral states. It should be noted in this context that all UN treaty-monitoring bodies that have considered this question have determined the applicability of the human rights covenants and conventions in the occupied Palestinian territories.

In the report of my visit to the region, November 2000, I also indicated that the full application of the Fourth Geneva Convention is essential to guarantee respect for fundamental human rights.

Mr. Chairman,

Since my last visit to the region in November 2000, I have been following closely the developments in Israel and the occupied Palestinian territories. I can honestly say that not a day goes by without my following events in detail, and I do so with growing anxiety.

The serious deterioration of the situation has had a terrible cost in terms of human lives. Since the end of September 2000, over 830 Palestinians, including many children, have been killed and 16,500 injured. More than 230 Israelis have been killed over the same period including in the horrific attacks in Jerusalem and Haifa only last week-end. Most of those killed and injured on both sides have been civilians. It is important to emphasize that neither the Israeli policy of targeted assassination of Palestinian civilians, nor Palestinian attacks against Israeli civilians, can be reconciled with provisions of international humanitarian law, including the Fourth Geneva Convention. Articles 27 and 32, in particular, seek to protect the lives of persons not taking a direct part in the hostilities. These practices also violate human rights norms that affirm the right to life and the prohibition on execution of civilians without trial and fair judicial process.

Collective punishments such as prolonged siege and closures of the territories and destruction of homes and agricultural land, has also led to increased poverty and a steady economic decline in the West Bank and in Gaza.

Te consequences of collective punishments are manifold: Palestinian workers cannot reach their places of work in Israel, Palestinian producers are prevented from exporting their products, unemployment increased, pupils and students are denied their right to education, and injured and sick people are deprived of their right to health-care. All of this has had grave effects on economic, social and cultural life in the Palestinian territories in general. It has adversely impacted on an already weak Palestinian economy. There has been a dramatic loss of income for a large section of the population, and medical and humanitarian aid has been impeded.

Today there are more than 150 settlements in the West Bank and <u>Gaza</u> inhabited by approximately 380,000 settlers, of whom some 180,000 live in East Jerusalem. Although resolutions of the Security Council, the General Assembly and the Commission on Human Rights have stated that these settlements violate article 49 (6) of the Fourth Geneva Convention, the settlements have undergone considerable expansion since the start of the Oslo Peace process in September 1993. Settlements have become a catalyst for violence. They are protected by the Israeli Defense Forces and are exempt from the jurisdiction of the courts of the Palestinian Authority. Settlers have committed numerous acts of violence against Palestinians.

Palestinian hostility against settlers has also grown alarmingly and Palestinians have killed a number of settlers. Despite the fact that the settlers presence in the occupied Palestinian territories is illegal, those who are not taking part in military hostilities remain civilians. Such killings are also contrary to the norms of international law. The increase in violence directed at settlers has been linked to an alarming rise in the incidence of hate speech and incitement.

Mr. Chairman,

The protection of the victim should be the overriding concern of the UN and its agencies and programmes. However, the failure to resolve the fundamental problem of occupation - an occupation which has continued for over 34 years - combined with the failure by successive Israeli governments to comply with the provisions of the Fourth Geneva Convention and international human rights standards, has left the population of the occupied Palestinian territories in a vulnerable situation, lacking protection and exposed to a wide range of violations.

Protection needs to be accorded to the people of the occupied territories in strict compliance with the Fourth Geneva Convention. My mandate obliges me to seek resolution of, and remedies for, human rights violations whenever and wherever they occur, and to prevent further violations if possible. I strongly believe that ensuring respect for the international human rights standards set out in the Universal Declaration of Human Rights and the Fourth Geneva Convention is crucial in order to prevent human suffering and in the search for comprehensive solutions for peace. Article I of the Convention places a duty on the High Contracting Parties "to respect and ensure respect of" the provisions of the Convention "in all circumstances". To meet this challenge, legal and diplomatic mechanisms are available under the United Nations Charter, in addition to those created by the Convention itself.

I would like to reiterate my call for the establishment of an international monitoring presence in the occupied Palestinian territories. I urge both Israelis and Palestinians to work towards ending the mutually destructive cycle of violence and to seek a return to negotiations, the aim of which should be to achieve peace through a just and durable solution, in conformity with fundamental standards of international human rights and humanitarian law.

COMMISSION ON HUMAN RIGHTS ADOPTS RESOLUTION CRITICIZING ISRAELI SETTLEMENT POLICIES

Commission on Human Rights
58th session
12 April 2002
Afternoon

Debate Continues on Civil and Political Rights

The Commission on Human Rights approved by roll-call vote this afternoon a resolution expressing concern over the continued establishment of settlements by Israel in the occupied Arab territories and urging the Government of Israel to reverse its settlement policy.

The measure, adopted by a vote of 52 in favour and 1 opposed — Guatemala - also expressed concern at closures of and within the Palestinian territories and at restrictions on the freedom of movement of Palestinians. It strongly condemned all acts of violence, in particular indiscriminate terrorist attacks over past weeks that had killed and injured civilians.

The Commission carried on this afternoon with its debate on civil and political rights, hearing from a series of national delegations and non-governmental organizations (NGOs). The Republic of Korea, Switzerland, Georgia and Denmark called for greater efforts to eradicate torture. Switzerland said an end had to be put to impunity for such acts — that Governments in all countries must ensure that persons guilty of torture were punished wherever they were. The Republic of Korea and Denmark expressed support for an optional protocol to the Convention against Torture that would allow visits by international experts to places of detention.

Others delivering statements were Nicaragua, Egypt, the Holy See, the United States, Liechtenstein, Ireland, Slovenia, Romania, Turkey, Cyprus, Belarus, Bosnia and Herzegovina, and the NGOs Women's International League for Peace and Freedom; Coordination francaise pour le Lobby Europeen des Femmes; United Nations Association of China; and Agir ensemble pour les droits de l'homme.

The Commission will reconvene at 10 a.m. on Monday, 15 April, to continue its debate on civil and political rights and to act on outstanding resolutions under its agenda items on racism and racial discrimination and the question of the violation of human rights in the occupied Arab territories.

Action on Resolutions

MARCOS GOMEZ MARTINEZ (Spain), speaking on behalf of the EU, said that it regretted it was not able to support resolution L.2, adopted this morning, on the occupied Syrian Golan. While the resolution was not completely in line with the corresponding General Assembly resolution, the main concern for the Union was a different one. The EU felt that in order for the Union to support the text in this forum, it would need a stronger focus on human rights. The EU also noted with regret that this year no opportunity had been given by the main sponsor of this resolution to engage in negotiations intended to improve the text.

In a resolution (E/CN.4/2002.L.17) on Israeli settlements in the occupied Arab territories, adopted by a roll-call vote of 52 in favour and 1 opposed, the Commission expressed grave concern at the dramatic escalation of the IsraeliPalestinian conflict, which had led to a spiral of hatred, anger, and further violence, and to increased suffering for both Israelis and Palestinians; expressed concern at continuing Israeli settlement activities; strongly condemned all acts of violence, in particular indiscriminate terrorist attacks over the past weeks, killing and injuring civilians; expressed concern at closures of and within the Palestinian territories and the restriction of the freedom of movement of Palestinians; urged the Government of Israel to comply fully with previous Commission resolutions on the subject; to reverse its settlement policy in the occupied territories; to prevent any new installation of settlers in the occupied territories; to implement the recommendations of the High Commissioner for Human Rights regarding the settlements; to confiscate arms and take other measures with the aim of preventing illegal acts of violence by Israeli settlers; and it urged the parties to implement immediately Security Council resolutions 1397 (2002) and 1402 (2002), and called for the Israeli and Palestinian sides and their leaders to cooperate in the implementation of the Security Implementation Work Plan and the recommendations of the Mitchell Report aimed at resuming negotiations.

The vote was as follows:

In favour: Algeria, Argentina, Armenia, Austria, Bahrain, Belgium, Brazil, Burundi, Cameroon, Canada, Chile, China, Costa Rica, Croatia, Cuba, Czech Republic, Democratic Republic of the Congo, Ecuador, France, Germany, India, Indonesia, Italy, Japan, Kenya, Libyan Arab Jamahiriya, Malaysia, Mexico, Nigeria, Pakistan, Peru, Poland, Portugal, Republic of Korea, Russian Federation, Saudi Arabia, Senegal, Sierra Leone, South Africa, Spain, Sudan, Swaziland, Sweden, Syrian Arab Republic, Thailand, Togo, Uganda, United Kingdom of Great Britain and Northern Ireland, Uruguay, Venezuela, Viet Nam, Zambia.

Against: Guatemala

Abstentions: None

E/CN.4/2004/6

Report of the Special Rapporteur of the Commission on Human Rights, John Dugard, on the situation of human rights in the Palestinian territories occupied by Israel since 1967, submitted in accordance with Commission resolution 1993/2A

Summary

The situation in the Occupied Palestinian Territory (OPT) continues to be a matter of grave concern. Although the road map promoted by the Quartet offers some prospect of peace in the region, it is important to record that the past six months have seen continued violations of human rights and international humanitarian law.

The Government of Israel has justified its actions in the OPT on the grounds of self-defence and portrayed them as anti-terrorism measures. That Israel has legitimate security concerns cannot be denied. On the other hand, some limit must be placed on the violation of human rights in the name of counter-terrorism. A balance must be struck between respect for human rights and the interests of security.

During the past few months the construction of the Wall, separating Israel from the West Bank, has been frenetically pursued. The Wall does not follow the Green Line, which marks the de facto boundary between Israel and Palestine. Instead, it incorporates substantial areas of the West Bank into Israel. Over 210,000 Palestinians will be seriously affected by the Wall. Palestinians living between the Wall and the Green Line will be effectively cut off from their farmlands and workplaces, schools, health clinics and other social services. This is likely to lead to a new generation of refugees or internally displaced persons.

The Wall has all the features of a permanent structure. The fact that it will incorporate half of the settler population in the West Bank and East Jerusalem suggests that it is designed to further entrench the position of the settlers. The evidence strongly suggests that Israel is determined to create facts on the ground amounting to de facto annexation. Annexation of this kind, known as conquest in international law, is prohibited by the Charter of the United Nations and the Fourth Geneva Convention. The Special Rapporteur submits that the time has come to condemn the Wall as an unlawful act of annexation in the same way that Israel's annexation of East Jerusalem and the Golan Heights has been condemned as unlawful. Similarly, no recognition should be given by the international community to Israel's control over Palestinian territory enclosed by the Wall.

The restrictions on freedom of movement continue to create a humanitarian crisis in the OPT. Although curfews have not affected as many people in 2003 as in the previous year, they still disrupt Palestinian life on a broad scale. The number of checkpoints has increased during the past six months. These restraints on the movement of goods and persons give rise to unemployment, poverty, poor health care and interrupted education and, in addition, they result in the humiliation of the Palestinian people.

The death toll in the conflict continues to rise as a result of suicide bombings and military incursions. The Israeli practice of assassinating suspected terrorists has inflicted death and injury not only on those targeted but on a substantial number of innocent civilians in the vicinity of such actions. The legality of such measures is highly questionable.
There are some 6,000 Palestinians in Israeli prisons and detention centres. Although Israel has agreed to release 540 of them, its refusal to release more prisoners constitutes a major obstacle in the way of peace in the region. Sadly, allegations of torture and inhuman and degrading treatment continue to be made. The Special Rapporteur therefore calls for an independent inquiry into such allegations.

The destruction of property in the OPT continues unabated. During the past eight months, Gaza has been particularly affected by military action that has caused large-scale devastation to houses and agricultural land.

Israel's undertaking to curb the growth of settlements has not been implemented. On the contrary, settlements have continued to grow at an unacceptable pace. This phenomenon, together with the construction of the Wall, suggests that territorial expansion remains an essential feature of Israel's policies and practices in the OPT.

Item 8

E/CN.4/2004/6/Add.1

Report of the Special Rapporteur of the Commission on Human Rights, John Dugard, on the situation of Human Rights in the Palestinian territories occupied by Israel since 1967*

Summary

The situation in the Occupied Palestinian Territory (OPT) is characterized by serious violations of general international law, of human rights law and of international humanitarian law. It is not helpful to suggest that a solution can be found to the conflict in the region by ignoring norms of international law. A sustainable peace in the region must take place within the framework of international law and relevant resolutions of the United Nations.

Terrorism is a constant feature of the conflict in the OPT and neighbouring Israel. Both Palestinians and Israelis have been responsible for inflicting a reign of terror on innocent civilians. Measures must be taken to prevent terrorism, but not at the expense of fundamental principles of law. The Wall presently being constructed by Israel, insofar as it is built on Palestinian territory, cannot be justified as a legitimate or proportionate response to terrorism.

The present report focuses on the Wall in the West Bank. This should not result in a failure to pay proper attention to the situation in Gaza where death and destruction remain a feature of daily life. House demolitions continue unabated and the number of homeless persons rises steadily - particularly in the Rafah refugee camp. Moreover, the people of Gaza are subjected to regular military incursions in which scant regard is paid to civilian life.

The Wall being built by Israel in the name of security penetrates deep into Palestinian territory and has resulted in the creation of a zone between the Green Line (the de facto border between Israel and Palestine) and the Wall inside the OPT, which Israel has designated as "closed" to all Palestinians. Palestinians who live, farm, work or go to school within this closed zone require special permits from the Israeli authorities. Both the construction of the Wall and the operation of the permit system for the "Closed Zone" between the Wall and the Green Line have caused great hardships to Palestinians and violated norms of human rights law and international humanitarian law.

The construction of the Wall has resulted in the large-scale destruction of Palestinian property. Olive and citrus trees have been uprooted and agricultural land reduced to a wasteland. The seizure of land for the building of the Wall has taken place without due process of law. Notice of seizure of land has been served in an arbitrary manner and there is, in the circumstances, no real remedy available to landowners to contest the seizure of land. The Wall has infrequent gates for the purpose of crossing. Consequently, those farmers granted permits to farm their land have difficulty in accessing their land.

The permit system for the Closed Zone is administered in an arbitrary and humiliating manner. Permits are frequently withheld, even for landowners and residents of the Closed Zone, or granted for short periods only. The failure to grant permits to farmers to cultivate their lands will result in neglect and ultimate decay of fertile agricultural land. The permit system has also drastically interfered with education, health care and family life. This system, which subjects Palestinian freedom of movement to the whim of the Occupying Power, creates anger, anxiety and humiliation among the population. In the result, it is likely to create insecurity for Israel rather than security.

There is a real prospect that life will become so intolerable for those villagers living in the Closed Zone that they will abandon their homes and migrate to the West Bank. Farmers whose lands are in the Closed Zone are also likely to abandon their farms under pressure from an arbitrary permit system.

The main beneficiaries of the Wall are settlers: 54 settlements and 142,000 settlers (that is 63 per cent of the West Bank settlement population) will find themselves on the Israeli side of the Wall, with access to land separated from its Palestinian owners.

The Wall might have been justified as a legitimate security measure to prevent would-be suicide bombers from entering Israel had it followed the course of the Green Line. The manner in which it has been built - largely on Palestinian territory - cannot, however, be justified on security grounds. The building of the Wall, in such a way that it separates farmers from their land, isolates villages from employment, schools and health care, brings settlers within the de facto borders of Israel and confirms the unlawful annexation of East Jerusalem, suggests that the main purpose of the Wall is the annexation, albeit by de facto means, of additional land for the State of Israel.

The Wall violates the prohibition on the acquisition of territory by forcible means, and seriously undermines the right to self-determination of the Palestinian people by reducing the size of a future Palestinian State. Moreover, it violates important norms of international humanitarian law prohibiting the annexation of occupied territory, the establishment of settlements, the confiscation of private land and the forcible transfer of people. Human rights norms are likewise violated, particularly those affirming freedom of movement, the right to family life and the right to education and health care.

(Footnotes)
* In accordance with General Assembly resolution 53/208 B, paragraph 8, this document is submitted late so as to include the most up-to-date information possible.

Index

Symbols

A

F

Malcolm Baldrige National Quality Award 102
Mandamus 99
Mandela Institute 200
McCartin v. Norton 100
McCaul, Elizabeth 132
Mead, Walter Russell 88
Mediterranean 148
Meier, Gideon 8
Mein Kampf 20
Meir, Gideon 120
Merrill Ditch-Liners, Inc. v. Pablo 115
Microsoft 82
Middle Ages 25
Middle East 86
"Militants" 174
Military Assistance to Foreign Nations 97
Ministry of Immigrants Absorption 140
Mishlav, Yosef 116
Mizrahi 141
Mofaz, Shaul 120
Morag 141
"Moral turpitude" 110, 113
Mordechai, Fuli 45
Motoc, Mihnea 50
Mozart 156
Muhammad Juma 40
Munich 90
Munich Agreement 20
Munir Akram 50
Munoz 10
Murder 110
Murder 86
Muslims 10, 131
Mussolini, Benito 19, 24

N

Nablus 5, 25, 230
NAKBA 31, 43
NASA 82
Nasser Al-kidwa 51
National Bank Act 125
National Space and Aeronautics Agency 82
Nationally Preferred Areas 140
Naturalization 114
Naveh, Dan 32
Naveh, Yair 120

Nazis 132, 174
Nefesh B'Nefesh 156
Negev 27
Netanyahu, Benjamin 32
Netzarem 141
New York Banking Law 130
New York City 133
New York State Banking Department 129
Nongovernmental organizations (NGO) 98
Norway 10
Nuremberg 7, 134
Nuremberg Tribunal 134
NYC Comptroller 134

O

Observer for Palestine 51
Occupied Territories 24, 83, 111, 124, 138, 226, 227, 236, 250
Occupying Power 10, 25
Ofer 275
Olmert, Ehud 120
Omar Mansour Muhammad Mansour 4, 12
One Israel Fund 159
Operation Defensive Shield 271
Operation Rainbow 32
Oppenheimer, Yariv 26
Outlaws 18
Owens 106

P

Pakistan 50
Palestine 82
Palestinian Authority 19
Palestinian Center for Human Rights 192, 315
Palestinian State 24
Palestinians 25, 131
Parkview Corp. v. Department of the Army 100
Partisans 174
Pataki, George E. 132
Pazner, Avi 120
PCRS 215
Peace Now 26, 98
Phantom Fighter 95
Philadelphi Corridor 36, 37
Philadelphia University 5
Philippines 10

Pinochet 7
PRCS 211
Pre-Military Mechina Program 151
Pro-Israel vote 24
Public Committee Against Torture in Israel 195
Purssell, Richard 104

Q

Qalqilya 6, 231
Qetziot 275

R

Rafah 31, 37, 46, 55, 101
Rahameh Rashid Sahiin 3, 12
Ramallah 25
Rantisi 4, 26, 95, 101, 110
Rapid Response Team 150
Rawam Abu Zaed 33
Rawam Mohammed Abu Zaed 34
Regev, Gil 116
Rehnquist, J. 167
Resistance fighters 174
Resolution No.1544 42, 46
Resolution No.607 89
Resolution No.242 22, 86, 89, 284
Resolution No.452 22, 285
Resolution No.605 287
Resolution No.607 289
Resolution No.799 290
"Right of Return;" 20
Robinson, Mary 310, 319, 340
Romania 10, 50
Romero, Archbishop Oscar 172 et seq.
Rotz, Jay H. 147
Russia 10, 148, 294
Ryan, Richard 9

S

Sachs, Ron 104
Sachsenhausen 115
Samer al-Arja 34
Scalia, Justice 82, 84
Scalia, udge 167
Schick, Tom 94
Secretary of State 98

Tel al-Sultan 32, 34, 41
"Terrorist Activities," 111
The Alien Tort Law 84
The Church of Scientology 149
Thomas, J. 167
<u>TM Systems, Inc. v. United States</u> 100
Torture 86, 168, 175
Torture Victim Protection Act 1 et seq., 81, 101, 160, 173
TVPA 2, 11, 81

U

UN 37 See also United Nations etc.
UN Charter 139, 169
UN Commission on Human Rights 23, 110
UN General Assembly 168
UN Security Council 22, 83
UN Security Council Resolutions 139
Union Bank 141
Union Bank of Israel 138
Union Bank of Switzerland 131
United Jewish Appeal 159
United Mizrahi 138
United Nations 82, 97, 148
United Nations Charter 2
United Nations Commission on Human Rights 9, 89, 99, 310, 322, 340,
United Nations General Assembly 168
United States State Department 161
UNWRA 227
US Defense Department 93
US State Department's Annual Report on Human Right 26
US Supreme Court 81

V

Vietnam 28, 83
Visas 113
Volker Commission 133

W

Wagner 156
Wall 167
        See also Security Fence
Weapons 93
West Bank 13, 20, 24, 83
World Bank 27, 88
World Council of Churches 318

THE AUTHORS

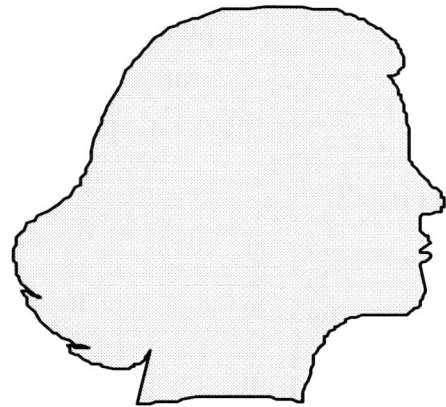

D. Cellini

L. Meier

Printed by BoD™in Norderstedt, Germany

9 780974 636610